Lemon Chicken 84

THE COMPLETE
CHICKEN
COOKBOOK

THE COMPLETE
CHICKEN
COOKBOOK

MEREHURST

Chicken Burger with Tangy Garlic Mayonnaise, page 138

Tagliatelle with Chicken Livers and Cream, page 118

Fried Crispy Noodles (Mee Grob), page 96

Contents

Chicken and Ham Pie, page 182

You will find the following cookery ratings on the recipes in this book:

A single pot symbol indicates a recipe that is simple and generally straightforward to make—perfect for beginners.

Two symbols indicate the need for just a little more care and a little more time.

Three symbols indicate special recipes that need more investment in time, care and patience—but the results are worth it.

Hainan Chicken Rice, page 52

Chicken and Corn Soup, page 33

Vietnamese Pawpaw and Chicken Salad, page 66

Baked Chicken and Artichoke Pancakes, page 172

Chicken Basics

Chicken is a versatile food, which lends itself to many different types of recipes, methods of cooking and styles of cuisine. This comprehensive guide to cooking with chicken, including information on the different types of chicken cuts available, purchasing, storing and cooking chicken, will help you to prepare successful and delicious chicken dishes.

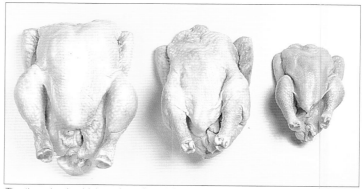

The three basic chicken sizes, from left to right: large boiling fowl; roasting chicken; baby chicken or poussin.

Here is advice on how to get the best out of chicken: what to look for when buying and how to store and prepare your purchase prior to cooking. There's also information on how to make stock and gravy, jointing and boning chickens, and the art of carving.

PURCHASING

There is a wide variety of chickens and chicken cuts available.

Young tender birds are good for grilling, barbecuing, frying and roasting. Chickens over 1.8 kg (3 lb 10 oz) are usually only suitable for poaching, braising or boiling because of their tough flesh (although they have excellent flavour) and are labelled as boiling fowls. Unless you specifically want a very large bird, buy two smaller chickens rather than one large.

Whole baby chickens (or poussins) weigh about 500 g (1 lb) and serve one person. Chickens under 1.5 kg (3 lb) serve two to four people. Whole roasting chickens weighing over 1.5 kg (3 lb) should serve at least four people.

Chickens are sold cleaned, with their innards removed. The neck is usually tucked inside. Sometimes the giblets are in the cavity, contained in a plastic bag, so be sure to remove them before cooking or freezing.

Whole birds are marketed by weight, and the weight becomes the number of the chicken. For example, a No. 10 chicken weighs 1 kg (2 lb); a No. 16 chicken weighs 1.6 kg (3¼ lb), and so on.

When buying chicken by weight, check whether the giblets are with the bird. Giblets weigh approximately 175 g (6 oz) and will affect the number of portions you get after cooking.

FRESH CHICKEN

Fresh chicken has better flavour and texture than frozen. Look for skin that is light pink and moist, rather than wet, with no dry spots. It should be unbroken and free from blemishes and bruises. The breast should be plump and well rounded; on a young bird the point of the breastbone will be flexible.

At speciality poultry shops you can buy free-range, grain-fed, and corn-fed chickens (with yellow skin and flesh).

Chicken can also be purchased cooked. Hot take-away barbecued, roasted or chargrilled chicken has become a mainstay of busy people as the basis for quick and satisfying meals. Cooked, smoked chicken is available whole, chilled, from delicatessens and supermarkets.

Chicken cuts include: double or single breasts on the bone, with skin or without; breast fillets; tenderloins (the part just behind the breast); marylands (the whole thigh and leg); thigh cutlets; thigh fillets; wings; and drumsticks (the bottom part of the leg). Buy the appropriate cut of chicken for the cooking process you will be using. Chicken is very versatile, and it is not always necessary to buy the most expensive fillets to produce an excellent result. Here is a guide to the cuts used in this book.

For roasting – whole roasting chickens, baby chickens, whole breasts, wings, marylands, drumsticks, thighs.

Chicken leg cuts, clockwise from left: thigh (underside view), drumstick, maryland, thigh fillet, thigh.

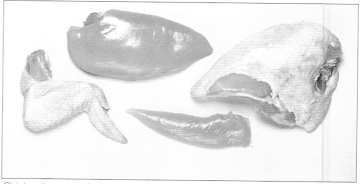

Chicken breast and wing cuts, clockwise from left: wing, single breast fillet, whole breast with bone, tenderloin.

For grilling – chicken halves and quarters, wings, drumsticks, marylands, thigh cutlets.

For barbecuing – chicken halves, whole breasts, wings, drumsticks, marylands, thigh cutlets, tenderloins.

For stir-frying – breast fillets, thigh fillets, tenderloins, livers.

For pan-frying – marylands, breast fillets, tenderloins, livers.

For deep-frying – drumsticks, wings, thighs, chicken pieces.

For casseroles/braising – whole chickens, chicken pieces, thighs, thigh cutlets, drumsticks, wings.

For poaching – whole chickens, whole breasts, breast fillets, thighs, drumsticks.

For stock – bones, necks, giblets, boiling fowls.

Storing fresh chicken: Chicken must be transported home as quickly as possible. Do not leave it sitting in the sun in the car or car boot. The internal temperature of a car left closed in full sun spells disaster to all chicken products. The longer that food spends between 5°C (41°F) and 60°C (140°F), the greater the likelihood of rapid growth of harmful bacteria that may result in food poisoning.

Keep chicken away from any strong-smelling items such as cleaning agents and petrol that you may have stored in your vehicle; chicken will absorb the smells.

Make it your policy to purchase chicken or meat as the last item on your round of shopping. In hot weather, use an insulated chiller bag to keep it cold.

It is particularly important to store poultry carefully to avoid contamination by salmonella bacteria, which can cause food poisoning. Always wash hands, chopping boards, knives and cooking implements in very hot soapy water after handling raw chicken. Always keep cooked and raw chicken separate.

Before storing uncooked whole chicken, discard the tight plastic wrappings and pour off any juices. Remove the neck and giblets from whole birds (sometimes these are in a plastic bag inside the cavity). Giblets should be cooked immediately or stored separately. Use the neck and giblets for stock; chop the liver to flavour a sauce, gravy or stuffing.

Loosely wrap the chicken in plastic wrap or place in a plastic bag, place the package on a plate and refrigerate on the bottom shelf of the refrigerator. Never place uncooked chicken where the juices could drip on or otherwise come into contact with other foodstuffs. A fresh, cleaned and wrapped chicken can be stored in the refrigerator for up to two days.

To store fresh chicken pieces or cuts, remove them from trays or other packaging, pour off any juices and loosely wrap in plastic wrap or place in a plastic bag. Refrigerate for up to two days.

Storing cooked chicken: Chicken should stand no more than an hour at room temperature after cooking. If keeping longer than this, store it loosely wrapped in the refrigerator and use within three days. The chicken does not have to be cold when it goes into the refrigerator. If the chicken has a sauce or stuffing, it should be eaten within 24 hours of cooking. Stuffing and gravy should be stored separately.

FROZEN CHICKEN

Make sure that any frozen chicken you buy from the supermarket freezer is solid and completely enclosed in its packaging. Do not purchase any that appear semi-soft and that are sitting in their own juices, as this indicates that they have been in the display cabinet for longer than is ideal.

Uncooked, home-frozen chicken (without giblets) will keep for up to nine months in good condition. Remove the giblets before freezing as they will begin to deteriorate after eight weeks.

If a package has partly defrosted it must never be refrozen; defrost fully in the refrigerator and cook promptly. Stuffed birds should never be frozen, as the filling will not freeze enough to prevent the development of harmful bacteria.

Freezing fresh chicken: Have the freezer temperature at minus 15°C or lower. Use heavy-gauge polythene bags and good-quality plastic wrap to package fresh chicken.

Label each package with the details of the contents, the date it was packaged and stored and either the number of people it will feed or the unfrozen weight. Use a waterproof pen or wax crayon.

It is important to expel as much air as possible from the packaging; oxygen left behind will speed up the process of oxidisation of any fat, resulting in an unpleasant taste after prolonged storing. If you do a lot of freezing, it may be worthwhile investing in a vacuum freezer pump to efficiently expel air.

Secure freezer bags by twisting the tips and closing them with masking tape; this is preferable to metal twist ties. Or, clip a metal band in place with a clipping device.

To freeze uncooked chicken, wrap in heavy-duty plastic bags.

To freeze cooked dishes, place into plastic or aluminium containers.

STUFFING AND TRUSSING

Make up the stuffing according to the recipe. Spoon the stuffing mixture into the tail cavity of the chicken, filling loosely to allow for the stuffing to expand during cooking. Secure the skin across the cavity with a skewer, or truss the chicken as described below. The stuffing can also be pushed under the skin of the breast and into the neck cavity. The stuffing must be completely cooked through to prevent contamination by salmonella bacteria.

Trussing a whole chicken, or securing with kitchen string, keeps the stuffing in place in the cavity and holds the chicken together compactly, so that the legs or wing tips do not overcook, and so that the cooked chicken sits neatly, ready for carving.

When the chicken has been filled with the stuffing, pull the skin down over the cavity. Turn the chicken over onto its breast and tie a long length of kitchen string right around the wings, securing them neatly. Turn the chicken over, taking the string over the legs and crossing it underneath the chicken. Tuck the tail (the parson's nose) into the cavity and tie the legs together firmly. After the chicken has been cooked, leave it to rest for 10 minutes, then remove all of the string and carve.

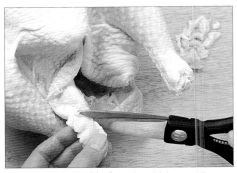

Trim any pockets of fat from the chicken cavity before cooking.

Spoon the stuffing mixture into the tail cavity, allowing for expansion during cooking.

Secure the skin across the cavity with a skewer, or truss the chicken.

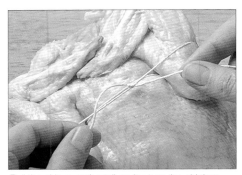

Pull the skin over the tail cavity, turn the chicken onto its breast and tie string around the wings.

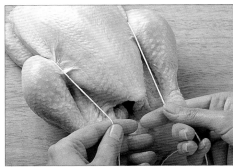

Turn the chicken over again, taking the string over the legs.

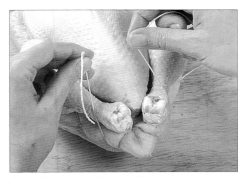

Cross the string underneath the chicken and bring it up beside the legs.

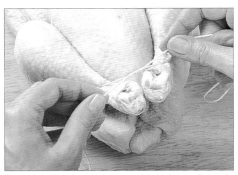

Tuck the tail (the parson's nose) into the cavity and tie the legs together.

Wrap the chicken in heavy-gauge freezer bags or good-quality plastic wrap, then in aluminium foil, expelling air. Label and freeze. Remove the giblets and neck and pack separately to be used for stock.

Commercially frozen whole chickens without giblets can be kept for nine months, or according to instructions on the package. If the chicken is still frozen hard, place it in the freezer in its original wrappings as soon as possible after purchase. If it has started to thaw, place it in the refrigerator to completely thaw out, cook it promptly, cool quickly, wrap and refreeze it. Never refreeze thawed, uncooked poultry.

Whole chickens can be trussed before freezing to be ready for cooking when thawed. To provide convenient serving portions and to save space, cut the chicken into four, eight or 10 pieces before freezing. Wrap each joint individually in plastic wrap, expelling air, and then combine in a larger package in a sturdy plastic bag. Seal, tape the end of the bag to the package, label and freeze.

Chicken cuts such as legs or wings can be frozen either as individual portions or in amounts to serve several people. Wrap portions individually in plastic wrap, expelling air, then place them in a larger plastic bag. Seal and tape the end of the bag to the package. Label and freeze.

Boneless cuts can be cut into strips or cubes before freezing. Weigh out meal-sized portions and place in heavy-duty plastic bags. Fill right to the corners with chicken. Flatten the package (so it will defrost quickly) and expel the air. Seal, label and freeze.

The same procedure applies to chicken mince.

Freezing cooked chicken: Cooked whole chickens or chicken pieces can be frozen with or without bones, for up to two weeks. After this time it will tend to dry out.

Moist chicken dishes such as stews, casseroles, curries and soups are all suitable for freezing. Quickly reduce the temperature of the cooked item by placing it in the refrigerator or by plunging the base of the dish into cold water, then cool completely in the refrigerator. Line cake tins or other suitable containers with a heavy-duty plastic bag. Spoon portions into the bag and expel the air. Seal, label and freeze. Place the bag in its tin into the freezer. When frozen, remove from the tin, reseal to remove as much air as possible and return, labelled, to the freezer.

Or, simply spoon the meat directly into plastic or aluminium containers and seal, label and freeze. As a general rule, freeze cooked chicken for a maximum of two months.

Defrosting: Frozen chicken must be completely thawed in the refrigerator before cooking; allow two to three hours per 500 g (1 lb). A frozen chicken should be cooked within 12 hours of thawing. Do not thaw chicken at room temperature. Never keep perishable food at room temperature for longer than two hours, particularly on hot days. This includes time to prepare, serve and eat.

Microwave defrosting is not recommended for whole frozen chickens because of uneven thawing. However, smaller packages of cuts or pre-cooked meals can be successfully thawed in the microwave using the defrost setting. Always remove chicken from wrapping before defrosting. Stir casseroles occasionally to distribute heat evenly. Separate joints or pieces as they soften.

PREPARATION

Before cooking a chicken, remove the neck, giblets and fat pockets from the cavity. Discard the fat and use the neck and giblets for stock. Remove any excess fat and sinew from chicken pieces.

Raw poultry should be wiped with a damp cloth, rather than washed, before cooking. Wipe frozen chickens with

JOINTING

Jointing a whole chicken is an easy process, once you know how. Large birds can be cut into four, six, eight or 10 pieces. Use a sharp, heavy knife or poultry shears.

To cut a bird into six pieces, remove the leg by cutting around the end of the thigh joint. Twist the leg sharply outwards to break the joint, and then cut through the joint. Turn the bird around and repeat on the other side. Remove the wings by bending them outwards and snipping around the joint. Cut up one side of the body and open it out flat. Cut the body into two pieces. Cut down the centre of the breast.

To make eight portions, separate the thigh from the drumstick. To make 10 portions, cut the breast pieces in half.

Always keep in mind that the dark meat of a chicken (legs and thighs) takes longer to cook than the white meat of a chicken (breasts).

Twist the leg sharply outwards to break the joint, and then cut through the joint.

Remove the wings by bending them outwards and snipping around the joint.

Carefully cut up one side of the body and open it out flat.

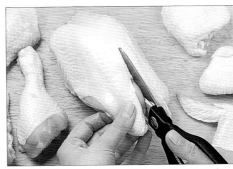
Cut down the centre of the breast to separate the two halves.

To make eight portions of chicken, separate the thigh from the drumstick.

To make ten portions of chicken, cut the breast pieces in half.

paper towels to absorb excess moisture.

Use a cook's knife for jointing uncooked chickens. Poultry shears are excellent for dividing whole chickens into serving portions, expecially for splitting the breastbone, cutting the backbone and rib bones and cutting the breast and legs in half.

To marinate, pour the liquid over the chicken in a non-metallic dish.

Stuffing a whole chicken before roasting adds extra flavour and plumps up the chicken. Do not stuff a chicken more than three hours before cooking. If using warm stuffing, the chicken must be cooked immediately. Stuffed, or stuffed and trussed chickens take a little longer to cook than unstuffed chickens. The juices from the cavity of the chicken will soak into the stuffing, so the stuffing must be cooked through to prevent contamination by harmful salmonella bacteria.

Some people prefer chicken without the skin. Removing the skin eliminates much of the fat from the chicken, as the fat lies in a layer just underneath the skin. Usually the skin is removed after cooking, but drumsticks can be skinned and then cooked. To remove the skin from drumsticks, use a small sharp knife. Begin by carefully loosening the skin from the flesh at the large joint end. Then pull the skin down and away from the flesh. Some chicken shops sell drumsticks with the skin already removed.

Boning a whole chicken is a technique used for special-occasion dishes. With bones removed, the chicken makes a meaty casing for a luxurious stuffing and the cooked chicken is much easier to carve or slice than a whole chicken. Chicken presented in this way is often served cold. Chicken wings can also be boned and stuffed, making an easy-to-eat appetizer or finger food for parties.

Marinating chicken gives it extra flavour and moisture. Marinades usually contain at least one acid ingredient, such as wine, vinegar, lemon juice or even yoghurt, to tenderize, plus other ingredients to flavour and colour the chicken.

BONING WHOLE CHICKEN

Using a small, sharp knife, cut through the skin on the centre back. Separate the flesh from the bone down one side to the breast, being careful not to pierce the skin. Follow along the bones closely with the knife, gradually easing the meat from the thigh, drumstick and wing. Cut through the thigh bone and cut off the wing tip. Repeat on the other side, then lift the rib cage away, leaving the flesh in one piece. Scrape all the meat from the drumstick and wings; discard the bones. Turn the wing and drumstick flesh inside the chicken and lay the chicken out flat, skin-side down. The chicken is now ready to be stuffed and rolled according to the recipe.

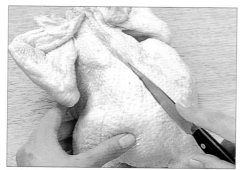
Using a small sharp knife, cut through the chicken skin and along the backbone.

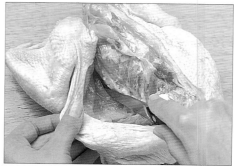
Using the tip of the knife, scrape against the bone down the length of the cut.

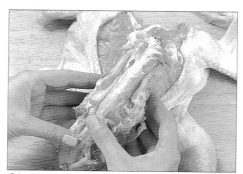
Cut through the thigh bone and cut off the wing tip, then lift out the rib cage.

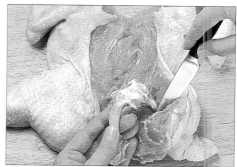
Scrape all of the flesh from the drumsticks and wings and discard the bones.

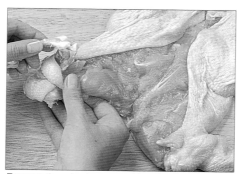
Remove the wing bones and turn the flesh inside the chicken.

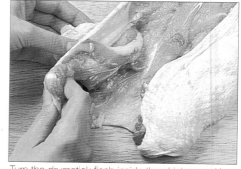
Turn the drumstick flesh inside the chicken and lay the chicken out flat.

Marinating is ideal to use in conjunction with quick-cooking methods. Frozen chicken should be thawed before marinating.

Place chicken in a shallow ceramic or glass (not metal) container and pour in the marinade. Stir well to make sure the chicken is well coated. Cover with plastic wrap and refrigerate, usually for at least two to eight hours, or preferably overnight, turning occasionally. When ready to cook, drain the chicken and reserve the liquid (or discard, according to the particular recipe) for basting

BONING WINGS

Boned chicken wings can be stuffed with a variety of ingredients and are easier to eat than unboned wings. Smaller wings make excellent barbecued or pan-fried entrees. Use larger wings for main course dishes.

Using a small sharp knife and starting at the drumstick end, slip the knife down the sides of the bone towards the joint, without piercing the skin. Snap the bone free and proceed with the next joint in the same way, taking care not to pierce the elbow. Remove the bones and reshape the wing ready for stuffing.

Starting at the drumstick end, slip the knife down the sides of the bone toward the joint.

Snap the bone free and carefully remove, without piercing the skin.

Slip the knife down the sides of the final bones, remove and reshape the wings.

during cooking and for making a sauce to serve with the finished dish, but make sure any sauces are boiled before serving. Honey or sugar should be used sparingly in marinades as sweet mixtures easily scorch during cooking.

COOKING TECHNIQUES

Chicken must always be eaten thoroughly cooked. To test when roasted, grilled or barbecued poultry is cooked, insert a skewer into the thickest part of the chicken (the thigh). If the juices run clear, the chicken is done. You can also test for doneness by twisting or jiggling the leg. If it moves easily in its socket, the chicken is cooked. Pan-fried, grilled or barbecued chicken is cooked when the meat is tender enough to fall easily off the bone when tested with a fork.

There are two basic cooking methods—using either dry heat or moist heat.

Dry heat cookery comprises oven roasting, barbecuing and grilling, stir-frying and pan-frying. With these methods, timing is important to prevent a tough, dry result.

Moist heat cookery comprises braising, casseroling, pot roasting, poaching and steaming. The less tender cuts are ideal here because they benefit from the long, slow cooking process.

Roasting: Stuff and truss the whole chicken if desired. Preheat the oven and have the chicken ready at room temperature. Use a shallow ovenproof pan that fits the chicken comfortably without squeezing it in. Place the chicken on a wire rack in the pan and pour a little wine or water into the bottom of the pan, if liked, to prevent the chicken from drying out. Brush the chicken all over with melted butter or oil. If the breast is browning too quickly, cover loosely with a piece of aluminium foil. Cook the chicken according to the directions in the recipe, basting occasionally. After roasting, let the chicken rest for 10 minutes, covered loosely with foil, before carving.

Barbecuing: Allow plenty of time for the barbecue to heat up, so that the chicken is cooking over glowing coals rather than flames. The cooking time of the chicken will depend on the thickness of the chicken pieces. There is a tendency for the outside of the chicken to cook too quickly when it is barbecued. If this happens, move the pieces further away from the heat, or brown the outside and then continue cooking, wrapped in aluminium foil. Serve the chicken wrapped in foil to preserve the juices. Brush any unwrapped pieces of chicken with marinade, butter or oil occasionally during cooking to prevent them from drying out.

To roast, place the chicken on a rack in a baking dish and brush with melted butter or oil.

If the juices run clear when a skewer is inserted into the thigh, the chicken is cooked.

To barbecue, place the chicken on a preheated grill and brush with marinade.

CARVING

Let the cooked bird stand for 10 minutes in a warm place, covered loosely with foil. (This rests the meat and makes it easier to carve.) Place on a carving board or secure surface. Using a two-pronged fork to hold the bird and a sharp carving knife, cut around the leg, taking in a reasonable amount of flesh from the sides, firstly cutting through the skin and then using the tip of the knife to separate the bone at the joint. Cut above the wing joint, through the breastbone. Separate the legs by cutting into the thigh and drumstick. Carve breast meat in slices parallel to the rib cage. Place pieces on a warmed serving platter with vegetables or directly onto serving plates. Give each person some white and dark meat.

Cut around the leg, cutting through the skin and then using the tip of the knife to separate the bone.

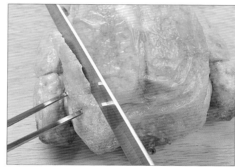
Next, cut the chicken above the wing joint, through the breastbone.

Separate the legs from the thighs by cutting into the thigh and drumstick.

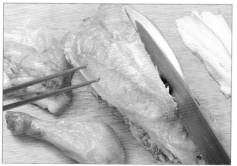
Carve the breast meat in even slices, parallel to the rib cage.

Pan-frying: This method of cooking is best for small, tender chicken pieces. Heat some oil or butter in a heavy-based pan over high heat, add the chicken pieces and cook for 2–3 minutes on each side to brown the chicken and seal in the juices, turning with tongs. Reduce the heat, cover the pan if necessary and cook as directed in the recipe. Do not crowd the pan or the chicken will stew. Use a wide, heavy-based pan or two smaller pans so that the chicken will fit in a single layer rather than trying to fit too much into one pan. If the chicken is cooked without a coating, pat the pieces dry with paper towels before cooking. Put any pieces with a bone in flesh-side first, as the side that cooks first looks the best when serving.

Grilling: Preheat the grill and place the chicken pieces on a cold, oiled grill pan. Arrange the pieces skin-side down and cook about 10 cm (4 inches) from the heat source for 15–20 minutes, then turn and cook the second side until the juices run clear when tested with a skewer. Brush with marinade during cooking to prevent the chicken from drying out. If you are not using a marinade, the chicken can be brushed with butter, herb butter or oil during the cooking process.

Deep-frying: Preheat a deep pan half filled with oil. Test the oil by dropping a square of dry bread into it. If the bread browns within 15 seconds and the oil bubbles and sizzles, it is hot enough for cooking. Chicken pieces should be of equal size so that they will cook at the same time. Dip chicken pieces in flour and/or breadcrumbs, then lower into the hot oil. When cooked, lift out with tongs and drain on paper towels.

Stir-frying: This is the traditional Asian way of cooking meat. This rapid method uses neatly cut strips of chicken, trimmed of fat and sinew. The strips must be evenly cut so that they cook at the same rate. Heat a little oil in a wok or large heavy-based frying pan and swirl it around the pan so that the bottom and side are evenly coated. Stir-fry by tossing the chicken quickly in small batches over high heat until cooked.

To stir-fry, toss even-sized pieces of chicken over high heat in a wok or pan.

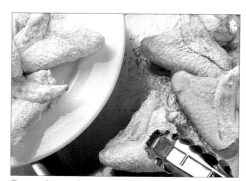
To pan-fry, cook the chicken in a single layer without crowding the pan.

To deep-fry, cook the chicken pieces in hot oil, then remove and drain.

To casserole or braise, chicken is first browned quickly to seal in the juices.

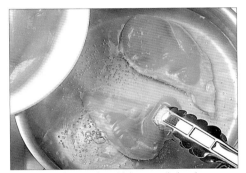

To poach, simmer the chicken gently in wine or water until tender.

Casseroling and braising: This long, slow cooking process brings out the best in chicken, and will transform even a 'tough old bird' into a meltingly delicious dish. The chicken should be gently simmered, never boiled, in the cooking liquid—boiling will make the chicken flesh tough. Brown whole birds or chicken pieces in butter or oil, then transfer to an oven- or flame-proof dish, with vegetables and cooking liquids such as stock and wine. If cooked on top of the stove the dish is covered, brought quickly to the boil, then the heat is reduced to a simmer—small bubbles should gently break the surface. For oven cooking, cover the pot and cook at a temperature low enough to prevent the liquid from boiling.

Poaching: In this method, the chicken is gently simmered in water, stock or wine, sometimes with vegetables and herbs added for flavour. The cooking liquid must never boil. This is a suitable method for cooking large chickens. If using a smaller bird, reduce the cooking time. After cooking, the liquid is strained and used to make a sauce to accompany the chicken or reserved for stock. Because of the low fat content, especially if the skin is removed, poached chicken is ideal for dieters.

TRADITIONAL CHICKEN GRAVY

A rich, delicious gravy to serve with roast chicken is easily achieved. This recipe makes enough gravy to serve 4–6 people. A little white wine, marsala, or chopped fresh herbs or mushrooms can be added to the recipe. Store any leftover gravy separately from chicken, in the refrigerator.

To make gravy: Sprinkle 2 tablespoons plain flour evenly over a baking tray. Place under a hot grill until the flour is golden. Add the flour to the pan juices from the roasting chicken and stir over low heat for 2 minutes. Add 3/4 cup (185 ml/6 fl oz) chicken stock gradually to the pan, stirring until the mixture is smooth. Stir constantly over medium heat for 5 minutes, or until the gravy boils and thickens. Boil for a further 1 minute, then remove from the heat. Pour the gravy into a warmed sauce boat and serve hot with chicken.

CHICKEN STOCK

Many recipes in this book call for chicken stock. This pantry basic is easy to prepare at home and imparts the best flavour to the dishes it is used in.

Chicken stock can be refrigerated or frozen in convenient amounts for up to eight weeks. Fill ice-cube trays with stock and freeze so that you can use a small amount. For recipes that call for large amounts of stock, such as soups or stews, measure the stock into plastic containers, label them and freeze.

Chicken carcasses for making stock can be purchased from butchers and speciality chicken stores. The neck and giblets removed from a whole roasting chicken can also be added for extra flavour.

If light chicken stock is specified in a recipe, dilute the basic stock with one-third water or until it reaches the desired strength.

Chicken stock can be purchased frozen from some speciality chicken shops or packaged in tetra-packs from supermarkets. Tinned consommé can be substituted. Chicken stock cubes and powder are also available.

Chicken Stock
Makes 1 litre

500 g (1 lb) chicken bones
1 large onion, chopped
2 bay leaves
6 peppercorns
1 carrot, chopped
1 celery stick with leaves, chopped
1–1.25 litres water

1 Preheat the oven to moderate 180°C (350°F/Gas 4). Place the chicken bones and onion in a baking dish. Bake for 50 minutes, or until well browned. Transfer to a large pan or stock pot.

2 Wrap the bay leaves and peppercorns in muslin to make a bouquet garni. Add the remaining ingredients with the bouquet garni to the pan. Bring to the boil, then reduce the heat and simmer, uncovered, for 40 minutes, adding a little more water if necessary. Strain the stock, discarding the bones and vegetables. Cool quickly and refrigerate or freeze. After refrigeration, skim any hard fat from the surface. Use the stock as indicated in the recipe.

Bake the chicken bones and onion for 50 minutes, or until well browned.

Add the carrot, celery, water and bouquet garni to the pan with the chicken bones and onion.

Soups

CHICKEN CURRY LAKSA

Preparation time: 30 minutes
Total cooking time: 25 minutes
Serves 4

500 g (1 lb) chicken breast fillets
1 large onion, roughly chopped
5 cm (2 inch) piece ginger, chopped
8 cm (3 inch) piece galangal, peeled
   and chopped
1 stem lemon grass, white part only,
   roughly chopped
2 cloves garlic
1 red chilli, seeded and chopped
2 teaspoons oil
2 tablespoons mild curry paste
2 cups (500 ml/16 fl oz) chicken
   stock
60 g (2 oz) rice vermicelli
50 g (1³/4 oz) dried egg noodles
400 ml (13 fl oz) light coconut milk
10 snow peas, halved
3 spring onions, finely chopped
1 cup (90 g/3 oz) bean sprouts
¹/2 cup (15 g/¹/2 oz) fresh coriander
   leaves

1 Cut the chicken into bite-sized cubes. Process the onion, ginger, galangal, lemon grass, garlic and chilli in a food processor until finely chopped. Add the oil and process until the mixture is a paste-like consistency.

Spoon into a large wok, add the curry paste and stir over low heat for 1–2 minutes, or until aromatic. Take care not to burn the mixture.
2 Increase the heat to medium, add the chicken and stir for 2 minutes, or until the chicken is well coated. Stir in the chicken stock and mix well. Bring slowly to the boil, then simmer for 10 minutes, or until the chicken is cooked through.
3 Meanwhile, cut the vermicelli into shorter lengths using scissors. Cook the vermicelli and egg noodles separately in large pans of boiling water for 5 minutes each. Drain and rinse under cold water.
4 Just prior to serving, add the light coconut milk and snow peas to the chicken mixture and heat through. To serve, divide the vermicelli and noodles among four warmed serving bowls. Pour the hot laksa over the top and garnish with the spring onion, bean sprouts and coriander leaves.

NUTRITION PER SERVE
Protein 30 g; Fat 8 g; Carbohydrate 4.5 g;
Dietary Fibre 3 g; Cholesterol 65 mg;
945 kJ (225 cal)

HINT: If you prefer a more fiery laksa, use a medium or hot brand of curry paste or increase the amount of chilli.

Stir the curry paste into the onion mixture, over low heat, until aromatic.

Just before serving, stir the coconut milk into the chicken mixture until heated.

CREAMY SPINACH AND CHICKEN SOUP

Preparation time: 40 minutes
Total cooking time: 55 minutes
Serves 6

1 tablespoon oil
1 kg (2 lb) chicken pieces
1 carrot, chopped
2 celery sticks, chopped
1 onion, chopped
6 black peppercorns
2 cloves garlic, chopped
1 bouquet garni
800 g (1 lb 10 oz) white sweet potato, chopped

2 bunches (about 500 g/1 lb) English spinach
1/2 cup (125 ml/4 fl oz) cream

1 Heat the oil in a large pan, add the chicken pieces in batches and brown well. Drain on paper towels. Pour off the excess fat, leaving 1 tablespoon in the pan. Return the chicken to the pan with the carrot, celery, onion, peppercorns, garlic, bouquet garni and 1.5 litres of water.
2 Bring the soup to the boil, reduce the heat and simmer for 40 minutes. Strain, returning the stock to the pan. Pull the chicken meat from the bones, shred and set aside.
3 Add the sweet potato to the stock in the pan. Bring to the boil, then reduce the heat and simmer until tender. Add the spinach leaves and cook until wilted. Process in batches in a food processor until finely chopped.
4 Return the spinach to the pan, add the shredded chicken and stir in the cream. Season to taste. Reheat gently before serving but do not allow the soup to boil.

NUTRITION PER SERVE
Protein 40 g; Fat 15 g; Carbohydrate 25 g; Dietary Fibre 4 g; Cholesterol 110 mg; 1720 kJ (410 cal)

To make a bouquet garni, tie parsley, thyme and a bay leaf with string.

Brown the chicken in batches, then drain on paper towels.

Add the spinach leaves to the soup and cook, stirring, until just wilted.

COCK-A-LEEKIE

Preparation time: 10 minutes
   + 2 hours refrigeration
Total cooking time: 1 hour 40 minutes
Serves 4–6

1.5 kg (3 lb) chicken
250 g (8 oz) chicken giblets, optional
   (see Note)
1 onion, sliced
2 litres chicken stock
4 leeks, thinly sliced
1/4 teaspoon ground coriander
pinch nutmeg
1 bouquet garni

12 pitted prunes
pinch cayenne pepper
3 fresh thyme sprigs
fresh thyme sprigs, extra, to serve

1 Put the chicken in a large pan and add the giblets, onion and stock. Bring to the boil, skimming the surface as required. Add the leek, coriander, nutmeg and bouquet garni. Reduce the heat, cover and simmer for 1¼ hours.
2 Remove the chicken and bouquet garni from the pan and lift out the giblets with a slotted spoon. Cool the stock, then refrigerate for 2 hours. Spoon off the fat from the surface and

discard. Remove the chicken meat from the bones and shred. Discard the skin and carcass.
3 Return the chicken to the soup with the prunes, cayenne pepper and thyme. Simmer for 20 minutes. Season to taste and garnish with the extra thyme sprigs.

NUTRITION PER SERVE (6)
Protein 60 g; Fat 6 g; Carbohydrate 7 g;
Dietary Fibre 1 g; Cholesterol 125 mg;
1310 kJ (315 cal)

NOTE: The chicken giblets are optional but will give great flavour.

Trim the ends from the leeks and slice thinly, including some green parts.

Add the chicken stock to the pan with the chicken, giblets (if using) and onion.

Add the cayenne pepper, prunes and thyme sprigs to the soup and stir to combine.

THAI-STYLE CHICKEN AND BABY CORN SOUP

Preparation time: 30 minutes
Total cooking time: 15 minutes
Serves 4

150 g (5 oz) whole baby corn
   (see Note)
1 tablespoon oil
2 stems lemon grass, white part only,
   very thinly sliced
2 tablespoons finely grated fresh
   ginger
6 spring onions, chopped
1 red chilli, finely chopped

1 litre chicken stock
1 1/2 cups (375 ml/12 fl oz) coconut
   milk
250 g (8 oz) chicken breast fillets,
   thinly sliced
130 g (4 1/2 oz) creamed corn
1 tablespoon soy sauce
2 tablespoons finely chopped fresh
   chives, to serve
1 red chilli, thinly sliced, to serve

1 Cut the baby corn in half or quarters lengthways, depending on their size.
2 Heat the oil in a pan over medium heat. Cook the lemon grass, ginger, spring onion and chilli for 1 minute, stirring. Add the stock and coconut milk and bring to the boil—do not cover or the coconut milk will curdle.
3 Stir in the corn, chicken and creamed corn and simmer for 8 minutes, or until the corn and chicken are just tender. Add the soy sauce, season well and serve garnished with the chives and chilli.

NUTRITION PER SERVE
Protein 20 g; Fat 25 g; Carbohydrate 15 g;
Dietary Fibre 3 g; Cholesterol 30 mg;
1520 kJ (360 cal)

NOTE: Canned baby corn can be substituted for fresh corn. Add during the last 2 minutes of cooking.

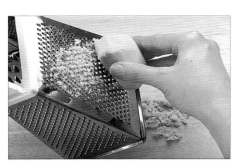

Grate the peeled ginger using the fine side of the grater.

Cut the baby corn lengthways into halves or quarters, depending on size.

Add the baby corn, chicken and creamed corn to the pan.

CHICKEN NOODLE SOUP

Preparation time: 15 minutes
+ 1 hour refrigeration
Total cooking time: 1 hour 20 minutes
Serves 4–6

1.25 kg (2¹/₂ lb) chicken wings
2 celery sticks, chopped
1 carrot, chopped
1 onion, chopped
1 bay leaf
1 fresh thyme sprig
4 fresh parsley sprigs
45 g (1¹/₂ oz) dried fine egg noodles

250 g (8 oz) chicken breast fillets,
    finely chopped
2 tablespoons chopped fresh parsley
chopped fresh chives, to serve

1 Rinse the chicken wings and place in a large pan with the celery, carrot, onion, bay leaf, thyme, parsley, 1 teaspoon salt and 2 litres of water. Bring to the boil slowly, skimming the surface as required. Simmer, covered, for 1 hour. Allow to cool slightly, then strain and discard the chicken and vegetables.
2 Cool the stock further, then cover and refrigerate for at least 1 hour, or

until fat forms on the surface of the stock and can be spooned off.
3 Place the stock in a large pan and bring to the boil. Gently crush the noodles and add to the soup. Return to the boil and simmer for 8 minutes, or until tender. Add the chopped chicken and parsley and simmer for a further 4–5 minutes, or until the chicken is cooked through. Serve topped with the chives.

NUTRITION PER SERVE (6)
Protein 45 g; Fat 8 g; Carbohydrate 8 g;
Dietary Fibre 2 g; Cholesterol 135 mg;
1205 kJ (290 cal)

Using a skimmer or slotted spoon, skim the surface of the stock as required.

Using a spoon, remove the fat that forms on the surface of the chilled stock.

Add the crushed noodles, then simmer for 8 minutes, or until tender.

CHICKEN AND VEGETABLE SOUP

Preparation time: 1 hour +
 refrigeration
Total cooking time: 1 hour 25 minutes
Serves 6–8

1.5 kg (3 lb) chicken
2 carrots, roughly chopped
2 celery sticks, roughly chopped
1 onion, quartered
4 fresh parsley sprigs
2 bay leaves
4 black peppercorns
50 g (1³/4 oz) butter
2 tablespoons plain flour
2 potatoes, chopped
250 g (8 oz) butternut pumpkin, cut
 into bite-sized pieces
2 carrots, extra, cut into matchsticks
1 leek, cut into matchsticks
3 celery sticks, extra, cut into
 matchsticks
100 g (3¹/2 oz) green beans, cut into
 short lengths, or baby green
 beans, halved
200 g (6¹/2 oz) broccoli, cut into small
 florets
100 g (3¹/2 oz) sugar snap peas,
 trimmed
50 g (1³/4 oz) English spinach leaves,
 shredded
¹/2 cup (125 ml/4 fl oz) cream
¹/4 cup (15 g/¹/2 oz) chopped fresh
 parsley

1 Place the chicken in a large pan with the carrot, celery, onion, parsley, bay leaves, 2 teaspoons of salt and the peppercorns. Add 3 litres of water. Bring to the boil, then reduce the heat and simmer for 1 hour, skimming the surface as required. Allow to cool for at least 30 minutes. Strain and reserve the liquid.

2 Remove the chicken and allow to cool until it is cool enough to handle. Discard the skin, then cut or pull the flesh from the bones and shred into small pieces. Set the chicken meat aside.

3 Heat the butter in a large pan over medium heat and, when foaming, add the flour. Cook, stirring, for 1 minute. Remove from the heat and gradually stir in the stock. Return to the heat and bring to the boil, stirring constantly. Add the potato, pumpkin and extra carrot and simmer for 7 minutes. Add the leek, extra celery and beans and simmer for a further 5 minutes. Finally, add the broccoli and sugar snap peas and cook for a further 3 minutes.

4 Just before serving, add the chicken, spinach, cream and chopped parsley. Reheat gently but do not allow the soup to boil. Keep stirring until the spinach has wilted. Season to taste with salt and freshly ground black pepper. Serve the soup immediately.

NUTRITION PER SERVE (8)
Protein 50 g; Fat 15 g; Carbohydrate 15 g;
Dietary Fibre 6 g; Cholesterol 130 mg;
1700 kJ (400 cal)

HINT: Do not overcook the vegetables. They should be tender yet crispy.

NOTE: The chicken stock (up to the end of Step 1) can be made 1 day ahead and kept, covered, in the refrigerator. This can, in fact, be beneficial—before reheating the stock, spoon off the fat which will have formed on the surface.

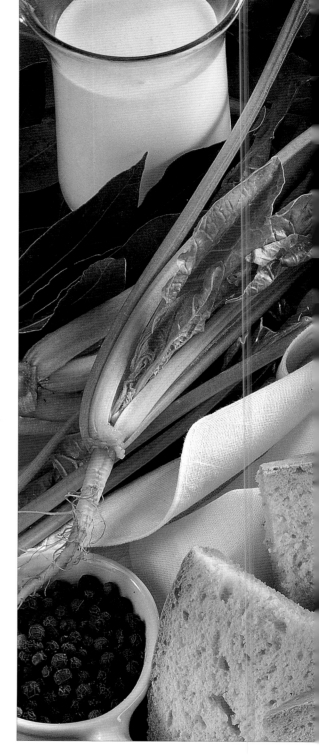

Cut the extra celery into short lengths, then into matchsticks.

Using a knife, trim the tops from the sugar snap peas, pulling down to remove the string.

Add the parsley sprigs and bay leaves to the chicken and vegetables in the pan.

Remove the skin from the cooled chicken, then shred the meat.

Add the potato, pumpkin and extra carrot to the boiling soup.

Pour in the cream and stir until the spinach has just wilted.

LEMON CHICKEN SOUP

Preparation time: 10 minutes
Total cooking time: 10 minutes
Serves 4

2 chicken breast fillets
1 lemon
1 litre chicken stock (see Hint)
2 fresh lemon thyme sprigs, plus extra,
    to serve (see Note)

1 Trim any excess fat from the chicken. Using a vegetable peeler, cut 2 strips of rind from the lemon and remove the pith. Place the stock, rind and lemon thyme in a shallow pan and slowly bring almost to the boil. Reduce to simmering point, add the chicken and cook, covered, for 7 minutes, or until the meat is tender.
2 Remove the chicken from the pan, transfer to a plate and cover with foil.
3 Strain the stock into a clean pan through a sieve lined with 2 layers of damp muslin. Finely shred the chicken and return to the soup. Reheat gently and season to taste with salt and freshly ground black pepper. Serve immediately, garnished with the extra sprigs of lemon thyme.

NUTRITION PER SERVE
Protein 25 g; Fat 3 g; Carbohydrate 0 g;
Dietary Fibre 0 g; Cholesterol 55 mg;
535 kJ (130 cal)

NOTE: You can use ordinary thyme if lemon thyme is not available.

HINT: If you don't have time to make your own stock, poultry shops or butchers sometimes sell their own. These may have more flavour and contain less salt than stock cubes.

Using a small knife, remove the white pith from the lemon rind.

Pour the stock into a clean pan through a sieve lined with damp muslin.

Finely shred the chicken into thin pieces and return to the soup.

FAST CHICKEN NOODLE SOUP

Preparation time: 20 minutes
Total cooking time: 20–25 minutes
Serves 4–6

2.25 litres chicken stock
1¹/₃ cups (235 g/7¹/₂ oz) finely
    shredded cooked chicken
1 cup (90 g/3 oz) broken thin
    noodles

¹/₄ cup (15 g/¹/₂ oz) chopped fresh
    chives
³/₄ cup (45 g/1¹/₂ oz) chopped fresh
    parsley

1 Put the stock in a pan and bring to the boil. Add the shredded chicken.
2 Add the noodles, chives and parsley to the pan and simmer over low heat for 15–20 minutes, or until the chicken is cooked and the noodles are tender. Season with salt and pepper, spoon into bowls and serve immediately.

NUTRITION PER SERVE
Protein 20 g; Fat 5.5 g; Carbohydrate 8 g; Dietary Fibre 1.5 g; Cholesterol 47 mg; 658 kJ (157 cal)

HINTS: The soup must be served as soon as it is ready, otherwise the noodles will soften too much and become soggy.
This soup can also be made very quickly using shredded barbecued chicken and broken 2-minute noodles.

To finely shred the cooked chicken, pull it apart with a fork.

Add the thin noodles to the pan of stock and shredded chicken.

Simmer until the chicken is cooked and the noodles are tender.

CHICKEN AND COUSCOUS SOUP

Preparation time: 25 minutes
Total cooking time: 30 minutes
Serves 6

1 tablespoon olive oil
1 onion, sliced
1/2 teaspoon ground cumin
1/2 teaspoon paprika
1 teaspoon grated fresh ginger
1 clove garlic, crushed
2 celery sticks, sliced
2 small carrots, sliced
2 zucchini, sliced
1.125 litres chicken stock
2 chicken breast fillets, sliced
pinch saffron threads, optional
1/2 cup (95 g/3 oz)
     instant couscous
2 tablespoons chopped
     fresh parsley

1 Heat the oil in a large heavy-based pan. Add the onion and cook over medium heat for 10 minutes, or until very soft, stirring occasionally. Add the cumin, paprika, ginger and garlic and cook, stirring, for 1 minute further.
2 Add the celery, carrot and zucchini and stir to coat with the spices. Stir in the stock. Bring to the boil, then reduce the heat and simmer, partially covered, for about 15 minutes, or until the vegetables are tender.
3 Add the chicken and saffron to the pan and cook for about 5 minutes, or until the chicken is just tender; do not overcook. Stir in the couscous and chopped parsley and serve.

NUTRITION PER SERVE
Protein 19 g; Fat 5.5 g; Carbohydrate 12 g;
Dietary Fibre 2 g; Cholesterol 37 mg;
712 kJ (170 cal)

HINT: Add the couscous to the soup just before serving because it absorbs liquid quickly and becomes very thick.

Add the spices to the pan with the onion and stir to thoroughly combine.

Stir the chicken stock into the vegetable and spice mixture.

Stir the chicken and saffron threads into the soup mixture.

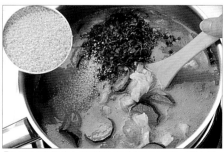

Do not stir in the parsley and couscous until just before the soup is served.

HERBED CHICKEN SOUP

Preparation time: 30 minutes
Total cooking time: 30 minutes
Serves 6

1 chicken breast fillet
1 bay leaf
6 black peppercorns
1 whole clove
4 fresh parsley sprigs
2 tablespoons olive oil
1 onion, finely chopped
1 small carrot, finely chopped
1 celery stick, finely chopped
1 large potato, finely chopped
1 teaspoon finely chopped fresh
    rosemary, or 1/4 teaspoon dried
1 teaspoon chopped fresh thyme, or
    1/2 teaspoon dried
1 teaspoon chopped fresh marjoram,
    or 1/2 teaspoon dried
1 litre chicken stock
310 g (10 oz) can creamed corn
1/4 cup (15 g/1/2 oz) finely chopped
    fresh parsley

1 Trim the chicken breast of excess fat and sinew. Put 2 cups (500 ml/16 fl oz) water in a pan and bring to a simmer. Add the chicken, bay leaf, peppercorns, clove and parsley and cook for 5 minutes, or until the chicken is tender. Remove the chicken from the liquid and cool slightly before shredding. Discard the bay leaf, peppercorns, clove and parsley, and reserve the cooking liquid.
2 Heat the oil in a large, heavy-based pan. Add the onion, carrot and celery and cook over medium heat for 5 minutes, or until the onion is soft. Add the potato, rosemary, thyme and marjoram and cook, stirring, over medium heat for 1 minute.

3 Add the stock and reserved cooking liquid. Season with salt and pepper and bring to the boil. Reduce the heat and simmer for 15 minutes, or until the potato and carrot have softened. Add the creamed corn and shredded chicken and stir for 2 minutes, or until heated through. Stir in the parsley.

NUTRITION PER SERVE
Protein 11 g; Fat 7.5 g; Carbohydrate 15 g;
Dietary Fibre 3 g; Cholesterol 18 mg;
695 kJ (166 cal)

HINT: Use shredded barbecued chicken if you prefer—add extra stock to make up the liquid.

Simmer the chicken breast with the bay leaf, peppercorns, clove and parsley until tender.

Add the potato and herbs to the vegetable mixture and cook over medium heat.

Add the shredded chicken and creamed corn to the soup.

SPICY CHICKEN BROTH WITH CORIANDER PASTA

Preparation time: 40 minutes
Total cooking time: 50 minutes
Serves 4

350 g (11 oz) chicken thighs or wings,
    skin removed
2 carrots, finely chopped
2 celery sticks, finely chopped
2 small leeks, finely chopped
3 egg whites
1.5 litres chicken stock
Tabasco sauce

CORIANDER PASTA
1/2 cup (60 g/2 oz) plain flour
1 egg
1/2 teaspoon sesame oil
small bunch coriander leaves

1 Put the chicken, carrot, celery and leek in a large heavy-based pan. Push the chicken to one side and add the egg whites to the vegetables. Using a wire whisk, beat for 1 minute, or until frothy (take care not to use a pan that can be scratched by the whisk).
2 Warm the stock in another pan, then add gradually to the first pan, whisking constantly to froth the egg whites. Continue whisking while slowly bringing to the boil. Make a hole in the top of the froth with a spoon and leave to simmer, uncovered, for 30 minutes without stirring.
3 Line a large strainer with a damp tea towel or double thickness of muslin and strain the broth into a clean bowl. Discard the chicken pieces and vegetables. Season to taste with salt, ground black pepper and Tabasco sauce. Set aside.

4 To make the coriander pasta, sift the flour into a bowl and make a well in the centre. Whisk the egg and oil together and pour into the well. Mix together to make a soft pasta dough and knead on a lightly floured surface for 2 minutes, or until smooth.
5 Divide the pasta dough into four even portions. Roll one portion out very thinly and cover with a layer of evenly spaced coriander leaves. Roll out another portion of pasta and lay this on top of the leaves, then gently roll the layers together. Repeat with the remaining pasta and coriander.
6 Cut out squares of pasta around the coriander leaves. The pasta may then be left to sit and dry out if it is not needed immediately. Just before serving, heat the chicken broth gently in a saucepan. As the broth simmers, add the pasta and cook for 1 minute. Serve immediately.

NUTRITION PER SERVE
Protein 23 g; Fat 4 g; Carbohydrate 17 g;
Dietary Fibre 3 g; Cholesterol 80 mg;
832 kJ (200 cal)

HINT: Try to use a pasta machine for making this fine, delicate pasta. A rolling pin will suffice, but roll the pasta as thinly as possible.

NOTE: The egg whites make the broth very clear rather than leaving it with the normal cloudy appearance of chicken stock. This is called clarifying the stock. When you strain the broth, don't press the solids to extract the extra liquid or the broth will become cloudy. It is necessary to make a hole in the froth on top to prevent the stock from boiling over.

Use a wire whisk to beat the egg whites with the vegetables.

Use a metal spoon to make a hole in the froth on top of the soup.

Strain the broth through a damp tea towel or double thickness of muslin.

Knead the dough on a lightly floured surface until it is smooth.

Lay a second layer of thin pasta over the coriander leaves.

Cut out neat squares of the pasta around each coriander leaf.

TOM KHA GAI (CHICKEN AND COCONUT SOUP)

Preparation time: 20 minutes
Total cooking time: 20 minutes
Serves 4

5 cm (2 inch) piece galangal (see Hint)
2 cups (500 ml/16 fl oz) coconut milk
1 cup (250 ml/8 fl oz) chicken stock
3 chicken breast fillets, cut into
    thin strips
1–2 teaspoons finely chopped red
    chilli

2 tablespoons fish sauce
1 teaspoon soft brown sugar
1/4 cup (7 g/1/4 oz) fresh coriander
    leaves
fresh coriander sprigs, to serve

1 Peel the galangal and cut it into thin slices. Combine the galangal, coconut milk and stock in a medium pan. Bring to the boil and simmer, uncovered, over low heat for 10 minutes, stirring occasionally.
2 Add the chicken strips and chilli to the pan and simmer for 8 minutes.
3 Stir in the fish sauce and brown sugar. Add the coriander leaves and serve immediately, garnished with the fresh coriander sprigs.

NUTRITION PER SERVE
Protein 40 g; Fat 30 g; Carbohydrate 6.5 g; Dietary Fibre 2.5 g; Cholesterol 83 mg; 1876 kJ (448 cal)

HINT: If fresh galangal is not available, you can use 5 large slices of dried galangal instead. Prepare by soaking the slices in a little boiling water for 10 minutes and then cutting them into shreds. Add the soaking liquid to the chicken stock to make 1 cup (250 ml/ 8 fl oz) and use it in the recipe.

Break the galangal so you have a piece measuring about 5 cm (2 inches).

Add the chicken strips and chilli to the simmering coconut milk mixture.

Just before serving, add the fresh coriander leaves to the pan.

ASIAN CHICKEN AND NOODLE SOUP

Preparation time: 20 minutes
Total cooking time: 25 minutes
Serves 4

CHILLI PASTE
4 dried chillies, roughly chopped
1 teaspoon coriander seeds
1 teaspoon grated fresh ginger
1 spring onion, chopped
1/2 teaspoon ground turmeric

3 cups (750 ml/24 fl oz) coconut milk
350 g (11 oz) chicken breast fillets,
    thinly sliced
2 tablespoons soy sauce
2 cups (500 ml/16 fl oz) chicken stock
400 g (13 oz) dried egg noodles
peanut oil, for deep-frying
spring onion, to serve
red chillies, to serve

1 To make the chilli paste, put the chilli, coriander seeds, ginger, spring onion and turmeric in a small pan. Stir over low heat for 5 minutes, or until fragrant. Transfer to a mortar and pestle or food processor and grind until smooth.
2 Heat 1 cup (250 ml/8 fl oz) of the coconut milk in a pan. Add the chilli paste and stir for 2–3 minutes. Add the chicken and soy sauce and cook for 3–4 minutes. Stir in the remaining coconut milk and the stock. Bring to the boil, then simmer for 10 minutes.
3 Break a quarter of the noodles into large pieces. Fry in the hot peanut oil until crisp, then drain on paper towels. Cook the remaining noodles in boiling water until just tender, then drain.
4 Place the boiled noodles in serving bowls and ladle the soup over the top. Garnish with the fried noodles and serve with spring onion and chilli.

NUTRITION PER SERVE
Protein 35 g; Fat 35 g; Carbohydrate 75 g;
Dietary Fibre 3 g; Cholesterol 60 mg;
2025 kJ (480 cal)

Grind the spices for the chilli paste in a mortar and pestle.

Add the chicken and soy sauce to the pan and stir to combine.

Fry a quarter of the noodles in hot peanut oil until crisp. Drain on paper towels.

Cook the remaining noodles in boiling water until just tender.

MULLIGATAWNY

Preparation time: 30 minutes
Total cooking time: 1 hour 20 minutes
Serves 6

1 kg (2 lb) chicken pieces
2 tablespoons plain flour
2 teaspoons curry powder
1/2 teaspoon ground ginger
1 teaspoon ground turmeric
60 g (2 oz) butter
12 black peppercorns
6 whole cloves
1.5 litres chicken stock
1 large apple, peeled, cored and
    chopped
2 tablespoons lemon juice
1/2 cup (125 ml/4 fl oz) cream
steamed rice, to serve

1 Trim the chicken pieces of excess fat and sinew. Combine the flour, curry powder, ginger and turmeric, and rub into the chicken.

2 Heat the butter in a large pan and cook the chicken until lightly browned on all sides. Tie the peppercorns and cloves in a small piece of muslin and add to the pan with the stock. Bring to the boil, then reduce the heat slightly and simmer, covered, for 1 hour. Add the apple and cook for a further 15 minutes.

3 Remove the chicken from the pan and discard the muslin bag. When cool enough to handle, remove the skin from the chicken and finely shred the flesh. Skim any fat from the surface of the soup.

4 Return the chicken to the pan. Stir in the lemon juice and cream, and heat through gently. Serve with rice.

NUTRITION PER SERVE
Protein 25 g; Fat 25 g; Carbohydrate 10 g;
Dietary Fibre 1 g; Cholesterol 130 mg;
1405 kJ (440 cal)

Combine the flour, curry powder, ginger and turmeric in a bowl.

Tie the cloves and peppercorns together in a piece of muslin.

Remove the skin and bones from the chicken and finely shred the flesh.

Stir the lemon juice and cream into the soup and gently heat through.

ROASTED CAPSICUM AND SMOKED CHICKEN SOUP

Preparation time: 20 minutes
Total cooking time: 30 minutes
Serves 6–8

4 large red capsicums
1 long green chilli
1 tablespoon olive oil
1 large onion, roughly chopped
2 cloves garlic, crushed
1/2 teaspoon cayenne pepper
1 teaspoon ground coriander
1 teaspoon ground cumin
2 litres chicken stock
315 g (10 oz) smoked chicken, cubed
1/4 cup (7 g/1/4 oz) fresh coriander
    leaves
sour cream and tortilla chips, to serve

1 Remove the seeds and membrane from the capsicums and the chilli, and cut into large flattish pieces. Cook, skin-side up, under a hot grill until the skin blackens and blisters. Remove from the heat, place in a plastic bag and leave to cool, then peel away the skin. Roughly chop the capsicum, and finely slice the chilli.

2 Heat the olive oil in a large pan over medium heat. Add the onion and garlic, and fry for 2–3 minutes. Mix in the cayenne pepper, coriander and cumin and cook for a further 1 minute, stirring constantly. Add the stock, roasted capsicum and chilli and bring to the boil. Reduce the heat and simmer gently for 15 minutes.

3 Remove from the heat, leave to cool slightly, then purée in a blender or food processor in batches until it becomes a smooth soup. Return the soup to the pan.

4 Reheat the soup over medium heat for 10 minutes. Stir in the chicken and season with pepper. When the soup is hot and ready to serve, add the coriander leaves. Ladle the soup into serving bowls and top each with sour cream. Serve with the tortilla chips.

NUTRITION PER SERVE (8)
Protein 35 g; Fat 30 g; Carbohydrate 20 g;
Dietary Fibre 5 g; Cholesterol 155 mg;
2120 kJ (505 cal)

When the capsicum has cooled, peel away the blackened skin with your fingers.

Add the stock, roasted chopped capsicum and chilli to the pan.

Reduce the heat and simmer the mixture gently for 15 minutes.

Transfer the mixture to a food processor in batches and purée until smooth.

CHINESE MUSHROOM AND CHICKEN SOUP

Preparation time: 20 minutes +
  10 minutes soaking
Total cooking time: 10 minutes
Serves 4

3 dried Chinese mushrooms
185 g (6 oz) thin dried egg noodles
1 tablespoon oil
4 spring onions, julienned
1 tablespoon soy sauce
2 tablespoons rice wine, mirin or
  sherry (see Note)
1.25 litres chicken stock
1/2 small barbecued chicken,
  shredded

50 g (1³/4 oz) sliced ham, cut into
  strips
1 cup (90 g/3 oz) bean sprouts
fresh coriander leaves, to serve
thinly sliced red chilli, to serve

1 Soak the mushrooms in boiling water for 10 minutes to soften them. Squeeze dry then remove the tough stem from the mushrooms and slice them thinly.
2 Cook the noodles in a large pan of boiling water for 3 minutes, or according to the manufacturer's directions. Drain and cut the noodles into shorter lengths with scissors.
3 Heat the oil in a large heavy-based pan. Add the mushrooms and spring onion. Cook for 1 minute, then add

the soy sauce, rice wine and stock. Bring slowly to the boil and cook for 1 minute. Reduce the heat then add the noodles, shredded chicken, ham and bean sprouts. Heat through for 2 minutes without allowing the soup to boil.
4 Use tongs to divide the noodles among four bowls, ladle in the remaining mixture, and garnish with coriander leaves and sliced chilli.

NUTRITION PER SERVE
Protein 25 g; Fat 10 g; Carbohydrate 35 g;
Dietary Fibre 3 g; Cholesterol 80 mg;
1426 kJ (340 cal)

NOTE: Rice wine and mirin are available at Asian food stores.

Use a fork to shred the meat from the barbecued chicken.

Put the mushrooms in a bowl, cover with boiling water and leave to soak.

Cut the noodles into shorter lengths to make them easier to eat.

CHICKEN AND CORN SOUP

Preparation time: 15 minutes
Total cooking time: 20 minutes
Serves 6

3 corn cobs
1 tablespoon oil
4 spring onions, finely chopped
2 teaspoons grated fresh ginger
1 litre chicken stock
1 tablespoon rice wine, mirin or sherry
1 tablespoon soy sauce
1/2 small barbecued chicken, shredded

1 tablespoon cornflour
1 teaspoon sesame oil
420 g (13 oz) can creamed corn
fresh thyme sprigs, to garnish

1 Cut the corn kernels from the cobs—you will need about 2 cups (400 g/13 oz). Heat the oil in a large pan, and add the spring onion and ginger. Cook for 1 minute, or until softened, then add the corn, stock, rice wine and soy sauce. Bring slowly to the boil, then reduce the heat and simmer for 10 minutes, or until the corn is cooked through. Add the chicken.
2 In a bowl, blend the cornflour with 3 tablespoons water or stock to make

a smooth paste. Add to the soup with the sesame oil and simmer, stirring constantly, until slightly thickened. Stir in the creamed corn and heat for 2–3 minutes without allowing to boil. Season and serve hot, garnished with the thyme sprigs.

NUTRITION PER SERVE
Protein 14 g; Fat 8 g; Carbohydrate 30 g; Dietary Fibre 5 g; Cholesterol 45 mg; 1077 kJ (255 cal)

NOTE: If fresh corn is unavailable, use a 440 g (14 oz) can of drained corn kernels.

Use a fork to shred the meat from the barbecued chicken.

Remove the husks from the corn cobs and cut off the kernels.

Blend the cornflour and water or stock to make a smooth paste.

JUNGLE SOUP

Preparation time: 10 minutes
Total cooking time: 35 minutes
Serves 4

2 teaspoons oil
1 medium onion, finely sliced
225 g (7 oz) butternut pumpkin,
    peeled and diced
225 g (7 oz) fresh pineapple or
    mango, chopped
1 clove garlic, crushed
1 dried red chilli, finely chopped

2 teaspoons grated fresh ginger
1 litre chicken stock
2 tablespoons lime juice
350 g (11 oz) chicken breast fillet, cut
    diagonally into thin strips
chopped fresh coriander, to serve
chilli sauce, to serve

1 Heat the oil in a large heavy-based pan and cook the onion over medium heat for 5 minutes, or until golden brown. Add the pumpkin to the pan and cook for a further 5 minutes, or until just browned. Add the pineapple, garlic, chilli and ginger and toss the contents of the pan together.

2 Add the stock and lime juice, bring to the boil, then reduce the heat to simmer for 20 minutes, or until the pumpkin is nearly tender.

3 Add the chicken to the soup and simmer for a further 5 minutes, or until the chicken is cooked through. Serve immediately, garnished with the chopped coriander and chilli sauce.

NUTRITION PER SERVE
Protein 22 g; Fat 5 g; Carbohydrate 10 g;
Dietary Fibre 2.5 g; Cholesterol 44 mg;
743 kJ (178 cal)

Peel the pineapple and chop the flesh into bite-sized pieces.

Add the pumpkin to the onion in the pan and cook until browned,

Use two wooden spoons to toss the contents of the pan together.

CREAM OF CHICKEN AND VEGETABLE SOUP

Preparation time: 20 minutes
Total cooking time: 1 hour 45 minutes
Serves 6

STOCK
1.1 kg (2 lb 3¹/₂ oz) chicken
¹/₂ celery stick, chopped
6 peppercorns
1 bay leaf
1 clove garlic, chopped
1 small onion, chopped

1 tablespoon oil
1 onion, sliced
1 carrot, cut into matchsticks
200 g (6¹/₂ oz) button mushrooms, sliced

¹/₄ cup (30 g/1 oz) plain flour
²/₃ cup (170 ml/5¹/₂ fl oz) milk
1 cup (250 ml/8 fl oz) cream
100 g (3¹/₂ oz) snow peas, thinly sliced
3 tomatoes, peeled, seeded and chopped
1 tablespoon soy sauce

1 To make the stock, remove any excess fat from the chicken. Pat the chicken dry with paper towels. Cut the chicken into breast, thigh, leg and wing pieces. Pour 1.5 litres water into a large heavy-based pan and add the celery, peppercorns, bay leaf, garlic, onion and chicken pieces. Bring to the boil, then reduce the heat and simmer, covered, for 1¹/₄ hours. Remove from the heat and cool slightly. Strain the stock, reserving the chicken and discarding the onion mixture.

2 Heat the oil in a large heavy-based pan. Add the onion, carrot and mushrooms and cook, stirring, over low heat until the onion is tender. Stir in 1.125 litres of the stock and the combined flour and milk. Bring to the boil. Reduce the heat and simmer, stirring, until the soup is slightly thickened.

3 Cut the reserved chicken into thin strips. Add the chicken, cream, snow peas, tomato and soy sauce to the soup. Stir until heated through, then season to taste.

NUTRITION PER SERVE
Protein 44 g; Fat 26 g; Carbohydrate 12 g;
Dietary Fibre 3.5 g; Cholesterol 144 mg;
1915 kJ (457 cal)

Cut the chicken into pieces using a pair of poultry shears.

Add the onion, carrot and mushrooms to the pan and cook until tender.

Add the soy sauce to the soup and stir until heated through.

Starters & Snacks

CHICKEN TIKKA

Preparation time: 30 minutes
  + overnight marinating
Total cooking time: 15 minutes
Makes 10 skewers

1/4 onion, chopped
2 cloves garlic, crushed
1 tablespoon grated fresh ginger
2 tablespoons lemon juice
1 teaspoon grated lemon rind
3 teaspoons ground coriander
3 teaspoons ground cumin
3 teaspoons garam masala
1/3 cup (90 g/3 oz) plain yoghurt
1 teaspoon salt
750 g (1 1/2 lb) chicken thigh fillets, cut
    into cubes

1 Soak 10 wooden skewers in water for 30 minutes to prevent burning.
2 In a food processor, finely chop the onion, garlic, ginger, lemon juice, rind, coriander, cumin and garam masala. Stir in the yoghurt and salt.
3 Thread 4–5 chicken cubes onto each skewer and place in a large shallow dish. Coat the skewers with the spice mixture. Marinate for several hours or overnight, covered, in the refrigerator.
4 Cook the skewers in batches on a barbecue or chargrill pan, or under a hot grill, for 3–4 minutes on each side, or until golden brown and cooked.

NUTRITION PER SKEWER
Protein 15 g; Fat 4 g; Carbohydrate 1 g;
Dietary Fibre 0 g; Cholesterol 55 mg;
420 kJ (100 cal)

Soak the skewers in water so that they do not burn during cooking.

Finely chop the onion, garlic, ginger, lemon juice, lemon rind and spices in a food processor.

Take the skewers and thread 4–5 pieces of chicken onto each one.

Cook the skewers for 3–4 minutes on each side, or until golden brown.

CHICKEN LIVER PATE WITH PISTACHIO NUTS AND PROSCIUTTO

Preparation time: 20 minutes +
    3 hours refrigeration
Total cooking time: 15 minutes
Serves 10

6 very thin slices prosciutto
2 tablespoons butter
1/4 cup (60 ml/2 fl oz) olive oil
80 g (2 3/4 oz) finely diced bacon
1 onion, finely chopped
2 cloves garlic, crushed
500 g (1 lb) chicken livers
3 bay leaves
1/3 cup (80 ml/2 3/4 fl oz) sherry or
    brandy
125 g (4 oz) butter, extra, softened
1/3 cup (50 g/1 3/4 oz) pistachio nuts,
    toasted

1 Line a 1.5 litre loaf tin with foil. Then line with the prosciutto so that it hangs over the sides, making sure each slice overlaps. Heat the butter and oil and cook the bacon, onion and garlic for 5–6 minutes, or until the onion is softened but not browned.
2 Trim the chicken livers of any fat and veins. Add them to the pan with the bay leaves. Increase the heat to hot and cook for 3–4 minutes, or until the livers are brown on the outside, but still pink on the inside.
3 Add the sherry and simmer, stirring, for 3 minutes, or until the liquid has almost disappeared. Remove the bay leaves. Process the mixture in a food processor until very fine. Gradually add the butter and blend until smooth. Season, then stir in the pistachios.
4 Spoon the pâté mixture into the tin and fold the prosciutto over to enclose it. Refrigerate for at least 3 hours before serving. Cut into slices to serve.

NUTRITION PER SERVE
Protein 4 g; Fat 20 g; Carbohydrate 2 g;
Dietary Fibre 0.5 g; Cholesterol 48 mg;
938 kJ (224 cal)

NOTE: The flavour, colour and texture of the pâté will improve after 2 days, and it will also become easier to slice. Keep refrigerated for 3–4 days.

Line the loaf tin with the prosciutto with each slice overlapping.

Remove the fat and veins from the chicken livers before cooking.

Add the sherry and simmer until most of the liquid has disappeared.

Stir the toasted pistachio nuts through the chicken liver mixture.

POTTED CHICKEN

Preparation time: 15 minutes
    + 2 hours refrigeration
Total cooking time: 1 hour
Serves 6

6 chicken thighs, skin removed
1 onion, sliced
1 carrot, sliced
6 peppercorns
1 bay leaf
pinch ground mace
pinch cayenne pepper
$1/4$ teaspoon freshly grated nutmeg
200 g ($6^1/2$ oz) unsalted butter,
    softened

1 Place the chicken thighs, onion, carrot, peppercorns and bay leaf in a pan and add 2 cups (500 ml/16 fl oz) of water. Bring to the boil, skimming off any foam. Reduce the heat, then cover and simmer for 30 minutes, or until the chicken is tender and cooked through.
2 Remove the chicken, then rapidly boil the remaining liquid until it has reduced to about $1/4$ cup (60 ml/ 2 fl oz). Strain through a fine sieve and allow to cool.
3 Remove the chicken flesh from the bones. Place the flesh in a food processor with the liquid and process until smooth. Add the mace, cayenne pepper, nutmeg and 150 g (5 oz) of the butter. Season to taste with salt and pepper and process until combined and smooth.
4 Put the chicken mixture in a 3-cup (750 ml/24 fl oz) ceramic dish. Melt the remaining butter in a small pan and pour the yellow clarified butter onto the surface of the chicken, leaving the white milk solids in the pan. Refrigerate for 2 hours, or until the butter sets.

NUTRITION PER SERVE
Protein 25 g; Fat 30 g; Carbohydrate 1.5 g; Dietary Fibre 0.5 g; Cholesterol 140 mg; 1590 kJ (380 cal)

Strain the liquid through a fine sieve and leave to cool.

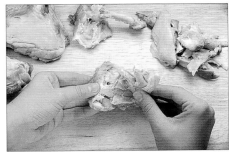

When cool enough to handle, pull the chicken flesh off the bones.

Process the chicken flesh with the butter and spices until smooth.

Carefully pour the yellow clarified butter over the potted chicken.

PUMPKIN AND PESTO CHICKEN IN FILO PASTRY

Preparation time: 30 minutes
Total cooking time: 50 minutes
Serves 4

4 chicken breast fillets
1 tablespoon oil
250 g (8 oz) pumpkin
1 bunch English spinach
12 sheets filo pastry
100 g (3^1/$_2$ oz) butter, melted
^{1}/$_4$ cup (25 g/^{3}/$_4$ oz) dry breadcrumbs
100 g (3^1/$_2$ oz) ricotta
^{1}/$_3$ cup (90 g/3 oz) pesto (see Note)
1 tablespoon pine nuts, chopped

1 Preheat the oven to moderately hot 200°C (400°F/Gas 6). Season the chicken fillets with salt and pepper. Heat half the oil in a frying pan and fry the chicken until browned on both sides, then remove from the pan.
2 Cut the peeled pumpkin into 5 mm (^{1}/$_4$ inch) slices. Heat the remaining oil in the same pan and fry the pumpkin until lightly browned on both sides. Allow to cool.
3 Put the spinach leaves into a bowl of boiling water and stir until just wilted. Drain well and pat dry with paper towels. Layer 3 sheets of filo pastry, brushing each with some of the melted butter, sprinkling between layers with some of the breadcrumbs.
4 Wrap each chicken breast in a quarter of the spinach and place on one short side of the filo, leaving a 2 cm (^{3}/$_4$ inch) gap. Top the chicken with a quarter of the pumpkin slices, then spread a quarter of the ricotta down the centre of the pumpkin. Top with a tablespoon of the pesto.

5 Fold the sides of the pastry over the filling, then roll the parcel up until it sits on the unsecured end. Repeat with the remaining ingredients. Place the parcels on a lightly greased baking tray, brush with any remaining butter and sprinkle with the pine nuts. Bake for 15 minutes, then cover loosely with foil and bake for a further 20 minutes, or until the pastry is golden brown.

NUTRITION PER SERVE
Protein 35 g; Fat 40 g; Carbohydrate 30 g; Dietary Fibre 2.5 g; Cholesterol 132 mg; 2635 kJ (630 cal)

NOTE: Bottled pesto is not suitable for this recipe—you can either make your own or use fresh pesto from a delicatessen.

Remove the spinach from the bowl of boiling water and drain well.

Top the chicken breast fillet with a quarter of the pumpkin slices.

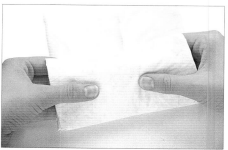

Fold the sides of the pastry over the filling, then roll up until it sits on the unsecured end.

THAI CHICKEN BALLS

Preparation time: 20 minutes
Total cooking time: 40 minutes
Serves 6

1 kg (2 lb) chicken mince
1 cup (80 g/2³⁄₄ oz) fresh
    breadcrumbs
4 spring onions, sliced
1 tablespoon ground coriander
1 cup (50 g/1³⁄₄ oz) chopped fresh
    coriander
¹⁄₄ cup (60 ml/2 fl oz) sweet chilli sauce

1–2 tablespoons lemon juice
oil, for frying

1 Preheat the oven to moderately hot 200°C (400°F/Gas 6). Mix the mince and breadcrumbs in a large bowl.
2 Add the spring onion, ground and fresh coriander, chilli sauce and lemon juice, and mix well. Using damp hands, form the mixture into evenly shaped balls that are either small enough to eat with your fingers or large enough to use as burgers.
3 Heat the oil in a deep frying pan, and shallow-fry the chicken balls in

batches over high heat until browned all over. Place the chicken balls on a baking tray and bake until cooked through. (The small chicken balls will take 5 minutes to cook and the larger ones will take 10–15 minutes.) This mixture also makes a delicious filling for sausage rolls.

NUTRITION PER SERVE
Protein 40 g; Fat 8 g; Carbohydrate 10 g; Dietary Fibre 1 g; Cholesterol 85 mg; 1160 kJ (275 cal)

Mix the spring onion, coriander, chilli sauce and lemon juice into the chicken mixture.

With damp hands, form the mixture into evenly shaped balls.

Fry the chicken balls in oil until they are browned on both sides.

CHICKEN QUESADILLAS

Preparation time: 45 minutes
  + 1 hour marinating
Total cooking time: 20–30 minutes
Serves 4

4 large green chillies
3 large red chillies
2 chicken breast fillets
3 tablespoons wholegrain mustard
2 tablespoons honey
4 flour tortillas
3 cups (375 g/12 oz) grated Cheddar
6 spring onions, thinly sliced
1–2 small red chillies, thinly sliced,
    optional
1–2 small green chillies, thinly sliced,
    optional
oilve oil, for cooking

GREEN CHILLI SALSA
3 long green chillies, thinly sliced
2 tomatoes, peeled, seeded and
    chopped
1 onion, finely chopped
1/3 cup (10 g/1/4 oz) fresh coriander
    leaves, finely chopped
2 tablespoons lime juice

1 Place the large chillies under a hot grill and cook for 5–8 minutes, turning frequently, until the skins are blackened. Place the chillies in a plastic bag and leave to cool. Remove the skin and seeds. Cut them in half, then slice the flesh into thin strips.
2 Place the chicken in a deep dish. Combine the mustard and honey and add to the chicken. Turn the meat until well coated with the mixture. Cover and refrigerate for 1 hour. Place the chicken under a hot grill and cook for 4 minutes each side, or until tender.

Cool slightly, then cut into thin strips.
3 To make the green chilli salsa, combine the chilli, tomato, onion, coriander and lime juice in a bowl and mix well, adding a little more lime juice if desired. Set aside to allow the flavours to combine.
4 Lightly grease a large, heavy-based frying pan and warm over medium heat. Place one tortilla in the pan and sprinkle with a quarter of the Cheddar and half the spring onion, roasted chilli, chicken and sliced chilli. Sprinkle with a third of the remaining Cheddar and top with another tortilla.
5 Brush lightly with a little oil, invert the quesadilla onto a plate and then slide back into the pan so that the top becomes the bottom. Cook for a few minutes longer, just until the Cheddar has melted and the underside looks golden and crisp. Slide the quesadilla onto a plate and keep warm.
6 Repeat with another tortilla, adding half of the remaining Cheddar, the remaining spring onion, roasted chilli, chicken and sliced chilli. Top with the rest of the Cheddar and the last tortilla. Serve immediately, cut into halves or triangles, with the salsa.

NUTRITION PER SERVE
Protein 45 g; Fat 35 g; Carbohydrate 40 g;
Dietary Fibre 5 g; Cholesterol 125 mg;
2665 kJ (635 cal)

NOTE: Flour tortillas are available from most supermarkets, in the bread section—they may need trimming slightly to fit in the frying pan.

Remove the blackened skins from the grilled, cooled chillies.

Turn the chicken to coat well with the mustard and honey mixture.

Combine all the salsa ingredients in a bowl and mix well.

Sprinkle one of the tortillas with a quarter of the grated Cheddar.

Cover the Cheddar, chicken, chilli and spring onion filling with another tortilla.

Invert the quesadilla onto a plate, then slide it back into the pan.

LEMON GRASS CHICKEN SKEWERS

Preparation time: 20 minutes
  + overnight marinating
Total cooking time: 15–20 minutes
Serves 4

4 chicken thigh fillets (400 g/13 oz)
1¹/₂ tablespoons soft brown
    sugar
1¹/₂ tablespoons lime juice
2 teaspoons green curry
    paste
18 kaffir lime leaves
2 stems lemon grass

MANGO SALSA
1 small mango, finely diced
1 teaspoon grated lime rind
2 teaspoons lime juice
1 teaspoon soft brown sugar
¹/₂ teaspoon fish sauce

1 Discard any excess fat from the chicken and cut in half lengthways. Combine the sugar, lime juice, curry paste and 2 of the kaffir lime leaves, shredded, in a bowl. Add the chicken and mix well. Cover and refrigerate for several hours or overnight.
2 Trim the lemon grass to 20 cm (8 inches), leaving the root end intact. Cut each stem lengthways into four pieces. Cut a slit in each of the remaining lime leaves and thread one onto each piece of lemon grass. Cut two slits in each piece of chicken and thread onto the lemon grass, followed by another lime leaf. Pan-fry or barbecue until cooked through.
3 To make the mango salsa, put the mango, lime rind, juice, sugar and fish sauce in a bowl and stir gently to combine. Serve with the lemon grass skewers.

NUTRITION PER SERVE
Protein 25 g; Fat 2.5 g; Carbohydrate 15 g;
Dietary Fibre 1 g; Cholesterol 50 mg;
710 kJ (170 cal)

Discard any excess fat from the chicken thighs and cut in half lengthways.

Cut each trimmed lemon grass stem lengthways into four pieces.

Thread a lime leaf, then the chicken and another lime leaf onto the lemon grass.

NEW POTATO, CHICKEN AND SPINACH FRITTATA

Preparation time: 30 minutes
Total cooking time: 1 hour 5 minutes
Serves 4–6

600 g (1¼ lb) new potatoes,
    unpeeled, sliced about 1 cm
    (½ inch) thick
oil, for brushing
1 small barbecued chicken
500 g (1 lb) English spinach leaves,
    stalks removed
125 g (4 oz) feta, crumbled
½ cup (50 g/1¾ oz) grated
    Parmesan
½ cup (15 g/½ oz) basil leaves,
    chopped
10 eggs, lightly beaten
12 semi-dried tomato quarters

1 Preheat the oven to moderate 180°C (350°F/Gas 4). Put the potato in a greased ovenproof dish, brush all over with a little oil and bake for 30 minutes, or until cooked. Turn the potato once or twice during baking. Allow to cool.
2 Remove the skin from the chicken, pull the flesh from the bones and roughly chop the meat.
3 Wash the spinach, put in a large pan, cover and steam for 2 minutes to wilt slightly. Drain and allow to cool, then squeeze out the moisture and chop. Mix with the chicken and stir in the feta, Parmesan and basil. Season with salt and pepper, to taste.
4 Brush a 24 cm (9½ inch) diameter non-stick pan with a little oil. Arrange half the potato slices over the base and spread half the chicken mixture on top, then repeat the layers. Season the beaten egg and pour over the top.

Arrange the tomato quarters on top. Cook over low heat for 25 minutes, or until the centre is almost cooked. Take care not to burn the base. Heat the frittata under a preheated grill for 7 minutes, or until set. Cut the

frittata into wedges to serve.

NUTRITION PER SERVE (6)
Protein 40 g; Fat 25 g; Carbohydrate15 g;
Dietary Fibre 4 g; Cholesterol 375 mg;
2080 kJ (500 cal)

Steam the spinach leaves for 2 minutes, then squeeze out all the moisture.

Build up the layers of sliced potato and chicken filling in the pan.

Place the frittata under a preheated grill until it has set.

YAKITORI

Preparation time: 20 minutes
  + soaking
Total cooking time: 10 minutes
Makes 25 skewers

1 kg (2 lb) chicken thigh fillets
1/2 cup (125 ml/4 fl oz) sake
3/4 cup (185 ml/6 fl oz) shoyu
   (Japanese soy sauce)
1/2 cup (125 ml/4 fl oz) mirin
2 tablespoons sugar
10 spring onions, diagonally cut into
   2 cm (3/4 inch) pieces

1 Soak 25 wooden skewers in water for about 20 minutes to prevent burning. Drain and set aside.
2 Cut the chicken thigh fillets into bite-sized pieces. Combine the sake, shoyu, mirin and sugar in a small pan. Bring the mixture to the boil and then set aside.
3 Thread the chicken pieces onto the wooden skewers alternately with the spring onion pieces. Place the chicken skewers on a foil-lined tray and cook them under a preheated grill, turning and brushing frequently with the sauce, for 7–8 minutes, or until the chicken is cooked through. Serve

immediately, garnished with a few spring onion pieces.

NUTRITION PER SKEWER
Protein 9.5 g; Fat 1 g; Carbohydrate 3 g;
Dietary Fibre 0 g; Cholesterol 20 mg;
270 kJ (64 cal)

NOTE: In Japan, Yakitori is usually served as a snack with beer. The addition of steamed rice and your favourite vegetables turns these delicious kebabs into a satisfying meal.

Use a sharp knife to cut the chicken thigh fillets into bite-sized pieces.

Thread the chicken pieces and spring onion alternately onto the skewers.

Frequently brush the chicken with the sauce as it cooks.

CHICKEN SATAY WITH PEANUT SAUCE

Preparation time: 40 minutes
 + 30 minutes marinating
Total cooking time: 15–20 minutes
Serves 4

500 g (1 lb) chicken thigh fillets, trimmed
1 onion, roughly chopped
2 stems lemon grass, white part only, thinly sliced
4 cloves garlic
2 red chillies, chopped
2 teaspoons ground coriander
1 teaspoon ground cumin
1/2 teaspoon salt
1 tablespoon soy sauce
1/4 cup (60 ml/2 fl oz) oil
1 tablespoon soft brown sugar
cucumber slices, to serve
chopped roasted peanuts, to serve

PEANUT SAUCE
1/2 cup (125 g/4 oz) crunchy peanut butter
1 cup (250 ml/8 fl oz) coconut milk
1–2 tablespoons sweet chilli sauce
1 tablespoon soy sauce
2 teaspoons lemon juice

1 Soak 20 wooden skewers in cold water for 30 minutes. Cut the chicken into thick flattish strips. Thread a strip of chicken onto each skewer, flattening it on the skewer.
2 Process the onion, lemon grass, garlic, chilli, coriander, cumin, salt and soy sauce in a food processor, in short bursts, until smooth, adding a little oil to assist the processing. Spread the lemon grass mixture over the chicken, cover and refrigerate for 30 minutes.
3 To make the peanut sauce, put the peanut butter, coconut milk, sweet chilli sauce, soy sauce and lemon juice in a heavy-based pan with 1/2 cup (125 ml/4 fl oz) water. Stir over low heat until the mixture boils. Remove from the heat. The sauce will thicken on standing.
4 Heat a chargrill or barbecue flatplate until very hot and brush with the remaining oil. Cook the chicken for 2–3 minutes on each side, sprinkling with a little oil and brown sugar (this will help produce a lovely flavour and colour). Serve topped with the peanut sauce and garnished with the cucumber and peanuts. Serve the remaining peanut sauce as a dipping sauce.

Thread one chicken strip onto each skewer, flattening it out on the skewer.

Add a little oil to the lemon grass paste to assist the processing.

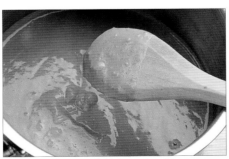

The peanut sauce will thicken when it has been standing.

During cooking, sprinkle the chicken with oil and brown sugar.

NUTRITION PER SERVE
Protein 40 g; Fat 45 g; Carbohydrate 14 g; Dietary Fibre 6 g; Cholesterol 60 mg; 2600 kJ (620 cal)

CHICKEN CURRY PUFFS

Preparation time: 1 hour 30 minutes
Total cooking time: 35–45 minutes
Makes about 36

2 tablespoons oil
400 g (13 oz) chicken mince
2 cloves garlic, crushed
1 onion, finely chopped
3 coriander roots, finely chopped
2 teaspoons ground turmeric
1 1/2 teaspoons ground cumin
3 teaspoons ground coriander
1 small potato, peeled and
    very finely diced
1 tablespoon chopped fresh coriander
    leaves and stems
3 teaspoons soft brown sugar
1/2 teaspoon ground black pepper
2 small red chillies, finely chopped
1/4 cup (60 ml/2 fl oz) fish sauce
1 tablespoon lime juice
oil, extra, for deep-frying
chilli sauce or satay sauce, to serve

PASTRY
1 1/2 cups (185 g/6 oz) plain flour
1/2 cup (90 g/3 oz) rice flour
1/2 teaspoon salt
60 g (2 oz) butter
1/2 cup (125 ml/4 fl oz) coconut milk

1 Heat the oil in a medium wok or pan. Add the mince and cook over high heat for 3 minutes, or until starting to brown. Break up any lumps of mince as it cooks. Add the crushed garlic, onion, coriander roots, ground turmeric, cumin and coriander, and the potato to the wok. Stir-fry over medium heat for about 5 minutes, or until the mince and potato are tender.
2 Add the fresh coriander, sugar, pepper, chilli, fish sauce and lime juice. Stir until well combined and most of the liquid has evaporated, then remove from the heat and allow to cool.
3 To make the pastry, sift the flours and salt into a medium bowl and rub in the butter until the mixture is fine and crumbly. Make a well in the centre, add the coconut milk and mix with a knife until the mixture forms a dough. Gently knead until the dough is smooth. Cover with plastic wrap and refrigerate for 30 minutes.
4 Divide the dough in half. Roll out one half on a lightly floured surface until it is about 3 mm (1/8 inch) thick and then cut into circles with an 8 cm (3 inch) cutter.
5 Place 2 teaspoons of the filling in the centre of each circle, brush the edges of the pastry lightly with water and fold over to enclose the filling; press the edges to seal. Repeat with the remaining half of the dough, re-rolling the scraps until the dough and the filling are all used.
6 Heat the oil in a large wok or pan. Do not put too much oil in the wok—it should be only half full. Deep-fry the puffs, in batches, until puffed and browned. Remove from oil with a wire mesh drainer, slotted spoon or tongs; drain on paper towels. Serve hot with chilli sauce or satay sauce.

NUTRITION PER SERVE (6)
Protein 3.5 g; Fat 4 g; Carbohydrate 7 g;
Dietary Fibre 0.5 g; Cholesterol 10 mg;
335 kJ (80 cal)

HINT: If time is short, use about eight sheets of ready-rolled puff pastry instead of making the pastry.

Use a spoon or fork to break up any lumps of mince as it cooks.

Stir the ingredients in the wok until well combined and the liquid has evaporated.

Add the coconut milk and mix with a knife until the mixture forms a dough.

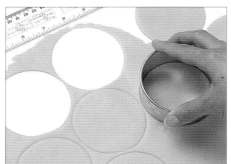

Cut the rolled out dough into circles, using an 8 cm (3 inch) cutter.

Fold the pastry over to enclose the filling and then press the edges to seal.

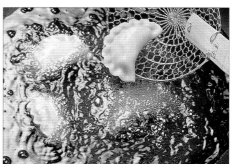

Add the curry puffs to the hot oil, cooking only a few at a time.

SAN CHOY BAU

Preparation time: 1 hour
  + 30 minutes soaking
Total cooking time: 10 minutes
Serves 4

8 dried Chinese mushrooms
1 small iceberg lettuce, washed
500 g (1 lb) chicken mince
1 tablespoon soy sauce
1 tablespoon oil
1/4 cup (40 g/1 1/4 oz) pine nuts
1 teaspoon minced garlic
4 spring onions, finely chopped
10 water chestnuts, chopped

SAUCE
3 teaspoons caster sugar
1 tablespoon bean paste
3 teaspoons cornflour
1 tablespoon oyster sauce
1/2 cup (125 ml/4 fl oz) chicken stock
    or water

1 Soak the mushrooms in hot water for 30 minutes. Drain, then squeeze to remove the excess liquid. Remove the stems and thinly slice the caps. Refrigerate the lettuce to crisp it.

2 Place the chicken in a bowl and stir in the soy sauce. Heat the oil in a wok, add the pine nuts and cook over medium heat until golden. Drain on paper towels. Add the garlic to the wok and cook gently until it is pale gold. Add the chicken mixture and cook over high heat, breaking up any lumps, for about 5 minutes, or until cooked through. Stir the mixture occasionally. Add the spring onion, mushrooms and water chestnuts, and cook for 1 minute.

3 To make the sauce, whisk the sugar, bean paste, cornflour, oyster sauce and chicken stock together until the sugar and cornflour have dissolved. Make a well in the centre of the chicken mixture and add the sauce, stirring until it thickens and comes to the boil. Transfer to a serving bowl and sprinkle with the nuts.

4 Separate the lettuce leaves and place in individual serving bowls. Spoon the chicken mixture into the lettuce leaves to roll up and eat with your fingers. Serve immediately.

Remove the stems from the drained mushrooms and thinly slice the caps.

Add the spring onion, mushrooms and water chestnuts to the chicken mixture.

Pour the sauce into the well in the centre of the chicken mixture.

Remove the core from the lettuce and separate the leaves.

NUTRITION PER SERVE
Protein 32 g; Fat 20 g; Carbohydrate 70 g; Dietary Fibre 2.5 g; Cholesterol 63 mg; 1360 kJ (325 cal)

HINT: There are numerous types of bean paste, varying in colour and intensity of flavour. Experiment until you find one of the piquancy you like.

STUFFED CHICKEN WINGS

Preparation time: 40 minutes
Total cooking time: 20 minutes
Makes 6

6 large chicken wings

FILLING
3 tablespoons chopped water
    chestnuts
1/2 teaspoon finely chopped garlic
1 tablespoon finely chopped fresh
    coriander leaves
1 1/2 tablespoons fish sauce
1/2 teaspoon ground black pepper
1 spring onion, finely chopped
250 g (8 oz) minced pork

1 Pat the chicken dry with paper towels. To bone the chicken wings, use a small, sharp knife. Starting at the drumstick end, slip the knife down the side of the bone, all the way to the joint, taking care not to pierce the skin. Snap the bone free. Start on the next joint with the point of the knife, taking care not to pierce the elbow.

2 Once the first part of these two bones has been freed, the bones can be pulled out and cut at the knuckle to release. Reshape the wings.

3 To make the filling, combine the water chestnuts, garlic, coriander leaves, fish sauce, pepper, spring onion and pork, mixing thoroughly. Using a teaspoon, stuff the wings evenly with the filling, taking care not to overfill or they will burst during cooking.

4 Place the chicken wings on a lightly oiled steamer, cover and steam over briskly boiling water for 10 minutes. Transfer the wings to a cold, lightly oiled grill tray. Cook the chicken wings under medium heat for 5 minutes on each side or until brown and cooked through.

NUTRITION PER CHICKEN WING
Protein 30 g; Fat 2.5 g; Carbohydrate 1.5 g;
Dietary Fibre 0.5 g; Cholesterol 62 mg;
610 kJ (145 cal)

Slip the knife down the side of the bone, taking care not to pierce the skin.

Pull the bones out and cut at the knuckle to release, then reshape the wings.

Combine the filling ingredients in a large bowl and mix thoroughly.

Place the chicken wings on a lightly oiled steamer and cover with a lid.

HAINAN CHICKEN RICE

Preparation time: 30 minutes
Total cooking time: 1 hour 30 minutes
Serves 4

1.5 kg (3 lb) chicken
1 sprig celery leaves
2 spring onions, roughly chopped
1 teaspoon salt
peppercorns
1/4 cup (60 ml/2 fl oz) peanut oil
1 tablespoon sesame oil
1 tablespoon finely grated fresh ginger
2 teaspoons finely grated garlic
1 large onion, thinly sliced
2 cups (440 g/14 oz) short-grain rice
1/2 cup (25 g/3/4 oz) finely shredded
   Chinese cabbage
2 tablespoons chopped fresh
   coriander

DIPPING SAUCES
1 tablespoon finely grated fresh ginger
2 tablespoons soy sauce
1 red chilli, chopped

1 Place the chicken in a large pan with the celery leaves, spring onion, salt and a few peppercorns. Cover with water. Bring to the boil, covered, reduce the heat and simmer for 15 minutes. Turn off the heat and leave, covered, for 45 minutes.
2 Heat the oils in a pan with a tight-fitting lid. Add the ginger, garlic and onion and cook until soft and golden. Set aside 1 tablespoon of the oil.
3 Add the rice and cook, stirring, for 2 minutes. Add 3 cups (750 ml/24 fl oz) of the chicken cooking liquid. Bring to the boil, then reduce the heat and simmer until holes appear in the rice. Cover the pan tightly and reduce the

heat to very low. Cook for 15 minutes. Remove the lid, and fluff up the rice with a fork.
4 While the rice is cooking, remove the chicken from the pan, retaining the stock. Cut the chicken into pieces, arrange on a platter and keep warm.
5 To make the dipping sauces, combine the reserved cooking oils with the ginger. For the second sauce, combine the soy sauce with the chilli.
6 Strain the remaining chicken cooking liquid into a pan. Bring to the boil, then add the Chinese cabbage. Pour the soup into a bowl and sprinkle with the coriander. Serve the chicken, rice and dipping sauces with the soup.

NUTRITION PER SERVE
Protein 65 g; Fat 25 g; Carbohydrate 84 g;
Dietary Fibre 4 g; Cholesterol 125 mg;
3465 kJ (828 cal)

Cook the ginger, garlic and onion in the oils until soft and golden.

Simmer the rice and stock mixture until holes appear in the rice.

Use poultry scissors to cut the chicken into pieces for serving.

TANDOORI CHICKEN TERRINE

Preparation time: 20 minutes
   + overnight refrigeration
Total cooking time: 1 hour 30 minutes
Serves 6–8

8 slices bacon, rind removed
30 g (1 oz) butter
1 onion, finely chopped
2 cloves garlic, crushed
1 teaspoon grated fresh ginger
1 kg (2 lb) chicken mince
250 g (8 oz) chicken livers
1 teaspoon ground turmeric
1 teaspoon ground sweet paprika
1 teaspoon garam masala

1/2 teaspoon ground cardamom
1 teaspoon ground coriander
2 tablespoons lemon juice
1 cup (250 g/8 oz) plain yoghurt
2 eggs, lightly beaten

1 Preheat the oven to moderate 180°C (350°F/Gas 4). Lightly oil a 27 x 10 cm (11 x 4 inch) terrine dish or tin and line with bacon, overlapping the sides. Melt the butter in a pan, add the onion, garlic and ginger and fry for 2–3 minutes. Remove from the heat.
2 Finely mince the chicken mince and livers in a food processor. Transfer to a large bowl and add the onion mixture, spices and lemon juice.
3 Whisk the yoghurt and eggs and stir into the chicken mixture. Spoon into the dish, pressing down firmly. Fold the bacon over the top of the terrine to enclose the mixture, cover with foil and place in a baking dish.
4 Pour in enough cold water to come halfway up the side of the terrine. Bake for 1–1 1/2 hours, or until the juices run clear when pierced with a skewer.
5 Remove the terrine from the oven and pour off the excess juice. Cover with foil and place a heavy weight on top of the terrine mixture to compress it. Refrigerate the terrine overnight.

NUTRITION PER SERVE (8)
Protein 18 g; Fat 9 g; Carbohydrate 3.5 g;
Dietary Fibre 0.5 g; Cholesterol 93 mg;
645 kJ (155 cal)

Line the dish with bacon, leaving the ends overlapping the sides of the dish.

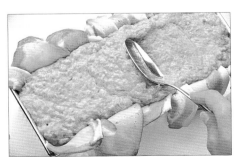

Spread the chicken mixture over the bacon, pressing down firmly.

Pour in enough cold water to come halfway up the sides of the terrine dish.

CHICKEN AND LIME HUMMUS TORTILLAS

Preparation time: 45 minutes
+ 30 minutes refrigeration
Total cooking time: 10–15 minutes
Serves 4

500 g (1 lb) chicken mince
1 red onion, finely chopped
3 cloves garlic, crushed
2 tablespoons chopped fresh mint
2 tablespoons chopped fresh parsley
2 tablespoons lime juice
2 eggs, lightly beaten
2 cups (160 g/5$^{1}/_{2}$ oz) fresh white
    breadcrumbs
2 teaspoons chicken stock powder
1$^{1}/_{2}$ cups (150 g/5 oz) dry
    breadcrumbs
oil, for shallow-frying
4 large flour tortillas
lettuce leaves, to serve
1 large ripe avocado, sliced

LIME HUMMUS
300 g (10 oz) can chickpeas, drained
2–3 tablespoons tahini
2 teaspoons sesame oil
2 cloves garlic, crushed
$^{1}/_{4}$ cup (60 ml/2 fl oz) lime juice
1 tablespoon finely chopped fresh
    mint
$^{1}/_{2}$ teaspoon sweet paprika

1 In a bowl, combine the chicken
mince, onion, garlic, herbs, lime juice,
1 egg, fresh breadcrumbs, stock
powder and some freshly ground
black pepper. Use your hands to mix
thoroughly. Shape 2 tablespoons of
the mixture at a time into round
patties, dip in the remaining beaten
egg, then toss in the dry breadcrumbs,
pressing them on firmly.

2 Arrange the patties on a tray, cover
and refrigerate for 30 minutes. Just
before serving, shallow-fry the patties
in moderately hot oil for 2–3 minutes
each side, or until golden and cooked
through. Drain on paper towels.

3 To make the lime hummus, process
the chickpeas, tahini, sesame oil,
garlic, lime juice and a little salt and
pepper in a food processor until the
mixture is a smooth, thick paste. Stir in
the mint and paprika.

4 To serve, toast the tortillas under a
grill or place in a dry pan until heated
and lightly browned on both sides.
Arrange lettuce leaves, a few chicken
patties and some sliced avocado on
each and top with the lime hummus.

NUTRITION PER SERVE
Protein 45 g; Fat 40 g; Carbohydrate 125 g;
Dietary Fibre 15 g; Cholesterol 30 mg;
4705 kJ (1124 cal)

Dip the patties in beaten egg and then coat with
the dry breadcrumbs.

Shallow-fry the patties for 2–3 minutes, or until
golden brown.

Process the chickpeas, tahini, oil, garlic, lime
juice and salt and pepper until smooth.

CHICKEN TERIYAKI PACKAGES

Preparation time: 50 minutes
 + 30 minutes soaking
Total cooking time: 25 minutes
Makes 24

5 dried Chinese mushrooms
1 tablespoon oil
2 cloves garlic, crushed
1 teaspoon finely grated fresh ginger
350 g (11 oz) chicken mince
1 small leek, thinly sliced
1 tablespoon soy sauce
2 tablespoons dry sherry
1 tablespoon sake
1 tablespoon sugar
1–2 teaspoons chilli sauce

100 g (3¹/₂ oz) fresh rice noodles,
 thinly sliced
15 sheets filo pastry
90 g (3 oz) butter, melted
2 tablespoons sesame seeds

1 Place the mushrooms in a heatproof bowl, cover with boiling water and soak for 30 minutes. Drain and chop finely. Heat the oil in a large pan, add the garlic, ginger, chicken mince and leek, and stir-fry for 4–5 minutes. Stir in the soy sauce, sherry, sake, sugar and chilli sauce. Fold in the mushrooms and rice noodles and remove the mixture from the heat. Preheat the oven to moderate 180°C (350°F/Gas 4).
2 Unfold the filo, remove 1 sheet and cover the rest with a damp tea towel to prevent them from drying out. Brush the filo lightly with melted butter. Top with another 2 sheets, brushing each with butter. Cut crossways into 7 cm (2³/₄ inch) strips and spoon 1 tablespoon of the filling onto one end of each strip. Fold the ends over to form a triangle and continue folding to the end of each strip. Repeat with the remaining pastry and filling.
3 Place the triangles on a lightly oiled baking tray, brush with melted butter and sprinkle with sesame seeds. Bake for 12–15 minutes, or until the triangles are light golden brown.

NUTRITION PER PACKAGE
Protein 4.5 g; Fat 5 g; Carbohydrate 6.5 g; Dietary Fibre 0.5 g; Cholesterol 17 mg; 395 kJ (94 cal)

Fold in the mushrooms and rice noodles and remove the mixture from the heat.

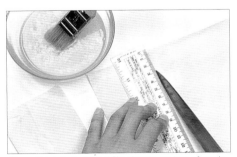

Place 3 lightly buttered filo sheets on top of each other and cut into strips.

Fold the ends over the filling to form a triangle, and keep folding to the end of the strip.

CHICKEN PANCAKES WITH CHARGRILLED VEGETABLES AND FETA

Preparation time: 40 minutes
+ 30 minutes marinating
Total cooking time: 30 minutes
Serves 4

CHARGRILLED VEGETABLES
1 red capsicum, thickly sliced
1 yellow capsicum, thickly sliced
1 kg (2 lb) baby bok choy, leaves
   separated
2 zucchini, cut into strips
8 small field mushrooms
1/4 cup (60 ml/2 fl oz) Italian salad
   dressing

1/2 cup (60 g/2 oz) plain flour
1 1/3 cups (350 ml/11 fl oz) buttermilk
2 eggs
1 teaspoon oil
2 smoked chicken breasts, thinly
   sliced
150 g (5 oz) Bulgarian feta
olive oil, to serve

1 To make the chargrilled vegetables, put the capsicum, bok choy, zucchini and mushrooms in a small bowl and pour in the salad dressing. Marinate for at least 30 minutes.

2 Sift the flour and a pinch of salt into a bowl and make a well in the centre. Whisk the buttermilk, eggs and oil in a jug and pour into the well, whisking until just combined. Add the sliced smoked chicken and mix gently.

3 Heat a small crepe or non-stick frying pan and brush lightly with melted butter or oil. Pour 1/4 cup (60 ml/2 fl oz) of the batter into the pan, quickly spreading the chicken to ensure it is evenly distributed

throughout the pancake. Cook over medium heat for 2 minutes, or until the underside is golden. Turn over and cook the other side. Transfer to a plate and cover while cooking the remaining batter. Cut each pancake into wedges.

4 Cook the vegetables on a hot barbecue or chargrill plate for 3 minutes, or until tender. Divide the vegetables among four serving plates and top with the pancake wedges and a little crumbled feta. Drizzle with the olive oil and sprinkle with cracked black pepper to serve.

NUTRITION PER SERVE
Protein 54 g; Fat 22 g; Carbohydrate 20 g;
Dietary Fibre 13 g; Cholesterol 179 mg;
2078 kJ (496 cal)

Cut the capsicums into thick slices, and carefully separate the leaves of the baby bok choy.

Add the slices of smoked chicken to the batter and mix gently to combine.

Quickly spread the chicken out so that it is evenly distributed through the pancake.

CHICKEN CURRY BAGS

Preparation time: 30 minutes
    + 30 minutes standing
Total cooking time: 1 hour
Makes 10

1 cup (125 g/4 oz) plain flour
1 egg
1 egg yolk
1¼ cups (315 ml/10 fl oz) milk
50 g (1¾ oz) butter, melted
½ cup (60 g/2 oz) finely grated
    Cheddar

CHICKEN FILLING
1 large, cooked chicken breast
60 g (2 oz) butter
1 red onion, chopped
1–2 teaspoons curry powder
2 tablespoons plain flour
1¼ cups (315 ml/10 fl oz) milk
¼ cup (60 ml/2 fl oz) cream
¼ cup (15 g/½ oz) chopped fresh
    parsley
2 hard-boiled eggs, chopped

1 Mix the flour, egg, egg yolk and half the milk in a food processor for 10 seconds. Add the remaining milk and 1 tablespoon of the melted butter and process until smooth. Transfer to a jug, cover and set aside for 30 minutes.
2 To make the chicken filling, chop the cooked chicken breast into small cubes. Melt the butter in a pan, add the onion and cook over medium heat until softened. Add the curry powder and flour and cook for 1–2 minutes. Gradually add the milk, stirring until smooth. Cook for 2–3 minutes, or until the sauce has boiled and thickened. Remove from the heat and add the cream, chicken, parsley and egg. Cover and set aside.

3 Heat a small crepe pan and brush lightly with melted butter. Pour about ¼ cup (60 ml/2 fl oz) batter into the pan, swirling the pan to cover the base. Pour the excess batter back into the jug, adding a little more milk to the batter if it is too thick. Cook for about 30 seconds, then turn over and cook until lightly brown. Remove to a plate while cooking the remaining batter.
4 Preheat the oven to moderate 180°C (350°F/Gas 4). Place 3 tablespoons of the chicken filling in the centre of each

crepe, then gather up into a bag. Tie loosely with a strip of foil, kitchen string or a couple of chives. Brush a large baking dish with melted butter, then brush each bag with melted butter and sprinkle with a little cheese. Bake for 10–15 minutes, or until the bags are heated and golden.

NUTRITION PER CURRY BAG
Protein 13 g; Fat 19 g; Carbohydrate 14 g; Dietary Fibre 1.6 g; Cholesterol 123 mg; 1159 kJ (277 cal)

Remove from the heat and add the cream, chicken, parsley and chopped eggs.

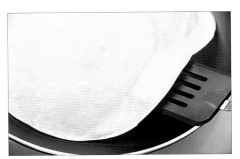

Use an egg slice to turn the crepe over and cook the other side.

Place 3 tablespoons of the chicken filling in the centre of each crepe.

CHICKEN AND LEEK PARCELS

Preparation time: 40 minutes
Total cooking time: 40 minutes
Makes 20

1 tablespoon oil
3 chicken thigh fillets (330 g/11 oz)
30 g butter
2 leeks, thinly sliced
1 slice bacon, finely chopped
1 clove garlic, crushed
1/4 cup (60 ml/2 fl oz) white wine
1/4 cup (60 ml/2 fl oz) cream
2 teaspoons wholegrain mustard
1/4 cup (25 g/3/4 oz) grated Parmesan
10 sheets filo pastry
80 g (23/4 oz) butter, extra, melted

1 Preheat oven to moderate 180°C (350°F/Gas 4). Brush a baking tray with melted butter or oil. Heat the oil in a heavy-based frying pan. Cook the chicken for 5 minutes on each side, or until browned and tender. Remove from the pan and drain on paper towels. Allow to cool, then chop the chicken finely.

2 Heat the butter in a large heavy-based pan. Add the leek, bacon and garlic, and cook for 3–4 minutes, or until the leek is soft and the bacon is crisp. Add the chicken, wine, cream and mustard. Cook, stirring constantly, for 4 minutes, or until thickened. Remove from the heat. Season to taste with salt and freshly ground black pepper, and stir in the Parmesan. Set aside to cool slightly.

3 Lay a sheet of filo pastry on a flat work surface and brush with melted butter. Top with another sheet of pastry and brush with butter. Cut the pastry lengthways into 4 strips. Place

1 tablespoon of the chicken mixture at the end of each strip. Fold the end diagonally over the filling, then continue folding to the end of the strip, forming a triangle. Repeat with the remaining pastry and filling. Place the triangles on the tray and brush with butter. Bake for 25 minutes, or until golden brown and heated through.

NUTRITION PER PARCEL
Protein 5.5 g; Fat 6.5 g; Carbohydrate 4 g; Dietary Fibre 0 g; Cholesterol 25 mg; 430 kJ (100 cal)

HINT: The uncooked parcels can be kept overnight in the refrigerator. To freeze, seal in an airtight container for two months. Cook just before serving.

Cook the chicken in the oil until browned and tender, then remove and drain on paper towels.

Add the chicken, wine, cream and mustard to the bacon mixture, and cook until thickened.

Place the chicken mixture at one end of the pastry and fold diagonally over the filling.

SPICY CHICKEN PASTIES

Preparation time: 30 minutes
Total cooking time: 30 minutes
Makes 20

2 tablespoons oil
1 small onion, finely chopped
1 clove garlic, crushed
1/2 teaspoon ground coriander
1/2 teaspoon ground cumin
1/4 teaspoon ground turmeric
1/4 teaspoon chilli powder
300 g (10 oz) chicken mince
1/3 cup (50 g/1³/4 oz) frozen peas
1 tablespoon finely chopped fresh
    coriander

5 sheets ready-rolled puff pastry
1 egg, lightly beaten

1 Preheat the oven to moderate 180°C (350°F/Gas 4). Line a baking tray with foil. Heat the oil in a heavy-based frying pan. Add the onion and garlic and cook over medium heat for 2 minutes, or until the onion is soft. Add all the spices and cook, stirring, for 1 minute.
2 Add the chicken mince to the pan and cook for 10 minutes, or until almost all the liquid has evaporated, stirring occasionally. Stir in the peas, coriander and salt, to taste. Remove from the heat and allow to cool.
3 Using a small plate or saucer as a

guide, cut 10 cm (4 inch) circles from the pastry with a sharp knife. Place a level tablespoon of the mixture in the centre of each circle. Fold over and pleat the edge to seal. Place on the tray and brush with beaten egg. Bake for 15 minutes, or until golden.

NUTRITION PER PASTIE
Protein 6 g; Fat 12 g; Carbohydrate 15 g;
Dietary Fibre 1 g; Cholesterol 27 mg;
811 kJ (194 cal)

HINT: The uncooked pasties can be prepared several hours ahead. Store, covered, in the refrigerator. Cook just before serving.

Add the spices to the onion and garlic mixture, and stir for 1 minute.

Stir the peas, coriander and salt into the chicken and spice mixture.

Fold the pastry over the filling, then pleat the edges to seal and brush with beaten egg.

Sandwich & Jaffle Fillings

CREAMY CHICKEN AND CELERY

Combine 2 cups (300 g/10 oz) chopped barbecued chicken, $1/3$ cup (80 g/$2^3/4$ oz) whole-egg mayonnaise, 2 tablespoons sweet chilli sauce, 4 finely chopped spring onions, 1 diced celery stick, 1 tablespoon finely chopped fresh coriander leaves, salt and freshly ground black pepper. Serve on four toasted bagel halves and sprinkle with snow pea sprouts. Cover with the remaining bagel halves. Serves 4.

CHICKEN, SEMI-DRIED TOMATO AND GRUYERE JAFFLE

Butter 8 slices of wholegrain bread on one side. Slice 250 g (8 oz) smoked chicken and divide among 4 slices of the bread, buttered-side down. Top with 100 g ($3^1/2$ oz) sliced semi-dried tomato and 100 g ($3^1/2$ oz) Gruyère cheese. Season with salt and pepper. Place the remaining slices of bread on top, buttered-side up and cook in a jaffle iron or sandwich maker for 3 minutes, or until golden brown. Serve immediately. Makes 4.

LEBANESE CHICKEN

Spread 200 g ($6^1/2$ oz) hummus over four Lebanese bread rounds. Combine 200 g ($6^1/2$ oz) cooked chopped barbecued chicken, $1^1/2$ cups (125 g/4 oz) ready-made tabouli, 1 teaspoon lemon juice and $1/2$ sliced red onion (optional). Divide the mixture among the Lebanese bread rounds, season with salt and freshly ground black pepper and roll up tightly. Cut in half on the diagonal and serve immediately. Serves 4.

CHICKEN WITH CRANBERRY AND CAMEMBERT

Combine $1/4$ cup (70 g/$2^1/4$ oz) cranberry sauce, 4 finely chopped spring onions, salt and freshly ground black pepper. Butter 8 slices of Turkish bread and divide 200 g ($6^1/2$ oz) thinly sliced processed chicken among 4 slices of bread, buttered-side up. Top with the cranberry mixture and divide 200 g ($6^1/2$ oz) sliced Camembert among the slices. Place the remaining slices of bread on top, buttered-side down, and cook in a sandwich maker or under a grill for 3 minutes, or until golden brown. Serve immediately. Serves 4.

MANGO CHICKEN

Combine 2 cups (300 g/10 oz) chopped smoked chicken, $1/4$ cup (70 g/$2^1/4$ oz) mango chutney, 2 teaspoons lime juice, $1/3$ cup (90 g/3 oz) natural yoghurt, salt and freshly ground black pepper. Divide the mixture down the centre of four large Lebanese bread rounds, top with rocket leaves and roll up tightly. Cut each roll into three and serve immediately. Serves 4.

CHICKEN AND CORN JAFFLE

Combine 200 g ($6^1/2$ oz) diced cooked chicken, 315 g (10 oz) can creamed corn, $1/2$ cup (60 g/2 oz) grated Cheddar, salt and freshly ground black pepper. Butter 8 slices of bread on one side and divide the chicken mixture among 4 slices, buttered-side down. Place the remaining slices of bread on top, buttered-side up, and cook in a jaffle iron or sandwich maker for 3 minutes, or until golden brown. Serve immediately with lime wedges. Serves 4.

Clockwise from top left: Creamy chicken and celery; Chicken with cranberry and Camembert; Mango chicken; Chicken and corn jaffle; Lebanese chicken; Chicken, semi-dried tomato and Gruyère jaffle.

Salads

SMOKED CHICKEN CAESAR SALAD

Preparation time: 25 minutes
Total cooking time: 15 minutes
Serves 4

GARLIC CROUTONS
1 thin baguette
45 g (1 1/2 oz) unsalted butter
1/2 cup (125 ml/4 fl oz) olive oil
4 cloves garlic, crushed

1 cos lettuce, tough outer leaves
    discarded
1 large smoked chicken (about
    950 g/1 lb 14 oz)
1 1/2 cups (150 g/5 oz) Parmesan
    shavings

DRESSING
2 eggs
2 cloves garlic, crushed
2 tablespoons lemon juice
2 teaspoons Dijon mustard
45 g (1 1/2 oz) can anchovy fillets,
    drained
1 cup (250 ml/8 fl oz) olive oil
1/4 teaspoon salt
1 teaspoon freshly ground black
    pepper

1 To make the garlic croutons, slice
the baguette diagonally into 1 cm

(1/2 inch) thick slices. Melt the butter
and olive oil in a large frying pan over
moderate heat. Stir in the crushed
garlic. Fry the bread slices, a few at a
time, until golden. Remove from the
pan and drain on paper towels.
2 Separate the lettuce leaves, wash
and dry thoroughly. Tear the larger
leaves into pieces and refrigerate until
well chilled. Cut the chicken into bite-
sized chunks. Refrigerate while
preparing the dressing.
3 To make the dressing, blend or
process the eggs, garlic, lemon juice,
mustard and anchovies. With the
motor running, gradually pour in the
oil in a thin stream and process until
thick. Season with the salt and pepper.
4 In a large bowl, combine the torn
lettuce leaves, chicken, about half of
the croutons and half the Parmesan.
Add the dressing and toss well.
Arrange 2–3 whole lettuce leaves in
each individual serving bowl, spoon in
the salad and sprinkle with the
remaining croutons and Parmesan.
Season liberally with freshly ground
black pepper and serve immediately.

NUTRITION PER SERVE
Protein 45 g; Fat 120 g; Carbohydrate 10 g;
Dietary Fibre 2 g; Cholesterol 235 mg;
5350 kJ (1275 cal)

Roughly chop the smoked chicken meat into
bite-sized chunks.

Process the eggs, garlic, lemon juice, mustard
and anchovies.

RED CURRY CHICKEN SALAD

Preparation time: 30 minutes
  + overnight marinating
Total cooking time: 20 minutes
Serves 4

500 g (1 lb) chicken thigh fillets,
  cut into thin strips
2 teaspoons Thai red curry paste
1 teaspoon chopped red chilli
1 clove garlic, crushed
1 stem lemon grass, white part only,
  finely chopped
cooking oil spray
1 red onion, thinly sliced
2 tomatoes, cut into wedges
1/2 cup (25 g/3/4 oz) chopped fresh mint
1/4 cup (15 g/1/2 oz) chopped fresh
  coriander
400 g (13 oz) mixed salad leaves
2 tablespoons roasted peanuts

DRESSING
11/2 tablespoons soft brown sugar
2 tablespoons fish sauce
2 tablespoons lime juice
2 kaffir lime leaves, shredded
2 teaspoons oil

1 Combine the chicken, curry paste, chilli, garlic and lemon grass. Cover and refrigerate overnight.
2 Lightly spray a non-stick frying pan with oil and cook the chicken in batches until tender and lightly browned; set aside. Add the onion to the pan and cook for 1 minute, or until just soft. Return the chicken and any juices to the pan and add the tomato, mint and coriander, stirring until heated. Set aside until just warm.
3 To make the dressing, put the sugar, fish sauce, lime juice, lime leaves and oil in a jug. Mix until combined. In a large bowl, toss the chicken mixture with the salad leaves and dressing. Sprinkle with the peanuts to serve.

NUTRITION PER SERVE
Protein 25 g; Fat 10 g; Carbohydrate 15 g;
Dietary Fibre 2.5 g; Cholesterol 50 mg;
1050 kJ (250 cal)

Remove the fat from the chicken fillets and cut the meat into strips.

If you find it easier, you can use your hands to mix the chicken and marinade.

Stir the tomatoes and herbs with the chicken, until heated through.

CHICKEN AND WATERCRESS SALAD

Preparation time: 40 minutes
Total cooking time: 10–15 minutes
Serves 4

3 small chicken breast fillets
    (350 g/11 oz)
1 Lebanese cucumber
1/2 red capsicum
150 g (5 oz) watercress
1/2 cup (10 g/1/4 oz) fresh mint leaves
2 tablespoons finely shredded fresh
    mint
2 chillies, thinly sliced
2 tablespoons crisp-fried onion

DRESSING
1/4 cup (60 ml/2 fl oz) lime juice
2 tablespoons coconut milk
1 tablespoon fish sauce
1 tablespoon sweet chilli sauce

1 Line a bamboo steamer with baking paper and steam the chicken, covered, over a wok or pan of simmering water, for 10 minutes or until the chicken is cooked through. Remove from the heat and set aside to cool. Thinly slice the cucumber and cut the slices in half. Slice the capsicum into thin strips.
2 While the chicken is cooling, pick over the watercress and separate the sprigs from the tough stems. Arrange the watercress and whole mint leaves on a serving plate. Using your fingers, tear the chicken into long, thin shreds. Gently toss the shredded chicken, cucumber and capsicum in a bowl. Arrange over the watercress bed.
3 To make the dressing, whisk the lime juice, coconut milk, fish sauce and sweet chilli sauce until combined.

4 Drizzle the dressing over the salad and sprinkle with the shredded mint, sliced chillies and crisp-fried onion.

NUTRITION PER SERVE
Protein 40 g; Fat 6 g; Carbohydrate 3 g;
Dietary Fibre 2.5 g; Cholesterol 82 mg;
966 kJ (230 cal)

NOTE: Crisp-fried, or sometimes deep-fried, onions are available in packets or small jars from Asian supermarkets.

Line a bamboo steamer with baking paper and cook the chicken.

Pick over the watercress to separate the sprigs from the tough stems.

When the chicken is cooked, tear it into shreds, using your fingers.

VIETNAMESE PAWPAW AND CHICKEN SALAD

Preparation time: 30 minutes
Total cooking time: 10 minutes
Serves 4

2 chicken breast fillets (350 g/11 oz)
1 large green pawpaw
1 cup (20 g/3/4 oz) fresh Vietnamese
   mint leaves
1/2 cup (15 g/1/2 oz) fresh coriander
   leaves
2 red chillies, seeded and thinly sliced
2 tablespoons fish sauce

1 tablespoon rice wine vinegar
1 tablespoon lime juice
2 teaspoons sugar
2 tablespoons chopped roasted
   peanuts

1 Place the chicken in a frying pan with enough water to just cover. Simmer over gentle heat for 10 minutes, or until cooked. Don't let the water boil—it should just gently simmer, to poach the chicken. Remove the chicken and allow to cool completely. Thinly slice the chicken.
2 Using a potato peeler, peel the pawpaw and then cut the flesh into

thin strips. Mix gently in a bowl with the mint, coriander, sliced chilli, fish sauce, vinegar, lime juice and sugar.
3 Arrange the pawpaw mixture on a serving plate and pile the sliced chicken on top. Scatter the peanuts over the top and serve immediately.

NUTRITION PER SERVE
Protein 22 g; Fat 6 g; Carbohydrate 6 g;
Dietary Fibre 1.5 g; Cholesterol 44 mg;
712 kJ (170 cal)

NOTE: Green pawpaw is underripe pawpaw, used for tartness and texture.

Gently simmer the chicken breast fillets until they are cooked through.

Use a sharp knife to cut the cooled chicken into thin slices.

Cut the peeled pawpaw into long, thin strips, using a very sharp knife.

VIETNAMESE CHICKEN AND CABBAGE SALAD

Preparation time: 40 minutes
Total cooking time: 5 minutes
Serves 4

4 cooked chicken thigh fillets
1 cup (125 g/4 oz) thinly sliced
    celery
2 carrots, cut into thin strips
1 cup (75 g/2¹/₂ oz) finely shredded
    cabbage
1 small onion, sliced
¹/₄ cup (7 g/¹/₄ oz) fresh coriander
    leaves
¹/₄ cup (15 g/¹/₂ oz) finely shredded
    fresh mint

DRESSING
¹/₄ cup (60 g/2 oz) caster sugar
1 tablespoon fish sauce
1 teaspoon crushed garlic
2 tablespoons white vinegar
1 red chilli, seeded and finely chopped

TOPPING
2 tablespoons peanut oil
1¹/₂ teaspoons chopped garlic
¹/₃ cup (50 g/1³/₄ oz) roasted peanuts,
    finely chopped
1 tablespoon caster sugar

1 Cut the chicken fillets into long, thin strips. Combine the chicken, celery, carrot, cabbage, onion, coriander and mint in a large bowl.
2 To make the dressing, put the sugar, fish sauce, garlic, vinegar, chilli and 2 tablespoons water in a small bowl. Whisk until the sugar has dissolved and the ingredients are well combined. Pour the dressing over the chicken mixture and toss to combine. Arrange on a serving plate.
3 To make the topping, heat the oil in a wok over moderate heat. Add the garlic and cook, stirring, until pale golden. Stir in the peanuts and sugar. Cool slightly. Sprinkle the topping over the salad just before serving.

NUTRITION PER SERVE
Protein 50 g; Fat 15 g; Carbohydrate 25 g;
Dietary Fibre 3 g; Cholesterol 110 mg;
1820 kJ (435 cal)

Combine the chicken, celery, carrot, cabbage, onion, coriander and mint.

Pour the dressing over the salad and gently toss to combine.

Gently stir the peanuts and sugar into the cooked garlic.

WARM CHICKEN SALAD

Preparation time: 15 minutes
Total cooking time: 15 minutes
Serves 4

2 teaspoons cumin seeds
1 tablespoon olive oil
1 red onion, thinly sliced
3 cloves garlic, finely chopped
2 teaspoons finely chopped red chilli
1½ teaspoons sweet paprika
600 g (1¼ lb) chicken tenderloins, cut
    into bite-sized pieces
2 tablespoons lemon juice

2 tablespoons chopped fresh
    coriander leaves
200 g (6½ oz) mixed salad leaves
2 Lebanese cucumbers, thinly sliced
12 Kalamata olives
2 tablespoons extra virgin olive oil

1 Fry the cumin seeds in a dry frying pan for 1–2 minutes, or until fragrant. Remove and set aside. Heat the olive oil in the frying pan, add the onion and cook over medium heat until soft.
2 Add the garlic, cumin seeds, chopped chilli and paprika. Cook, stirring, for 1 minute. Add the chicken and cook, stirring, for 5 minutes, or

until the chicken is tender.
3 Remove from the heat and cool slightly. Stir in the lemon juice and coriander, and season to taste with salt. Arrange the salad leaves, cucumber and olives on a serving platter, drizzle with the extra virgin olive oil and place the chicken mixture on top. Serve immediately.

NUTRITION PER SERVE
Protein 35 g; Fat 20 g; Carbohydrate 10 g;
Dietary Fibre 5 g; Cholesterol 105 mg;
1520 kJ (365 cal)

Heat the olive oil and cook the red onion over medium heat until soft.

Add the chopped chicken to the pan with the onion and spice mixture.

When the mixture has cooled slightly, stir in the lemon juice and coriander.

CHICKEN AND CITRUS SALAD WITH CURRY DRESSING

Preparation time: 20 minutes
Total cooking time: 15 minutes
Serves 4

4 chicken breast fillets
1 tablespoon olive oil
2 oranges
1 lettuce
250 g (8 oz) watercress
15 g (1/2 oz) fresh chives

CURRY DRESSING
3 teaspoons curry powder
2 spring onions, thinly sliced
2 tablespoons olive oil
2 tablespoons sunflower oil
1 tablespoon balsamic vinegar
2 teaspoons soft brown sugar
1 teaspoon chopped green chilli

1 Trim the chicken fillets of any fat and sinew. Heat the oil in a frying pan and cook the chicken over medium heat for about 7 minutes on each side, or until browned and tender. Allow to cool, then cut across the grain into thick strips.

2 To make the curry dressing, dry-fry the curry powder in a frying pan for 1 minute, or until fragrant. Cool slightly, then place in a small bowl with the spring onion, olive oil, sunflower oil, vinegar, sugar and chilli and whisk to combine. Season to taste with salt and black pepper. Set aside to allow the flavours to develop.

3 Peel the oranges, removing all the white pith. Cut into segments, between the membrane, and discard any pips.

4 Wash and dry the lettuce leaves and watercress and arrange on a large platter. Place the chicken pieces and orange segments on top. Whisk the dressing again, then drizzle it over the salad. Cut the chives into short lengths and scatter over the top.

NUTRITION PER SERVE
Protein 25 g; Fat 25 g; Carbohydrate 10 g; Dietary Fibre 2 g; Cholesterol 55 mg; 1590 kJ (380 cal)

Cook the chicken fillets until tender and browned on both sides.

Fry the curry powder in a dry frying pan for 1 minute, or until fragrant.

Carefully cut the oranges into segments between the membrane.

Whisk the curry dressing well before drizzling over the salad.

CHICKEN, PRAWN AND GRAPEFRUIT SALAD

Preparation time: 20 minutes
Total cooking time: Nil
Serves 4–6

1 small pink or yellow grapefruit
1/2 small green pawpaw or green
    mango (about 100 g/3 1/2 oz)
6 cooked prawns, peeled and
    deveined
2 Roma tomatoes, chopped
1 orange, peeled and segmented
125 g (4 oz) cooked chicken,
    shredded or cut into bite-sized
    pieces (see Note)
4 spring onions, sliced
2 cloves garlic, sliced
2 tablespoons coarsely chopped fresh
    coriander
1 tablespoon shredded coconut
lettuce leaves, to serve
1 tablespoon roasted, unsalted
    peanuts, finely chopped
2 teaspoons dried shrimp, finely
    chopped

DRESSING
2 teaspoons soft brown sugar
1 1/2 tablespoons fish sauce
1/4 cup (60 ml/2 fl oz) lime juice
2 teaspoons chilli sauce

1 Peel the grapefruit, discarding the pith, then cut it into thin segments. Peel the pawpaw and cut it into long, thin strips.
2 Combine the pawpaw, grapefruit, prawns, tomato, orange segments, chicken, spring onion, garlic, coriander and coconut in a bowl.
3 To make the dressing, combine the sugar, fish sauce, lime juice and chilli sauce in a jug and whisk until the sugar has dissolved. Pour the dressing over the salad and toss gently. Serve on a bed of lettuce leaves and sprinkle with the peanuts and dried shrimp.

NUTRITION PER SERVE (6)
Protein 9.5 g; Fat 1.5 g; Carbohydrate 8.5 g;
Dietary Fibre 2.5 g; Cholesterol 34 mg;
376 kJ (98 cal)

NOTE: Use leftover chicken, or pan-fry a chicken breast until tender.

Peel the grapefruit, removing all the white pith. Cut into thin segments.

Cut the peeled pawpaw into long, thin strips, using a sharp knife.

Combine the fruit, chicken, tomato, spring onion, garlic, coriander, coconut and prawns in a bowl.

Whisk the dressing ingredients in a small jug until the sugar has dissolved.

CORONATION CHICKEN

Preparation time: 20 minutes
Total cooking time: 30 minutes
Serves 4

4 chicken breast fillets
1 carrot, chopped
1 celery stick, chopped
1/2 small onion, chopped
4 whole peppercorns
1 bay leaf
1 tablespoon oil
1 onion, chopped
2 teaspoons curry powder
1 large tomato, peeled, seeded and
    finely chopped
1/2 cup (125 ml/4 fl oz) dry white wine
2 teaspoons tomato paste
1/2 cup (125 g/4 oz) thick plain yoghurt
1/2 cup (125 g/4 oz) mayonnaise
2 teaspoons lemon juice
2 tablespoons mango chutney

1 Place the chicken, carrot, celery, onion, peppercorns and bay leaf in a single layer in a large frying pan. Add enough water to just cover the chicken. Bring to the boil, then reduce the heat and simmer for 8 minutes, or until the chicken is tender. Leave to cool in the liquid, then remove the chicken and slice into thin strips.
2 Heat the oil in a frying pan and add the onion and curry powder. Cook, stirring, for a few minutes, or until the onion is translucent. Add the chopped tomato and wine, bring to the boil, then reduce the heat and simmer for 10 minutes.
3 Stir in the tomato paste, yoghurt, mayonnaise, lemon juice and mango chutney. Mix until well combined, then season well with salt and

freshly ground black pepper. Add the chicken and mix well. Serve on a bed of salad greens.

NUTRITION PER SERVE
Protein 30 g; Fat 20 g; Carbohydrate 15 g;
Dietary Fibre 3 g; Cholesterol 70 mg;
1570 kJ (375 cal)

NOTE: Coronation chicken is an English favourite and although traditionally served with a rice salad, it also makes a great sandwich filling. Use any variety of breads or crackers with some snow pea sprouts or salad greens to garnish.

Peel the tomato, remove the seeds, and finely chop the flesh.

Cover the chicken, carrot, celery, onion, peppercorns and bay leaf with water.

Stir in the tomato paste, yoghurt, mayonnaise, lemon juice and chutney.

PACIFIC CHICKEN SALAD

Preparation time: 20 minutes
Total cooking time: 15 minutes
Serves 4

1 cup (250 ml/8 fl oz) coconut milk
1 tablespoon fish sauce
1 tablespoon grated palm sugar
4 chicken breast fillets
2 mangoes, thinly sliced
4 spring onions, sliced
1/4 cup (7 g/1/4 oz) fresh coriander
    leaves
1/3 cup (45 g/11/2 oz) coarsely
    chopped roasted unsalted
    macadamia nuts

DRESSING
2 tablespoons oil
1 teaspoon finely grated lime rind
2 tablespoons lime juice

1 Place the coconut milk, fish sauce and palm sugar in a frying pan and bring to the boil, stirring. Reduce the heat, add the chicken fillets and gently simmer, covered, for 10 minutes, or until the chicken is just tender. Leave to cool in the coconut liquid, then remove and pour the liquid into a jug.
2 To make the dressing, put 1/2 cup (125 ml/4 fl oz) of the reserved coconut cooking liquid, the oil, lime rind and juice in a small bowl and whisk to combine. Season to taste with salt and pepper.
3 Cut each chicken fillet diagonally into long slices and arrange on individual serving plates or in a large serving bowl. Spoon the dressing over the chicken and top with the sliced mango, spring onion, coriander leaves and macadamia nuts.

NUTRITION PER SERVE
Protein 30 g; Fat 35 g; Carbohydrate 15 g; Dietary Fibre 2 g; Cholesterol 55 mg; 1965 kJ (465 cal)

NOTE: Palm sugar is obtained from either the palmyra palm or sugar palm, and is available in block form or in jars. It can be grated or gently melted before using. Soft brown sugar may be substituted.

Cut the mangoes into thin slices and carefully remove the skin.

Using a sharp knife, coarsely chop the macadamia nuts.

Put the coconut milk, fish sauce and palm sugar in a pan.

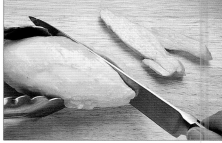

Cut each of the cooked chicken fillets into long diagonal slices.

TANDOORI CHICKEN SALAD

Preparation time: 20 minutes
  + overnight marinating
Total cooking time: 15 minutes
Serves 4

4 chicken breast fillets
2–3 tablespoons tandoori paste
200 g (6½ oz) thick plain yoghurt
1 tablespoon lemon juice
½ cup (15 g/½ oz) fresh coriander
  leaves
½ cup (60 g/2 oz) slivered almonds,
  toasted
snow pea sprouts, to serve

CUCUMBER AND YOGHURT DRESSING

1 Lebanese cucumber, grated
200 g (6½ oz) thick plain yoghurt
1 tablespoon chopped fresh mint
2 teaspoons lemon juice

1 Cut the chicken breast fillets into thick strips. Combine the tandoori paste, yoghurt and lemon juice in a large bowl, add the chicken strips and toss to coat well. Refrigerate and leave to marinate overnight.

2 To make the dressing, put the grated cucumber in a medium bowl. Add the yoghurt, chopped mint and lemon juice, and stir until well combined. Refrigerate until needed.

3 Heat a large non-stick frying pan, add the marinated chicken in batches and cook, turning frequently, until cooked through. Cool and place in a large bowl. Add the coriander leaves and toasted almonds, and toss until well combined. Serve on a bed of snow pea sprouts, with the dressing served separately.

NUTRITION PER SERVE
Protein 35 g; Fat 15 g; Carbohydrate 7 g;
Dietary Fibre 2 g; Cholesterol 70 mg;
1230 kJ (290 cal)

NOTE: The quality of the tandoori paste used will determine the flavour and look of the chicken. There are many home-made varieties available from supermarkets and delicatessens.

Combine the tandoori paste with the yoghurt and lemon juice.

Using a metal grater, coarsely grate the unpeeled Lebanese cucumber.

Cook the marinated chicken strips in batches, turning frequently.

CHILLI SALT CHICKEN SALAD

Preparation time: 35 minutes
Total cooking time: 20 minutes
Serves 4

1 red capsicum, cut into julienne strips
(see Note)
1 yellow capsicum, cut into julienne
strips
4 spring onions, cut into julienne strips
1 cup (20 g/³⁄₄ oz) fresh mint leaves
1 cup (30 g/1 oz) fresh coriander
leaves
3 chicken breast fillets
¹⁄₂ cup (60 g/2 oz) plain flour
1 tablespoon chilli powder
1 tablespoon onion powder
1 tablespoon garlic powder
1 tablespoon finely crushed
sea salt
oil, for deep-frying

DRESSING
1 tablespoon sugar
2 tablespoons lemon juice
¹⁄₄ cup (60 ml/2 fl oz) rice vinegar
¹⁄₄ cup (60 ml/2 fl oz) peanut oil

1 Put the capsicum and spring onion strips in a bowl with the mint and coriander leaves.
2 To make the dressing, put the sugar, lemon juice, vinegar and oil in a bowl and whisk to combine.
3 Cut the chicken fillets into thin strips. Combine the flour, chilli powder, onion powder, garlic powder and salt in a plastic bag or shallow bowl. Add the chicken in batches and toss to coat in the flour mixture. Remove the chicken and shake off any excess flour.
4 Half fill a large heavy-based pan with the oil. When the oil is hot, add the chicken in batches and deep-fry until it is golden brown. Drain well on paper towels. Add the chicken to the bowl with the vegetables and herbs, drizzle with the dressing and toss gently to combine. Serve immediately.

NUTRITION PER SERVE
Protein 20 g; Fat 30 g; Carbohydrate 20 g; Dietary Fibre 2 g; Cholesterol 40 mg; 1720 kJ (410 cal)

NOTE: Julienne strips are even-sized strips of vegetables, the size and shape of matchsticks.

Cut the capsicums and spring onions into julienne strips.

Remove the fat from the chicken and cut the fillets into long, thin strips.

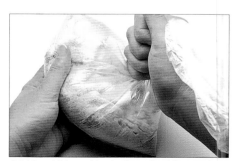
Add the chicken strips to the spiced flour and toss to coat.

CHICKEN SALAD

Preparation time: 30 minutes
Total cooking time: 15 minutes
Serves 6

150 g (5 oz) snow peas, trimmed
1 tablespoon oil
20 g (³/₄ oz) butter
4 chicken breast fillets
1 carrot, cut into julienne strips
2 celery sticks, cut into julienne strips
3 spring onions, cut into julienne strips
150 g (5 oz) button mushrooms, sliced
¹/₃ cup (7 g/¹/₄ oz) fresh flat-leaf
 parsley, chopped
1 tablespoon chopped fresh tarragon
150 g (5 oz) watercress or baby
 English spinach leaves
2 tablespoons almonds, chopped

DRESSING
¹/₄ cup (60 ml/2 fl oz) extra virgin
 olive oil
1 tablespoon white wine vinegar
¹/₂ teaspoon sugar
¹/₄ cup (60 g/2 oz) mayonnaise
2 tablespoons sour cream
1 tablespoon Dijon mustard

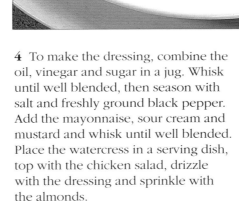

1 Plunge the snow peas into a pan of boiling water, return to the boil and cook for 1 minute, or until tender but still crisp. Rinse under cold water and drain well. Cut diagonally into strips.
2 Heat the oil and butter in a frying pan, add the chicken and cook for 7 minutes on each side over medium heat, or until tender and well browned all over. Drain on paper towels and allow to cool. Cut into thin slices.
3 Mix together the carrot, celery, spring onion, snow peas, chicken, mushrooms, parsley and tarragon, and season with salt and black pepper.

4 To make the dressing, combine the oil, vinegar and sugar in a jug. Whisk until well blended, then season with salt and freshly ground black pepper. Add the mayonnaise, sour cream and mustard and whisk until well blended. Place the watercress in a serving dish, top with the chicken salad, drizzle with the dressing and sprinkle with the almonds.

NUTRITION PER SERVE
Protein 20 g; Fat 25 g; Carbohydrate 5 g; Dietary Fibre 4 g; Cholesterol 60 mg; 1415 kJ (335 cal)

VARIATION: Add a sliced avocado and use fresh asparagus instead of snow peas.

Using a small knife, trim the mushrooms and cut into thin slices.

Cook the chicken over medium heat until well browned and tender.

Add the mayonnaise, sour cream and mustard and whisk until well blended.

THAI CHICKEN SALAD

Preparation time: 20 minutes
Total cooking time: 5 minutes
Serves 6

1 cos lettuce
2 tablespoons oil
750 g (1¹/₂ lb) chicken mince
4 fresh coriander sprigs, finely
    chopped
4 fresh mint sprigs, finely chopped
1 small red onion, sliced
3 spring onions, chopped
¹/₃ cup (80 ml/2³/₄ fl oz) lime juice
2 tablespoons soy sauce
2 tablespoons fish sauce

1 tablespoon sweet chilli sauce
2 cloves garlic, crushed
2 teaspoons soft brown sugar
1 tablespoon chopped fresh lemon
    grass, white part only
¹/₄ cup (40 g/1¹/₄ oz) roasted peanuts
1 tablespoon fresh coriander leaves
1 tablespoon chopped roasted
    peanuts

1 Wash and dry the lettuce leaves
thoroughly. Arrange on a platter.
2 Heat the oil in a heavy-based frying
pan. Add the chicken mince and
¹/₃ cup (80 ml/2³/₄ fl oz) water. Cook
over medium heat for 5 minutes, or
until the chicken is cooked and almost
all the liquid has evaporated. Break up

any lumps as the chicken cooks.
Remove from the heat.
3 Transfer the chicken to a bowl. Stir
in the chopped coriander, mint, onion
and spring onion.
4 Combine the lime juice, soy sauce,
fish sauce, sweet chilli sauce, garlic,
brown sugar and lemon grass in a
small bowl. Season with salt and mix
well. Stir into the chicken mixture.
Just before serving, stir in the peanuts.
Serve on the lettuce leaves, sprinkled
with the coriander leaves and peanuts.

NUTRITION PER SERVE
Protein 33 g; Fat 14 g; Carbohydrate 5 g;
Dietary Fibre 2.5 g; Cholesterol 62 mg;
1175 kJ (280 cal)

Break up any lumps of chicken with a fork as the
chicken cooks.

Add the coriander, mint, onion and spring onion
to the chicken.

Cut the onion into slices and finely chop the
coriander and mint.

ITALIAN-STYLE CHICKEN PASTA SALAD

Preparation time: 30 minutes +
  3 hours marinating
Total cooking time: 10 minutes
Serves 6–8

3 chicken breast fillets
1/4 cup (60 ml/2 fl oz) lemon juice
1 clove garlic, crushed
100 g (3 1/2 oz) thinly sliced prosciutto
1 Lebanese cucumber
2 tablespoons seasoned pepper
2 tablespoons olive oil
1 1/2 cups (135 g/4 1/2 oz) penne pasta,
  cooked
1/2 cup (80 g/2 3/4 oz) thinly sliced sun-
  dried tomatoes
1/2 cup (60 g/2 oz) pitted black olives,
  halved
1/2 cup (110 g/3 1/2 oz) halved bottled
  artichoke hearts
1/2 cup (50 g/1 3/4 oz) Parmesan
  shavings

CREAMY BASIL DRESSING
1/3 cup (80 ml/2 3/4 fl oz) olive oil
1 tablespoon white wine vinegar
1/4 teaspoon seasoned pepper
1 teaspoon Dijon mustard
3 teaspoons cornflour
2/3 cup (170 ml/5 1/2 fl oz) cream
1/3 cup (20 g/3/4 oz) shredded fresh
  basil

1 Remove the fat and sinew from the chicken. Flatten the chicken slightly with a mallet or rolling pin. Place the chicken in a bowl with the combined lemon juice and garlic. Cover and refrigerate for at least 3 hours or overnight, turning occasionally.
2 Cut the prosciutto into strips. Halve the cucumber lengthways, then slice.
3 Drain the chicken and coat with the seasoned pepper. Heat the oil in a large heavy-based frying pan. Cook the chicken for 4 minutes on each side, or until lightly browned and cooked through. Remove from the heat and cool. Cut into pieces.
4 To make the dressing, combine the oil, vinegar, pepper and mustard in a pan. Blend the cornflour with 1/3 cup (80 ml/2 3/4 fl oz) water until smooth, then add to the pan. Whisk over

Cut the cucumber in half lengthways, then cut into slices.

Cook the chicken until llightly browned, then cool and cut into pieces.

Add the cream, basil and salt to the pan and stir until heated through.

Combine the pasta, chicken, cucumber, prosciutto, tomato, olives and artichoke hearts.

medium heat for 2 minutes, or until the sauce boils and thickens. Add the cream, basil and salt. Stir until heated.
5 Combine the pasta, chicken, cucumber, prosciutto, tomato, olives and artichoke hearts in a large serving bowl. Pour in the dressing and toss gently to combine. Serve warm or cold, sprinkled with the Parmesan.

NUTRITION PER SERVE (8)
Protein 22 g; Fat 28 g; Carbohydrate 38 g;
Dietary Fibre 3.5 g; Cholesterol 64 mg;
2070 kJ (495 cal)

Pan-fries & Stir-fries

CHICKEN AND CASHEW STIR-FRY

Preparation time: 30 minutes
Total cooking time: 20 minutes
Serves 4–6

oil, for cooking
750 g (1 1/2 lb) chicken thigh fillets, cut into strips
2 egg whites, lightly beaten
1/2 cup (60 g/2 oz) cornflour
2 onions, thinly sliced
1 red capsicum, thinly sliced
200 g (6 1/2 oz) broccoli, cut into bite-sized pieces
2 tablespoons soy sauce
2 tablespoons sherry
1 tablespoon oyster sauce
1/3 cup (50 g/1 3/4 oz) roasted cashews
4 spring onions, diagonally sliced

1 Heat a wok until very hot, add 1 tablespoon of the oil and swirl it around to coat the side. Dip about a quarter of the chicken strips into the egg white and then into the cornflour. Add to the wok and stir-fry for 3–5 minutes, or until the chicken is golden brown and just cooked. Drain on paper towels and repeat with the remaining chicken, reheating the wok and adding a little more oil each time.

2 Reheat the wok, add 1 tablespoon of the oil and stir-fry the onion, capsicum and broccoli over medium heat for 4–5 minutes, or until the vegetables have softened slightly. Increase the heat to high and add the soy sauce, sherry and oyster sauce. Toss the vegetables well in the sauce and bring to the boil.

3 Return the chicken to the wok and toss over high heat for 1–2 minutes to heat the chicken and make sure it is entirely cooked through. Season well with salt and freshly cracked pepper. Toss the cashews and spring onion through the chicken mixture, and serve immediately.

NUTRITION PER SERVE (6)
Protein 35 g; Fat 15 g; Carbohydrate 15 g;
Dietary Fibre 3 g; Cholesterol 60 mg;
1375 kJ (330 cal)

NOTE: When choosing chicken, buy free range if you can as it has a better flavour and texture. Yellowish flesh indicates the chicken has been grain fed, but it is not necessarily free range.

Dip the chicken strips into the egg white, then into the cornflour.

Stir-fry the coated chicken in batches until it is golden brown.

PAN-FRIED CHICKEN TENDERLOINS WITH VEGETABLES

Preparation time: 25 minutes
Total cooking time: 20 minutes
Serves 4

2 tablespoons oil
6 slices prosciutto, cut crossways into
    1 cm strips
500 g (1 lb) chicken tenderloins
1 red onion, chopped
2 cloves garlic, crushed
1 small red chilli, chopped
1 tablespoon plain flour
1¹/₂ cups (375 ml/12 fl oz) chicken
    stock
150 g (5 oz) asparagus, halved
250 g (8 oz) beans, halved
¹/₄ cup (15 g/¹/₂ oz) chopped fresh
    chives

1 Heat 1 tablespoon of the oil in a frying pan. Stir-fry the prosciutto over medium-high heat for 2 minutes, or until crisp. Lift out with a slotted spoon and drain on paper towels.
2 Add the chicken to the pan and cook over high heat for 1 minute on each side, or until brown, turning once. Remove from the pan and drain on paper towels.
3 Heat the remaining oil in a pan. Add the onion, garlic and chilli and stir-fry over medium-high heat for 2 minutes, or until softened. Add the flour and stir for 1 minute.
4 Add the stock gradually, stirring over the heat until the mixture boils and thickens. Add the asparagus and beans and reduce the heat to low. Cook, covered, for 3–5 minutes, or until the vegetables are tender. Return the chicken tenderloins to the pan and cook for 1 minute, or until heated through. Stir in the chopped chives and serve hot, sprinkled with the prosciutto strips.

NUTRITION PER SERVE
Protein 4.5 g; Fat 10 g; Carbohydrate 6.5 g; Dietary Fibre 3 g; Cholesterol 2.5 mg; 263 kJ (135 cal)

HINT: Serve this dish with penne pasta or steamed potatoes.

Trim the asparagus spears and beans, then cut them in half.

Fry the chicken over high heat, then remove and drain on paper towels.

Sprinkle the flour over the onion mixture and stir for 1 minute.

Cook the asparagus and beans in the stock mixture until they are tender.

CHICKEN MARSALA

Preparation time: 10 minutes
Total cooking time: 25 minutes
Serves 4

4 chicken breast fillets
2 tablespoons oil
60 g (2 oz) butter
1 clove garlic, crushed
2 cups (500 ml/16 fl oz) chicken
    stock
1/3 cup (80 ml/2³/4 fl oz) Marsala
2 teaspoons plain flour
2 teaspoons Worcestershire
    sauce
1/4 cup (60 ml/2 fl oz) cream

1 Trim the chicken of excess fat and sinew. Heat the oil in a heavy-based frying pan and add the chicken. Cook over medium heat for 4 minutes on each side, or until cooked through and lightly golden. Remove the chicken, cover loosely with foil and keep warm. Drain off any fat from the pan.
2 Add the butter and garlic to the pan and stir over medium heat for 2 minutes. Add the combined stock and Marsala and bring to the boil. Reduce the heat and simmer for 10 minutes, or until the liquid has reduced by half.
3 Stir the flour, Worcestershire sauce and cream together. Add a little of the hot liquid and blend to a paste. Add to the pan and stir over medium heat until the sauce boils and thickens. Season to taste and then pour over the chicken fillets. Delicious with pasta.

NUTRITION PER SERVE
Protein 55 g; Fat 35 g; Carbohydrate 2 g;
Dietary Fibre 0 g; Cholesterol 180 mg;
2220 kJ (530 cal)

VARIATION: Marsala is a sweet wine and so makes a sweet-tasting sauce. Port or any dry red wine can be used instead. Boiling wine evaporates the alcohol, leaving the flavour but not the intoxicating qualities. Chicken thighs or drumsticks can be used instead of breast fillets.

Cook the chicken in a frying pan until lightly golden on each side.

Mix together the stock and Marsala, then add to the pan and bring to the boil.

Add the Worcestershire sauce mixture and stir over the heat until thickened.

HONEY CHICKEN

Preparation time: 15 minutes
Total cooking time: 25 minutes
Serves 4

oil, for cooking
500 g (1 lb) chicken thigh fillets,
    cut into cubes
1 egg white, lightly beaten
1/3 cup (40 g/1 1/4 oz) cornflour
2 onions, thinly sliced
1 green capsicum, cubed
2 carrots, cut into batons
100 g (3 1/2 oz) snow peas,
    sliced

1/4 cup (90 g/3 oz) honey
2 tablespoons toasted almonds

1 Heat a wok until very hot, add
1 1/2 tablespoons of the oil and swirl it
around to coat the side. Dip half of the
chicken into the egg white, then lightly
dust with the cornflour. Stir-fry over
high heat for 4–5 minutes, or until the
chicken is golden brown and just
cooked. Remove from the wok and
drain on paper towels. Repeat with the
remaining chicken, then remove all
the chicken from the wok.
2 Reheat the wok, add 1 tablespoon
of the oil and stir-fry the sliced onion
over high heat for 3–4 minutes, or until

slightly softened. Add the capsicum
and carrot, and cook, tossing, for
3–4 minutes, or until tender. Stir in the
snow peas and cook for 2 minutes.
3 Increase the heat, add the honey
and toss the vegetables until well
coated. Return the chicken to the wok
and toss until it is heated through and
is well coated in the honey. Remove
from the heat and season well with salt
and pepper. Serve immediately,
sprinkled with the almonds.

NUTRITION PER SERVE
Protein 35 g; Fat 20 g; Carbohydrate 35 g;
Dietary Fibre 4 g; Cholesterol 60 mg;
1815 kJ (435 cal)

Trim the excess fat from the chicken, and cut the
chicken into cubes.

Dip the chicken into the egg white, then lightly
dust with the cornflour.

Stir-fry the chicken pieces until golden brown and
just cooked.

CHICKEN IN TANGY LIME MARMALADE SAUCE

Preparation time: 25 minutes
Total cooking time: 20 minutes
Serves 4

500 g (1 lb) chicken thigh fillets, cut into strips
5 cm (2 inch) piece ginger, cut into paper-thin slices
4 spring onions, thinly sliced
oil, for cooking
1 red capsicum, thinly sliced
1 tablespoon mirin

1 tablespoon lime marmalade
2 teaspoons grated lime rind
2 tablespoons lime juice

1 Put the chicken, ginger, spring onion and some ground black pepper in a dish. Toss well to combine.
2 Heat a wok until very hot, add 1 tablespoon of the oil and swirl it around to coat the side. Stir-fry the chicken mixture in three batches over high heat for about 3 minutes, or until it is golden brown and cooked through. Reheat the wok in between each batch, adding more oil when necessary. Remove all the chicken from the wok and set aside.

3 Reheat the wok, add the capsicum and stir-fry for 30 seconds. Add the mirin, marmalade, lime rind and juice, and season with salt and freshly ground black pepper. Cover and steam for 1 minute. Add the chicken and cook, uncovered, for 2 minutes, or until heated through.

NUTRITION PER SERVE
Protein 30 g; Fat 10 g; Carbohydrate 5.5 g;
Dietary Fibre 0 g; Cholesterol 60 mg;
1050 kJ (250 cal)

HINT: Choose young ginger with thin skin as it will be tender and easy to slice.

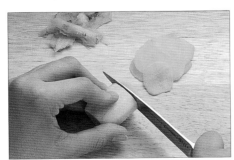

Peel the skin from the ginger, and cut it into paper-thin slices.

Remove the seeds and membrane from the capsicum, and cut it into thin slices.

Combine the chicken, ginger, spring onion and some black pepper.

very Good

More sauce & lemon

LEMON CHICKEN

Preparation time: 15 minutes
  + 30 minutes marinating
Total cooking time: 10 minutes
Serves 4

500 g (1 lb) chicken breast fillets
1 egg white, lightly beaten
2 teaspoons cornflour
1/2 teaspoon salt
1/4 teaspoon grated ginger
1/4 cup (60 ml/2 fl oz) oil

LEMON SAUCE
2 teaspoons cornflour
1½ tablespoons caster sugar

6   3/4 lemons
2 tablespoons lemon juice _ *but more*
3/4 cup (185 ml/6 fl oz) chicken stock
2 teaspoons soy sauce
1 teaspoon dry sherry

1 Pat the chicken dry with paper towels. Cut the chicken fillets on the diagonal into 1 cm (1/2 inch) wide strips. Combine the egg white, cornflour, salt and ginger and add the chicken strips, mixing well. Marinate in the refrigerator for 30 minutes.
2 Heat the oil in a wok or heavy-based frying pan, swirling to coat. Drain the chicken from the marinade, add to the pan and stir-fry over medium-high heat until just cooked but not browned. Place the chicken on

a plate to keep warm while preparing the sauce. Carefully pour the excess oil from the wok and discard.
3 To make the lemon sauce, mix the cornflour with 2 tablespoons water to form a smooth paste. Add to the wok with the sugar, lemon juice, chicken stock, soy sauce and sherry. Stir over high heat and boil for 1 minute. Add the chicken, stirring to coat it with the sauce. Transfer to a serving platter. Serve at once with steamed rice or noodles and stir-fried vegetables.

NUTRITION PER SERVE
Protein 29 g; Fat 17 g; Carbohydrate 8 g;
Dietary Fibre 0 g; Cholesterol 63 mg;
1280 kJ (306 cal)

Cut the chicken breast fillets on the diagonal into thin strips.

Stir-fry the marinated chicken until it is just cooked but not browned.

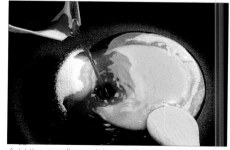

Add the cornflour mixture to the wok with the sugar, lemon juice, stock, soy sauce and sherry.

CRISP-SKINNED CHICKEN

Preparation time: 1 hour + cooling
Total cooking time: 25 minutes
Serves 4

1.3 kg (2 lb 10 oz) chicken
1 tablespoon honey
1 star anise
1 strip dried mandarin peel (see Note)
1 teaspoon salt
oil, for deep-frying
2 lemons, cut into wedges

FIVE-SPICE SALT
2 tablespoons sea salt
1 teaspoon white peppercorns
1/2 teaspoon five-spice powder
1/2 teaspoon ground white pepper

1 Place the chicken in a pan and cover with cold water. Add the honey, star anise, mandarin peel and salt, and bring to the boil. Reduce the heat and simmer for 15 minutes. Turn off the heat and leave the chicken, covered, for 15 minutes. Transfer the chicken to a plate, and cool. Cut the chicken in half lengthways. Place on paper towels, uncovered, in the refrigerator for 20 minutes.
2 Heat the oil in a wok or deep, heavy-based pan. It is hot enough to use when a piece of bread dropped into the oil turns brown in 30 seconds. Very gently lower in half the chicken, skin-side down. Cook for 6 minutes, then turn and cook for another 6 minutes, making sure all the skin comes in contact with the oil. Drain

on paper towels. Repeat with the remaining chicken.
3 To make the five-spice salt, put the sea salt and peppercorns in a pan and dry-fry until fragrant and the salt is slightly browned. Crush in a mortar and pestle. Mix with the five-spice powder and white pepper. Joint the chicken and serve sprinkled with the five-spice salt and with lemon wedges.

NUTRITION PER SERVE
Protein 45 g; Fat 15 g; Carbohydrate 7 g;
Dietary Fibre 1.5 g; Cholesterol 100 mg;
1482 kJ (355 cal)

NOTE: To make dried mandarin peel, remove all of the pith from strips of peel and bake in a moderate 180°C (350°F/Gas 4) oven for 15 minutes.

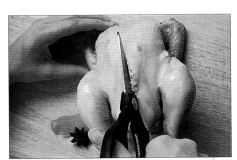
Use poultry scissors to cut the cooled chicken in half lengthways.

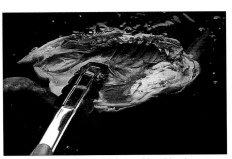
Gently lower half the chicken, skin-side down, into the oil.

Crush the sea salt and white peppercorns in a mortar and pestle.

GOAN-STYLE CHICKEN WITH SULTANAS AND ALMONDS

Preparation time: 20 minutes
Total cooking time: 20 minutes
Serves 3–4

2 teaspoons ground cumin
2 teaspoons ground coriander
1 teaspoon ground cinnamon
1/2 teaspoon cayenne pepper
1/2 teaspoon ground cardamom
oil, for cooking
1 large onion, cut into thin wedges
2 cloves garlic, finely chopped
500 g (1 lb) chicken breast fillets, cut into cubes
2 teaspoons finely grated orange rind
2 tablespoons orange juice
2 tablespoons sultanas
1 teaspoon soft brown sugar
1/4 cup (60 g/2 oz) thick plain yoghurt
1/3 cup (40 g/11/4 oz) slivered almonds, toasted

1 Dry-fry the spices in a wok over low heat for about 1 minute, or until fragrant, shaking the wok regularly.
2 Add 1 tablespoon oil to the wok and stir-fry the onion wedges and garlic over high heat for 3 minutes. Remove from the wok.
3 Reheat the wok, add 1 tablespoon of the oil and stir-fry the chicken in two batches until it is golden and just cooked. Return all the chicken to the wok with the onion mixture, orange rind, juice, sultanas and sugar. Cook for 1 minute, tossing until most of the juice evaporates.
4 Stir in the yoghurt and reheat gently, without boiling or the yoghurt will separate. Season well with salt and pepper. Serve garnished with the toasted almonds.

NUTRITION PER SERVE (4)
Protein 30 g; Fat 20 g; Carbohydrate 15 g; Dietary Fibre 2.5 g; Cholesterol 65 mg; 1500 kJ (360 cal)

NOTE: Yoghurt separates easily when heated due to its acid balance. Yoghurt also separates when shaken, whipped or stirred too much.

Toast the almonds by dry-frying them in the wok until golden brown.

Dry-fry the cumin, coriander, cinnamon, cayenne and cardamom over low heat until fragrant.

Stir-fry the onion wedges and garlic with the spices and oil.

Add the onion mixture, orange rind, juice, sultanas and sugar to the chicken.

CHICKEN WITH OLIVES AND SUN-DRIED TOMATOES

Preparation time: 20 minutes
Total cooking time: 15 minutes
Serves 4

olive oil, for cooking
600 g (1¼ lb) chicken breast fillets,
    cut diagonally into thin slices
1 red onion, thinly sliced
3 cloves garlic, finely chopped
2 tablespoons white wine vinegar
1 teaspoon sambal oelek
1 tablespoon lemon juice

12 Kalamata olives, pitted and
    quartered lengthways
¼ cup (40 g/1¼ oz) sun-dried
    tomatoes, cut into thin strips
¼ cup (15 g/½ oz) finely chopped
    fresh parsley
1 tablespoon shredded fresh basil

1 Heat a wok until very hot, add 2 teaspoons of the oil and swirl it around to coat the side. Stir-fry the chicken slices in two batches until browned and cooked through, adding more oil in between each batch. Remove all the chicken from the wok and keep warm.
2 Reheat the wok, add 1 tablespoon of the oil and stir-fry the onion until it is soft and golden. Add the garlic and cook for 1 minute. Return the warm chicken to the wok. Add the vinegar, sambal oelek and lemon juice, and toss well.
3 Stir in the olive pieces, sun-dried tomato, parsley and basil, and season with salt and ground black pepper. Heat through thoroughly.

NUTRITION PER SERVE
Protein 35 g; Fat 15 g; Carbohydrate 2.5 g; Dietary Fibre 1.5 g; Cholesterol 75 mg; 1420 kJ (335 cal)

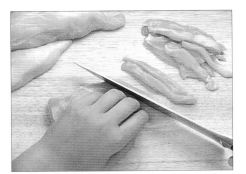

Trim the fat from the chicken breast fillets, and cut into thin diagonal slices.

Sambal oelek is a paste made from salt, vinegar and chilli.

Drain the sun-dried tomatoes and cut them into thin strips.

CHICKEN AND LEMON MEATBALLS

Preparation time: 20 minutes
  + 30 minutes refrigeration
Total cooking time: 10 minutes
Serves 4

500 g (1 lb) chicken mince
2 cloves garlic, crushed
1 cup (80 g/2³/₄ oz) fresh white
    breadcrumbs
1 teaspoon grated lemon rind
1 teaspoon fresh lemon thyme leaves
1 egg, lightly beaten

1 tablespoon olive oil
2 tablespoons lemon juice

YOGHURT MINT SAUCE
200 g (6¹/₂ oz) plain yoghurt
1 tablespoon shredded fresh mint
rinsed, chopped skin from
    ¹/₄ of a preserved lemon

1 Using your hands, mix the chicken mince, garlic, breadcrumbs, lemon rind, thyme, egg and some salt and black pepper together in a large bowl. Wet your hands and form tablespoons of the mixture into balls and place on a lined tray. Refrigerate for 30 minutes.

2 To make the yoghurt mint sauce, mix the yoghurt, mint and preserved lemon rind together.
3 Heat the oil in a non-stick frying pan and cook the chicken meatballs in two batches, until golden on all sides and cooked through. Sprinkle with the lemon juice, transfer to a serving dish and sprinkle with more salt. Serve with the yoghurt mint sauce.

NUTRITION PER SERVE
Protein 35 g; Fat 11 g; Carbohydrate 16 g;
Dietary Fibre 1 g; Cholesterol 116 mg;
1300 kJ (310 cal)

Combine the chicken, garlic, breadcrumbs, lemon rind, thyme, egg, salt and pepper.

Using wet hands, roll tablespoons of the mixture into balls.

Cook the meatballs in batches until golden and cooked through.

CHICKEN AND CHEESE BURGERS

Preparation time: 40 minutes
Total cooking time: 10–15 minutes
Makes 6

oil, for cooking
1 large onion, finely chopped
750 g (1¹/₂ lb) chicken mince
1 teaspoon paprika
1–2 teaspoons chopped red chilli
³/₄ cup (60 g/2 oz) fresh breadcrumbs
¹/₃ cup (90 g/3 oz) sour cream
2 tablespoons chopped fresh lemon
    thyme or chives
90 g (3 oz) Cheddar
30 g (1 oz) butter
1–2 cloves garlic, crushed

6 crusty bread rolls
lettuce, tomato, extra sour cream,
    pickled cucumbers and sweet chilli
    sauce, to serve

1 Heat a little oil in a frying pan. Add the onion and cook over medium heat until golden. Drain the onion on paper towels and cool slightly.

2 Using your hands, mix together in a large bowl the onion, chicken mince, paprika, chilli, breadcrumbs, sour cream, lemon thyme and some salt and freshly ground black pepper. Divide the mixture into 6 equal portions and shape into round balls. Cut the cheese into 6 pieces. Press a piece of cheese into the centre of each ball and mould the mixture to completely enclose the cheese. Flatten

the balls slightly to make patties.

3 Heat the butter and 1 tablespoon of oil in a large frying pan. Add the garlic. When the mixture is foaming, add the patties, pressing with a spatula to flatten slightly. Cook over medium heat for 2–3 minutes each side, or until the patties are browned and the cheese melted.

4 Split the bread rolls in half. Toast and spread with a little butter if you wish. Fill with lettuce and tomato slices, a chicken patty, sour cream, some pickled cucumbers and sweet chilli sauce.

NUTRITION PER BURGER
Protein 40 g; Fat 19 g; Carbohydrate 37 g;
Dietary Fibre 3 g; Cholesterol 107 mg;
2010 kJ (480 cal)

Transfer the cooked onion to a plate covered with paper towels, to drain.

Press a portion of cheese into the centre of each ball and completely enclose.

When the mixture is foaming, add the patties to the pan.

STIR-FRIED SESAME CHICKEN AND LEEK

Preparation time: 15 minutes
Total cooking time: 16 minutes
Serves 4–6

2 tablespoons sesame seeds
1 tablespoon oil
2 teaspoons sesame oil
800 g (1 lb 10 oz) chicken tenderloins, cut diagonally into strips
1 leek, white part only, julienned
2 cloves garlic, crushed
2 tablespoons soy sauce
1 tablespoon mirin
1 teaspoon sugar

1 Heat a wok until very hot, add the sesame seeds and dry-fry over high heat until they are golden. Remove the seeds from the wok.
2 Reheat the wok, add the oils and swirl them around to coat the side. Stir-fry the chicken strips in three batches over high heat, tossing constantly until just cooked. Reheat the wok before each addition. Return all the chicken to the wok.
3 Add the julienned leek and the garlic and cook for 1–2 minutes, or until the leek is soft and golden. Check that the chicken is cooked through; if it is not cooked, reduce the heat and cook, covered, for 2 minutes, or until it is completely cooked.
4 Add the soy sauce, mirin, sugar and toasted sesame seeds to the wok, and toss well to combine. Season with salt and black pepper, and serve immediately. Delicious with pasta.

NUTRITION PER SERVE (6)
Protein 2 g; Fat 8.5 g; Carbohydrate 2 g;
Dietary Fibre 1 g; Cholesterol 0 mg;
395 kJ (95 cal)

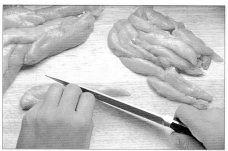
Use a sharp knife to cut the chicken tenderloins into thin diagonal strips.

Trim the ends of the leek, then cut the white part of the leek into julienne strips.

Dry-fry the sesame seeds over high heat, stirring, until golden.

STIR-FRIED CHICKEN, LEMON AND CAPERS

Preparation time: 15 minutes
Total cooking time: 15 minutes
Serves 4

olive oil, for cooking
1 red onion, cut into thin wedges
25 g (3/4 oz) butter
800 g (1 lb 10 oz) chicken breast
    fillets, cut into bite-sized pieces
rind of 1 lemon, cut into thin strips
2 tablespoons baby capers, rinsed
    well and drained
1/3 cup (80 ml/2 3/4 fl oz) lemon juice
1/4 cup (15 g/1/2 oz) shredded fresh
    basil

1 Heat a wok until very hot, add 2 teaspoons of the oil and swirl it around to coat the side. Add the red onion wedges and stir-fry until softened and golden. Remove from the wok and set aside.

2 Reheat the wok, add 2 teaspoons of the oil and half the butter, and stir-fry the chicken in two batches until it is browned, adding more oil and butter between batches. Return all the chicken to the wok with the onion.

3 Stir in the lemon rind, capers and lemon juice. Toss well and cook until warmed through. Add the shredded basil and season with salt and black pepper. Delicious served with creamy mashed potato.

NUTRITION PER SERVE
Protein 45 g; Fat 20 g; Carbohydrate 2.5 g;
Dietary Fibre 1 g; Cholesterol 115 mg;
1550 kJ (370 cal)

Peel the red onion, cut it in half and cut it into thin wedges.

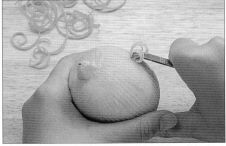

Use a citrus zester to remove thin strips of rind from the lemon.

Stir-fry the red onion wedges until they are soft and golden.

GINGER CHICKEN WITH BLACK FUNGUS

Preparation time: 25 minutes
Total cooking time: 15 minutes
Serves 4

1/4 cup (15 g/1/2 oz) black (wood)
    fungus (see Note)
1 tablespoon oil
3 cloves garlic, chopped
6 cm (21/2 inch) piece ginger, cut into
    thin shreds
500 g (1 lb) chicken breast fillets,
    sliced
4 spring onions, chopped

1 tablespoon Golden Mountain sauce
1 tablespoon fish sauce
2 teaspoons brown sugar
1/2 red capsicum, thinly sliced
1/2 cup (15 g/1/2 oz) fresh coriander
    leaves
1/2 cup (20 g/3/4 oz) shredded fresh
    Thai basil leaves

1 Soak the fungus in a bowl of hot water for 15 minutes, or until soft and swollen, then drain and chop roughly.
2 Heat the oil in a large wok, add the garlic and ginger and stir-fry for 1 minute. Add the chicken and stir-fry in batches over high heat until the chicken changes colour. Return all of the chicken to the wok. Add the spring onion and Golden Mountain sauce, and stir-fry for 1 minute.
3 Add the fish sauce, brown sugar and fungus to the pan. Stir thoroughly, then cover and steam for 2 minutes. Serve immediately, scattered with the capsicum, coriander and basil.

NUTRITION PER SERVE
Protein 30 g; Fat 8 g; Carbohydrate 3.5 g;
Dietary Fibre 1 g; Cholesterol 62 mg;
842 kJ (200 cal)

NOTE: Black (wood) fungus is a dried mushroom that swells to many times its size when soaked in hot water.

When the fungus is soft and swollen, drain it well and chop it with a sharp knife.

Add the spring onion and Golden Mountain sauce, and stir-fry for 1 minute.

Cover the wok and allow the mixture to steam for 2 minutes.

CURRIED RICE NOODLES WITH CHICKEN

Preparation time: 25 minutes
Total cooking time: 10–15 minutes
Serves 4–6

200 g (6½ oz) thick rice stick noodles (see Note)
1½ tablespoons oil
1 tablespoon red curry paste
3 chicken thigh fillets, cut into thin strips
1–2 teaspoons chopped red chilli
2 tablespoons fish sauce
2 tablespoons lime juice
100 g (3½ oz) bean sprouts
½ cup (80 g/2¾ oz) roasted chopped peanuts
¼ cup (20 g/¾ oz) crisp-fried onion
¼ cup (25 g/¾ oz) crisp-fried garlic
1 cup (30 g/1 oz) fresh coriander leaves

1 Cook the noodles in a pot of rapidly boiling water for 2 minutes. Drain and then toss with 2 teaspoons of the oil to prevent the strands from sticking together. Set aside.
2 Heat the remaining oil in a wok, add the curry paste and stir for 1 minute, or until fragrant. Add the chicken in batches and stir-fry for 2 minutes, or until golden brown. Return all of the chicken to the pan.
3 Add the chilli, fish sauce and lime juice. Bring to the boil and simmer for 1 minute. Add the bean sprouts and noodles and toss well. Arrange the noodles on a plate and sprinkle with the peanuts, onion, garlic and coriander leaves. Serve immediately.

NUTRITION PER SERVE (6)
Protein 32 g; Fat 20 g; Carbohydrate 12 g; Dietary Fibre 3 g; Cholesterol 55 mg; 1452 kJ (345 cal)

NOTE: Rice stick noodles are flat and are available from Asian food stores and some supermarkets.

Toss 2 teaspoons of oil through the noodles, using 2 wooden spoons.

Cook each batch of chicken for 2 minutes and return all of the chicken to the pan.

Add the bean sprouts and noodles to the wok and toss well to distribute evenly.

CHICKEN WITH BEANS AND ASPARAGUS

Preparation time: 25 minutes
  + 15 minutes marinating
Total cooking time: 15 minutes
Serves 4

1 stem lemon grass, white part only,
    chopped
5 cm (2 inch) piece ginger, peeled and
    chopped
2–3 small red chillies, seeded and
    chopped
1 teaspoon grated kaffir lime or lime
    rind
2–3 cloves garlic, chopped
1/2 teaspoon ground black pepper
2 tablespoons oil
375 g (12 oz) chicken breast fillets, cut
    into thin strips
250 g (8 oz) green beans, cut into
    short pieces
1 celery stick, cut into thick slices
185 g (6 oz) snow peas, halved
200 g (6 1/2 oz) asparagus, cut into
    short pieces
270 ml (9 fl oz) can coconut cream
2 tablespoons sweet chilli sauce
20 small fresh basil leaves

1 Place the lemon grass, ginger, chilli,
lime rind, garlic, pepper and oil in a
food processor or blender, and process
until the mixture forms a rough paste.
Combine the paste and chicken strips
in a glass or ceramic bowl, cover and
refrigerate for at least 15 minutes.
2 Briefly blanch the beans, celery,
snow peas and asparagus in a pan of
boiling water. Drain and plunge into
iced water. Drain again.
3 Heat the wok until very hot and stir-
fry the chicken mixture in batches over
high heat for 3–4 minutes, or until the
chicken is cooked through. Stir
constantly so the paste doesn't burn.
Return all of the chicken to the wok
with the vegetables, coconut cream,
sweet chilli sauce, to taste, and basil
leaves. Stir-fry until heated through.
Serve with rice or noodles.

NUTRITION PER SERVE
Protein 50 g; Fat 30 g; Carbohydrate 8 g;
Dietary Fibre 6 g; Cholesterol 95 mg;
1990 kJ (475 cal)

Grating rind is easier if you fit a piece of baking
paper over the grater first.

Process the lemon grass, ginger, chilli, lime rind,
garlic, pepper and oil to a paste.

CHICKEN WITH WALNUTS AND STRAW MUSHROOMS

Preparation time: 20 minutes
Total cooking time: 15 minutes
Serves 4

375 g (12 oz) chicken breast fillets or tenderloins, cut into thin strips
1/2 teaspoon five-spice powder
2 teaspoons cornflour
2 tablespoons soy sauce
2 tablespoons oyster sauce
2 teaspoons soft brown sugar
1 teaspoon sesame oil
oil, for cooking
75 g (2 1/2 oz) walnuts
150 g (5 oz) snake beans or green beans, chopped

6 spring onions, sliced
425 g (14 oz) can straw mushrooms, rinsed
230 g (7 1/2 oz) can sliced bamboo shoots, rinsed

1 Dry the chicken strips with paper towels and sprinkle with the five-spice powder. Mix the cornflour with the soy sauce in a bowl until smooth. Add 1/2 cup (125 ml/4 fl oz) water along with the oyster sauce, brown sugar and sesame oil.

2 Heat the wok until very hot, add 1 tablespoon of the oil and swirl it around to coat the side. Stir-fry the walnuts for 30 seconds, or until lightly browned. Drain on paper towels.

3 Reheat the wok over high heat. Add 1 tablespoon of the oil and stir-fry the chicken in batches for 2–3 minutes, or until just cooked through. Remove all of the chicken from the wok and set aside.

4 Add the snake beans, spring onion, straw mushrooms and bamboo shoots to the wok, and stir-fry for 2 minutes. Remove from the wok. Add the soy sauce mixture and heat for 1 minute, or until slightly thickened. Return the chicken and vegetables to the wok, and toss to coat with the sauce. Season well. Serve at once, sprinkled with the stir-fried walnuts.

NUTRITION PER SERVE
Protein 30 g; Fat 25 g; Carbohydrate 10 g; Dietary Fibre 6.5 g; Cholesterol 45 mg; 1675 kJ (400 cal)

Wash the straw mushrooms in a sieve under cold running water.

Top and tail the snake beans, and cut them into short pieces.

Stir-fry the walnuts in the hot oil until they are lightly browned.

FRIED CRISPY NOODLES (MEE GROB)

Preparation time: 30 minutes
Total cooking time: 20 minutes
Serves 4

100 g (3¹/₂ oz) rice vermicelli
2 cups (500ml/16 fl oz) oil, for deep-
    frying
100 g (3¹/₂ oz) fried bean curd, cut
    into matchsticks
2 cloves garlic, finely chopped
4 cm (1¹/₂ inch) piece ginger, grated
150 g (5 oz) chicken mince
100 g (3¹/₂ oz) raw prawn meat, finely
    chopped
1 tablespoon white vinegar
2 tablespoons fish sauce
2 tablespoons soft brown sugar
2 tablespoons chilli sauce
1 teaspoon chopped red chilli
2 small knobs pickled garlic, chopped
¹/₄ bunch fresh garlic chives, chopped
1 cup (30 g/1 oz) fresh coriander
    leaves

1 Place the vermicelli in a bowl of hot water for 1 minute. Drain and allow to dry for 20 minutes. Heat the oil in a wok or deep pan, add the bean curd in two batches and cook for 1 minute, or until golden and crisp. Drain.
2 Add the completely dry vermicelli to the wok in several batches and cook for 10 seconds, or until puffed and crisp. Remove from the oil immediately to prevent the vermicelli absorbing too much oil. Drain on paper towels and allow to cool.
3 Drain all but 1 tablespoon of the oil from the wok. Reheat wok over high heat and add the garlic, ginger, mince and prawn meat; stir-fry for 2 minutes or until golden brown. Add the vinegar, fish sauce, brown sugar, chilli sauce and chilli, and stir until boiling.
4 Just before serving, add the noodles and bean curd to the wok and toss thoroughly. Quickly toss through the pickled garlic, chives and coriander. Serve immediately.

NUTRITION PER SERVE
Protein 18 g; Fat 123 g; Carbohydrate 28 g;
Dietary Fibre 3 g; Cholesterol 56 mg;
5183 kJ (1238 cal)

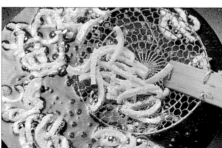
Cook the bean curd for 1 minute until golden brown. Remove with wire mesh strainer.

Add the vermicelli to the wok in batches and cook until puffed and crisp.

Add the chopped garlic, grated ginger, mince and prawn meat to the wok.

Just before serving, return the noodles and bean curd to the wok, and toss.

CHIANG MAI NOODLES

Preparation time: 20 minutes
Total cooking time: 15 minutes
Serves 4

500 g (1 lb) fresh egg noodles
1 tablespoon oil
3 French or Asian shallots, peeled and chopped
6 cloves garlic, chopped
2 teaspoons finely chopped red chilli, optional
1–2 tablespoons red curry paste
350 g (11 oz) lean chicken, thinly sliced

1 carrot, cut into fine, thin strips
2 tablespoons fish sauce
2 teaspoons soft brown sugar
3 spring onions, thinly sliced
1/4 cup (7 g/1/4 oz) fresh coriander leaves

1 Cook the noodles in a wok or pan of rapidly boiling water for 2–3 minutes, or until they are just tender. Drain and keep warm.
2 Heat the oil in a wok or large frying pan until it is very hot. Add the shallots, garlic, chilli and curry paste, and stir-fry for 2 minutes, or until the mixture is fragrant. Add the chicken in two batches and cook for 3 minutes,

or until the chicken changes colour.
3 Return all of the chicken to the wok. Add the carrot, fish sauce and brown sugar, and bring to the boil. Divide the noodles between serving bowls and mix in portions of the chicken mixture and spring onion. Top with the coriander leaves. Serve immediately.

NUTRITION PER SERVE
Protein 37 g; Fat 10 g; Carbohydrate 92 g; Dietary Fibre 4.5 g; Cholesterol 67 mg; 2565 kJ (612 cal)

HINT: This dish must be served as soon as it is cooked or the noodles and vegetables will go soggy.

Use a sharp knife to peel and finely chop the French shallots.

Cook the noodles in a wok or pan of rapidly boiling water until just tender.

Place all the chicken back into the wok. Add carrot, fish sauce and brown sugar.

CHICKEN WITH OYSTER SAUCE AND BASIL

Preparation time: 20 minutes
Total cooking time: 10 minutes
Serves 4

1/4 cup (60 ml/2 fl oz) oyster sauce
2 tablespoons fish sauce
1 tablespoon grated palm sugar
1 tablespoon oil
2–3 cloves garlic, crushed
1 tablespoon grated fresh ginger
1–2 red chillies, seeded and finely
    chopped
4 spring onions, finely chopped

375 g (12 oz) chicken breast fillets, cut
    into thin strips
250 g (8 oz) broccoli, cut into florets
230 g (7 1/2 oz) can water chestnuts,
    drained
230 g (7 1/2 oz) can sliced bamboo
    shoots, rinsed
20 fresh basil leaves, shredded

1 Put 1/4 cup (60 ml/2 fl oz) water in a small jug with the oyster sauce, fish sauce and palm sugar. Mix well.
2 Heat a wok until very hot, add the oil and swirl it around to coat the side. Stir-fry the garlic, ginger, chilli and spring onion for 1 minute over medium heat. Increase the heat to medium-high, add the chicken and stir-fry for 2–3 minutes, or until it is just cooked. Remove from the wok.
3 Reheat the wok and add the broccoli, water chestnuts and bamboo shoots. Stir-fry for 2–3 minutes, tossing constantly. Add the sauce and bring to the boil, tossing constantly. Return the chicken to the wok and toss until it is heated through. Stir in the basil and serve at once.

NUTRITION PER SERVE
Protein 30 g; Fat 3.5 g; Carbohydrate 35 g;
Dietary Fibre 8 g; Cholesterol 45 mg;
1205 kJ (285 cal)

Remove the seeds from the chillies and chop the chillies finely.

Stir-fry the garlic, ginger, chilli and spring onion over medium heat.

STIR-FRIED CHICKEN AND PASTA

Preparation time: 20 minutes
Total cooking time: 15 minutes
Serves 4–6

270 g (9 oz) jar sun-dried tomatoes
    in oil
500 g (1 lb) chicken breast fillets, cut
    into thin strips
2 cloves garlic, crushed
1/2 cup (125 ml/4 fl oz) cream

2 tablespoons shredded fresh basil
400 g (13 oz) penne pasta, cooked
2 tablespoons pine nuts, toasted

1 Drain the sun-dried tomatoes, reserving the oil. Thinly slice the sun-dried tomatoes.
2 Heat a wok until very hot, add 1 tablespoon of the reserved oil and swirl it around to coat the side. Stir-fry the chicken strips in batches, adding more oil when necessary.
3 Return all the chicken strips to the wok and add the garlic, sun-dried tomatoes and cream. Simmer gently for 4–5 minutes.
4 Stir in the basil and pasta, and heat through. Season well. Serve topped with the toasted pine nuts.

NUTRITION PER SERVE (6)
Protein 30 g; Fat 30 g; Carbohydrate 5 g;
Dietary Fibre 4 g; Cholesterol 70 mg;
2696 kJ (640 cal)

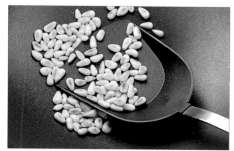

Toast the pine nuts by dry-frying them in the hot wok, stirring.

Drain the sun-dried tomatoes, reserving the oil, and thinly slice them.

Return the chicken to the wok with the garlic, sun-dried tomatoes and cream.

CHICKEN DOMBURI

Preparation time: 35 minutes
Total cooking time: 30 minutes
Serves 4

2 cups (440 g/14 oz) short-grain rice
2 tablespoons oil
2 small chicken breasts (about
    250 g/8 oz), cut into thin strips
2 onions, thinly sliced
1/3 cup (80 ml/2³/4 fl oz) shoyu
2 tablespoons mirin
1 teaspoon dashi granules
5 eggs, lightly beaten
2 sheets nori
2 spring onions, sliced

1 Wash the rice in a colander under cold running water until the water runs clear. Transfer the rice to a heavy-based pan, add 2¹/2 cups (600 ml/20 fl oz) water and bring to the boil over high heat. Cover the pan with a tight-fitting lid and reduce the heat to as low as possible (otherwise the rice in the bottom of the pan will burn) and cook for 15 minutes. Turn the heat to very high, for 15–20 seconds, remove the pan from the heat and set aside for 12 minutes, without lifting the lid or the steam will escape.
2 Heat the oil in a frying pan over high heat. Add the chicken and stir-fry until tender. Remove the chicken from the pan and set aside. Reheat the pan, add the onion and cook, stirring occasionally, for 3 minutes, or until beginning to soften. Add 1/3 cup (80 ml/2³/4 fl oz) water, the shoyu, mirin and dashi granules. Stir to dissolve the dashi, and bring to the boil. Cook for 3 minutes, or until the onion is tender.
3 Return the chicken to the pan and pour in the egg, stirring gently to break up. Cover and simmer over very low heat for 2–3 minutes, or until the egg is just set. Remove the pan from the heat. To make the nori crisp, hold it over low heat, moving it back and forward for about 15 seconds, and then crumble it into small pieces.
4 Transfer the rice to a serving dish, carefully spoon over the chicken and egg mixture and sprinkle with the nori. Garnish with the spring onion.

NUTRITION PER SERVE
Protein 32 g; Fat 18 g; Carbohydrate 90 g; Dietary Fibre 3.6 g; Cholesterol 256 mg; 2737 kJ (654 cal)

NOTES: Domburi is an earthenware dish, and food served in the dish is also known as domburi.
The Japanese technique of cooking rice uses a 'burst' of heat before the standing time. A rice cooker can be used to cook the rice if preferred.

Wash the rice well in a colander under cold running water.

Cook the onion for about 3 minutes, or until it begins to soften.

Pour the egg into the pan and stir gently to break it up.

CHICKEN WITH PINEAPPLE AND CASHEWS

Preparation time: 35 minutes
Total cooking time: 25 minutes
Serves 4

1/2 cup (80 g/2³/4 oz) raw cashews
2 tablespoons oil
4 cloves garlic, finely chopped
1 large onion, cut into large chunks
2 teaspoons chopped red chilli
350g (11 oz) chicken thigh fillets, chopped
1/2 red capsicum, chopped

1/2 green capsicum, chopped
2 tablespoons oyster sauce
1 tablespoon fish sauce
1 teaspoon sugar
2 cups (320 g/11 oz) chopped fresh pineapple
3 spring onions, chopped
2 tablespoons shredded coconut, toasted

1 Roast the cashews in a moderate 180°C (350°F/Gas 4) oven for 15 minutes, or until deep golden.
2 Heat the oil in a wok or large frying pan and stir-fry the garlic, onion and chilli over medium heat for 2 minutes. Remove from the wok. Increase the heat to high and stir-fry the chicken and capsicum, in two batches, tossing until the chicken is light brown. The heat must be very high so the chicken will be succulent.
3 Return the onion mixture to the wok with the oyster sauce, fish sauce, sugar and pineapple, and toss for 2 minutes. Toss the cashews through. Arrange on a serving plate and scatter with the spring onion and coconut. Serve immediately with rice.

NUTRITION PER SERVE
Protein 26 g; Fat 23 g; Carbohydrate 16 g; Dietary Fibre 4.5 g; Cholesterol 44 mg; 1556 kJ (372 cal)

Roast the cashews on a baking tray for 15 minutes, or until golden.

Stir-fry the chicken and capsicum until the chicken is light brown.

Return the onion mixture to the wok and stir through with a wooden spoon.

101

CHICKEN CHOW MEIN

Preparation time: 25 minutes
  + 1 hour marinating
Total cooking time: 20 minutes
Serves 4–6

500 g (1 lb) chicken thigh fillets,
    cut into small cubes
1 tablespoon cornflour
2 tablespoons soy sauce
1 tablespoon oyster sauce
2 teaspoons sugar
oil, for cooking
2 onions, thinly sliced
2 cloves garlic, finely chopped
1 tablespoon finely chopped fresh
    ginger
1 green capsicum, cubed
2 celery sticks, diagonally sliced
8 spring onions, cut into short pieces
100 g (3¹/2 oz) mushrooms, thinly
    sliced
¹/2 cup (80 g/2³/4 oz) water chestnuts,
    thinly sliced
2 teaspoons cornflour, extra
1 tablespoon sherry

¹/2 cup (125 ml/4 fl oz) chicken stock
1 tablespoon soy sauce, extra
90 g (3 oz) Chinese cabbage, finely
    shredded
200 g (6¹/2 oz) ready-prepared fried
    noodles

1 In a glass or ceramic bowl, combine the chicken with the cornflour, soy sauce, oyster sauce and sugar. Cover and refrigerate for 1 hour.

2 Heat the wok until very hot, add 1 tablespoon of the oil and swirl it around to coat the side. Stir-fry the chicken in two batches over high heat for 4–5 minutes, or until cooked. Add oil between batches. Remove all the chicken from the wok and set it aside.

3 Reheat the wok, add 1 tablespoon of the oil and stir-fry the onion over medium-high heat for 3–4 minutes, or until the onion is slightly softened. Add the garlic, ginger, capsicum, celery, spring onion, mushrooms and water chestnuts to the wok. Stir-fry over high heat for 3–4 minutes.

4 Combine the extra cornflour with the sherry, chicken stock and soy

sauce. Add to the wok and bring to the boil. Simmer for 1–2 minutes, or until the sauce thickens slightly. Stir in the cabbage and cook, covered, for 1–2 minutes, or until the cabbage is just wilted. Return the chicken to the wok and toss until heated through. Season with salt and pepper. Arrange the noodles around the edge of a large platter and spoon the chicken mixture into the centre. Serve immediately.

NUTRITION PER SERVE (6)
Protein 25 g; Fat 8.5 g; Carbohydrate 20 g;
Dietary Fibre 4 g; Cholesterol 55 mg;
1110 kJ (265 cal)

Combine the cornflour, sherry, stock and soy sauce, and pour into the wok.

GINGER CHICKEN WITH MUSHROOMS AND WHEAT NOODLES

Preparation time: 20 minutes + soaking
Total cooking time: 10 minutes
Serves 4

4 dried Chinese mushrooms
2 teaspoons cornflour
2 tablespoons soy sauce
2 tablespoons oyster sauce
1 tablespoon mirin or sweet sherry
200 g (6¹/2 oz) dried wheat noodles
1 teaspoon sesame oil
oil, for cooking
2–3 cloves garlic, crushed
8 cm (3 inch) piece fresh ginger, cut
    into matchsticks
375 g (12 oz) chicken breast fillets or
    tenderloins, cut into thin strips
1 red onion, cut into thin wedges
6 spring onions, cut into short lengths
185 g (6 oz) small field mushrooms,
    thickly sliced
1 cup (90 g/3 oz) bean sprouts
¹/3 cup (20 g/³/4 oz) chopped fresh
    mint

1 Place the dried mushrooms in a small bowl and cover with hot water. Leave to soak for 10 minutes, or until softened. Drain and squeeze dry, then discard the hard centre stem and chop the mushrooms finely.
2 Combine the cornflour with ¹/4 cup (60 ml/2 fl oz) water and mix to a fine paste. Add the soy sauce, oyster sauce and mirin.
3 Cook the noodles in a large pan of boiling salted water for 1–2 minutes, or according to the manufacturer's instructions. Drain and set aside.
4 Heat the wok until very hot, add the sesame oil and 1 tablespoon of the oil, and swirl it around to coat the side. Stir-fry the garlic, ginger and chicken strips in batches over high heat for 2–3 minutes, or until the chicken has cooked through. Remove from the wok and set aside.
5 Reheat the wok, add 1 tablespoon of the oil and stir-fry the red onion and spring onion for 1–2 minutes, or until softened. Add the dried and field mushrooms, then stir-fry the mixture for 1–2 minutes, or until tender.

Remove from the wok and set aside.
6 Add the soy sauce mixture to the wok and stir for 1–2 minutes, or until the sauce is well heated and slightly thickened. Return the chicken and vegetables to the wok with the bean sprouts, noodles and chopped mint.

Stir until the noodles are well coated with the sauce. Serve at once.

NUTRITION PER SERVE
Protein 30 g; Fat 9 g; Carbohydrate 45 g;
Dietary Fibre 6 g; Cholesterol 45 mg;
1650 kJ (395 cal)

Cover the dried mushrooms with hot water and leave to soak.

Cook the wheat noodles in a large pan of boiling salted water.

STIR-FRIED CHICKEN WITH LEMON GRASS, GINGER AND CHILLI

Preparation time: 30 minutes
Total cooking time: 15–20 minutes
Serves 4

2 tablespoons oil
2 brown onions, roughly chopped
4 cloves garlic, finely chopped
5 cm (2 inch) piece fresh ginger, finely grated
3 stems lemon grass, white part only, very thinly sliced
2–3 teaspoons chopped green chilli

500 g (1 lb) chicken thigh fillets, thinly sliced
2 teaspoons sugar
1 tablespoon fish sauce
sliced green chilli, to serve
fresh coriander leaves, to serve
fresh Vietnamese mint leaves, to serve

1 Heat the oil in a heavy-based frying pan or wok and add the onion, garlic, ginger, lemon grass and chilli. Stir for 3–5 minutes over medium heat, until the mixture is lightly golden. Be careful not to burn the mixture or it will be bitter.
2 Increase the heat, add the chicken slices and toss well. Sprinkle the sugar over the chicken and cook for

approximately 5 minutes, tossing regularly until just cooked.
3 Add the fish sauce, cook for another 2 minutes and serve garnished with sliced green chilli, fresh coriander and mint. Serve with steamed rice.

NUTRITION PER SERVE
Protein 1.5 g; Fat 9.5 g; Carbohydrate 5 g; Dietary Fibre 1.5 g; Cholesterol 0 mg; 472 kJ (113 cal)

HINTS: Be sure to cook this stir-fry quickly in a very hot wok, or the chicken will stew in its own juices. Lemon grass imparts a delightful lemony flavour to food. Make sure the stems you buy are not dried out.

Use a sharp knife to thinly slice the white part of the lemon grass.

Sprinkle the sugar over the chicken mixture and cook for about 5 minutes.

Just before serving, add the fish sauce and cook for another 2 minutes.

STUFFED CHICKEN BREASTS

Preparation time: 40 minutes
Total cooking time: 45 minutes
Serves 6

1 tablespoon olive oil
1 onion, finely chopped
2 cloves garlic, crushed
100 g (3¹/₂ oz) ham, finely chopped
1 green capsicum, finely chopped
2 tablespoons finely chopped pitted
    black olives
¹/₃ cup (35 g/1¹/₄ oz) grated
    Parmesan
6 chicken breast fillets

plain flour, to coat
2 eggs, lightly beaten
1¹/₂ cups (150 g/5 oz) dry
    breadcrumbs
¹/₄ cup (60 ml/2 fl oz) olive oil

1 Heat the oil in a pan and add the onion, garlic, ham and capsicum. Cook, stirring, over medium heat for 5 minutes, or until the onion is soft. Remove and place in a heatproof bowl. Add the olives and Parmesan.
2 Cut a deep pocket in the side of each chicken fillet, cutting almost through to the other side.
3 Fill each fillet with the ham mixture and secure with toothpicks along the opening of the pocket. Coat each fillet

with the flour, shaking off any excess. Dip into the beaten egg and then coat with the breadcrumbs. Heat the oil in a large pan and cook the fillets, in batches, over medium-high heat for 15–20 minutes, turning halfway through, until golden and cooked through. To serve, remove the toothpicks, then cut diagonally into thin slices.

NUTRITION PER SERVE
Protein 35 g; Fat 20 g; Carbohydrate 20 g;
Dietary Fibre 2 g; Cholesterol 115 mg;
1660 kJ (395 cal)

Cut a deep pocket in the side of each fillet, cutting almost through to the other side.

Spoon the filling into each fillet, securing the pocket openings with toothpicks.

Coat the chicken breasts in the beaten egg and breadcrumbs before cooking.

SZECHWAN PEPPER CHICKEN STIR-FRY

Preparation time: 25 minutes
  + 2 hours marinating
Total cooking time: 20 minutes
Serves 4

3 teaspoons Szechwan pepper
500 g (1 lb) chicken thigh fillets, cut
  into strips
2 tablespoons soy sauce
1 clove garlic, crushed
1 teaspoon grated fresh ginger
3 teaspoons cornflour
100 g (3¹/₂ oz) dried thin egg noodles
oil, for cooking
1 onion, sliced
1 yellow capsicum, cut into thin strips
1 red capsicum, cut into thin strips
100 g (3¹/₂ oz) sugar snap peas
¹/₄ cup (60 ml/2 fl oz) chicken stock

1 Heat a wok until very hot and dry-fry the Szechwan pepper for 30 seconds. Remove from the wok and crush with a mortar and pestle or in a spice mill or small food processor.
2 Combine the chicken pieces with the soy sauce, garlic, ginger, cornflour and Szechwan pepper in a glass or ceramic bowl. Cover and refrigerate for 2 hours.
3 Bring a large pan of water to the boil, add the egg noodles and cook for 5 minutes, or until tender. Drain, then drizzle with a little oil and toss it through the noodles to prevent them from sticking together. Set aside.
4 Heat the wok until very hot, add 1 tablespoon of the oil and swirl it around to coat the side. Stir-fry the chicken in batches over medium-high heat for 5 minutes, or until golden brown and cooked. Add more oil

when necessary. Remove from the wok and set aside.
5 Reheat the wok, add 1 tablespoon of the oil and stir-fry the onion, capsicum and sugar snap peas over high heat for 2–3 minutes, or until the vegetables are tender. Add the chicken stock and bring to the boil.
6 Return the chicken and egg noodles

to the wok and toss over high heat until the mixture is well combined. Serve immediately.

NUTRITION PER SERVE
Protein 35 g; Fat 15 g; Carbohydrate 25 g;
Dietary Fibre 3 g; Cholesterol 65 mg;
1515 kJ (360 cal)

Heat the wok until very hot, then dry-fry the Szechwan pepper.

Crush the Szechwan pepper with a mortar and pestle.

Toss the oil through the noodles to prevent them from sticking.

NASI GORENG

Preparation time: 25 minutes
Total cooking time: 15 minutes
Serves 4–6

5–8 long red chillies, seeded and
    chopped
2 teaspoons shrimp paste
8 cloves garlic, finely chopped
oil, for cooking
2 eggs, lightly beaten
350 g (11 oz) chicken thigh fillets, cut
    into thin strips
200 g (6^1/$_2$ oz) peeled raw prawns,
    deveined
8 cups (1.5 kg/3 lb) cooked rice
^{1}/$_3$ cup (80 ml/2^3/$_4$ fl oz) kecap manis
^{1}/$_3$ cup (80 ml/2^3/$_4$ fl oz) soy sauce
2 small Lebanese cucumbers, finely
    chopped
1 large tomato, finely chopped
lime wedges, to serve

1 Mix the chilli, shrimp paste and garlic in a food processor until the mixture resembles a paste.

2 Heat a wok until very hot, add 1 tablespoon of the oil and swirl it around to coat the side. Add the beaten eggs and, using a wok chan or metal egg flip, push the egg up the edges of the wok to form a large omelette. Cook for 1 minute over medium heat, or until the egg is set, then flip it over and cook the other side for 1 minute. Remove from the wok and cool before slicing into strips.

3 Reheat the wok, add 1 tablespoon of the oil and stir-fry the chicken and half the chilli paste over high heat until the chicken is just cooked. Remove the chicken from the wok.

4 Reheat the wok, add 1 tablespoon of the oil and stir-fry the prawns and the remaining chilli paste until the prawns are cooked. Remove from the wok and set aside.

5 Reheat the wok, add 1 tablespoon of the oil and the cooked rice, and toss constantly over medium heat for 4–5 minutes, or until the rice is heated through. Add the kecap manis and soy sauce, and toss constantly until all of the rice is coated in the sauces. Return the chicken and prawns to the wok, and toss until well combined and heated through. Season well with freshly cracked pepper and salt. Transfer to a large deep serving bowl and top with the omelette strips, cucumber and tomato. Serve with the lime wedges.

NUTRITION PER SERVE (6)
Protein 30 g; Fat 10 g; Carbohydrate 70 g; Dietary Fibre 3.5 g; Cholesterol 140 mg; 2105 kJ (505 cal)

Remove the seeds from the chillies and finely chop the flesh.

Slit the peeled prawns down the backs to remove the vein.

Process the chilli, shrimp paste and garlic until it forms a paste.

CURRY CHICKEN NOODLE STIR-FRY

Preparation time: 20 minutes
Total cooking time: 10 minutes
Serves 4

100 g (3¹/₂ oz) dried rice vermicelli
oil, for cooking
500 g (1 lb) chicken breast fillets, cut
    into thin strips
2 cloves garlic, crushed
1 teaspoon grated fresh ginger
2 teaspoons Asian-style curry powder
1 red onion, sliced
1 red capsicum, cut into short strips

2 carrots, cut into matchsticks
2 zucchini, cut into matchsticks
1 tablespoon soy sauce

1 Place the vermicelli in a large bowl, cover with boiling water and soak for 5 minutes. Drain well and place on a tea towel to dry.
2 Heat the wok until very hot, add 1 tablespoon of the oil and swirl it around to coat the side. Stir-fry the chicken in batches over high heat until browned and tender. Remove all the chicken and drain on paper towels.
3 Reheat the wok, add 1 tablespoon of the oil and stir-fry the garlic, ginger, curry powder and onion for

1–2 minutes, or until fragrant. Add the capsicum, carrot and zucchini to the wok, and stir-fry until well coated in the spices. Add 1 tablespoon water and stir-fry for 1 minute.
4 Add the drained noodles and chicken to the wok. Add the soy sauce and toss using two wooden spoons until well combined. Season well with salt and serve.

NUTRITION PER SERVE
Protein 30 g; Fat 15 g; Carbohydrate 25 g;
Dietary Fibre 4 g; Cholesterol 60 mg;
1495 kJ (355 cal)

Trim any excess fat from the chicken and cut the chicken into thin strips.

Cut the peeled carrots into strips, the size and shape of matchsticks.

Soak the dried rice vermicelli in boiling water for 5 minutes.

RICE STICKS STIR-FRIED WITH CHICKEN AND GREENS

Preparation time: 25 minutes
Total cooking time: 10 minutes
Serves 4

6 baby bok choy
8 stems Chinese broccoli
150 g (5 oz) dried rice stick noodles
2 tablespoons oil
375 g (12 oz) chicken breast fillets
    or tenderloins, cut into
    thin strips
2–3 cloves garlic, crushed
5 cm (2 inch) piece ginger, grated
6 spring onions, cut into short pieces
1 tablespoon sherry
1 cup (90 g/3 oz) bean sprouts

SAUCE
2 teaspoons cornflour
2 tablespoons soy sauce
2 tablespoons oyster sauce
2 teaspoons soft brown sugar
1 teaspoon sesame oil

1 Remove any tough outer leaves from the bok choy and Chinese broccoli. Cut into 4 cm (1¹/₂ inch) pieces across the leaves, including the stems. Wash well, then drain and dry thoroughly.
2 Place the rice stick noodles in a large heatproof bowl and cover with boiling water. Soak for 5–8 minutes, or until softened. Rinse, then drain. Cut into short lengths using scissors.
3 Meanwhile, to make the sauce, combine the cornflour and soy sauce in a small bowl. Mix to a smooth paste, then stir in the oyster sauce, brown sugar, sesame oil and ¹/₂ cup (125 ml/ 4 fl oz) water.
4 Heat a wok until very hot, add the oil and swirl it around to coat the side. Stir-fry the chicken strips, garlic, ginger and spring onion in batches over high heat for 3–4 minutes, or until the chicken is cooked. Remove from the wok and set aside.
5 Add the chopped bok choy, Chinese broccoli and sherry to the wok, cover and steam for 2 minutes, or until the vegetables are wilted. Remove from the wok and set aside.

Cut the bok choy and Chinese broccoli into pieces, including the stems.

Using a pair of scissors, cut the soaked noodles into short lengths.

Add the sauce to the wok and stir until the sauce is glossy and slightly thickened. Return the chicken, vegetables, noodles and bean sprouts to the wok, and stir until well combined and heated through. Serve at once.

NUTRITION PER SERVE
Protein 30 g; Fat 15 g; Carbohydrate 50 g; Dietary Fibre 4 g; Cholesterol 45 mg; 1855 kJ (445 cal)

NOTE: Broccoli and English spinach may be used as the greens.

NOODLES WITH CHICKEN AND FRESH BLACK BEANS

Preparation time: 15 minutes
Total cooking time: 15 minutes
Serves 2–3

2 teaspoons salted black beans
oil, for cooking
2 teaspoons sesame oil
500 g (1 lb) chicken thigh fillets, cut
    into thin strips
3 cloves garlic, very thinly sliced
4 spring onions, chopped
1 teaspoon sugar

1 red capsicum, sliced
100 g (3$^{1}/_{2}$ oz) green beans, cut into
    short pieces
300 g (10 oz) Hokkien noodles
2 tablespoons oyster sauce
1 tablespoon soy sauce

1 Rinse the black beans in running water. Drain and roughly chop.
2 Heat a wok until very hot, add 1 tablespoon of oil and the sesame oil and swirl it around to coat the side. Stir-fry the chicken in three batches, until well browned, tossing regularly. Remove from the wok and set aside.
3 Reheat the wok, add 1 tablespoon of the oil and stir-fry the garlic and spring onion for 1 minute. Add the black beans, sugar, capsicum and green beans, and cook for 1 minute. Sprinkle with 2 tablespoons of water, cover and steam for 2 minutes.
4 Gently separate the noodles and add to the wok with the chicken, oyster sauce and soy sauce, and toss well to combine. Cook, covered, for about 2 minutes, or until the noodles are just softened.

NUTRITION PER SERVE (3)
Protein 50 g; Fat 20 g; Carbohydrate 50 g;
Dietary Fibre 2 g; Cholesterol 85 mg;
2490 kJ (595 cal)

Cut the chicken thigh fillets into thin strips, removing any excess fat.

Roughly chop the rinsed and drained black beans with a sharp knife.

Add the black beans, sugar, capsicum and green beans to the garlic and spring onion mixture.

CHICKEN MINCE WITH HERBS AND SPICES

Preparation time: 30 minutes
Total cooking time: 50 minutes
Serves 4–6

1/4 cup (50 g/1³/4 oz) long-grain rice
1 kg (2 lb) chicken thigh fillets
2 tablespoons peanut oil
4 cloves garlic, crushed
2 tablespoons grated fresh galangal
2 small red chillies, finely chopped
4 spring onions, finely chopped
1/4 cup (60 ml/2 fl oz) fish sauce
1 tablespoon shrimp paste
1/4 cup (15 g/¹/2 oz) chopped fresh
    Vietnamese mint

2 tablespoons chopped fresh basil
1/3 cup (80 ml/2³/4 fl oz) lime juice
200 g (6¹/2 oz) chicken livers, optional

1 Spread the rice on a baking tray and roast it in a moderate 180°C (350°F/ Gas 4) oven for 15 minutes, or until golden. Cool slightly and process in a food processor until finely ground.
2 Meanwhile, process the chicken in a food processor until finely minced. Heat the oil in a wok or frying pan, add the garlic, galangal, chilli and spring onion and cook over medium heat for 3 minutes, or until golden.
3 Add the minced chicken to the wok and stir for 5 minutes or until browned. Break up any large lumps with a wooden spoon. Stir in the fish

sauce and shrimp paste, bring to the boil, then reduce the heat and simmer for 5 minutes.
4 Remove from the heat, stir in the mint, basil, rice and lime juice, and mix until well combined. If chicken livers are used, they should be cooked in 1/2 cup (125 ml/4 fl oz) of chicken stock for 5 minutes, or until tender, and then allowed to cool slightly before chopping. Fold them through at this stage. Garnish with split chillies. Serve with sticky rice.

NUTRITION PER SERVE
Protein 43 g; Fat 12 g; Carbohydrate 8.5 g;
Dietary Fibre 1 g; Cholesterol 178 mg;
1333 kJ (320 cal)

Roast the uncooked rice on a baking tray until lightly golden.

Process the chicken thigh fillets in a food processor until finely minced.

Stir-fry the minced chicken with the garlic, galangal, chilli and spring onion until browned.

CHICKEN DIANE

Preparation time: 10 minutes
Total cooking time: 15 minutes
Serves 4

8 (880 g/1 lb 13 oz) chicken thigh
    fillets
90 g (3 oz) butter
2 cloves garlic, crushed
1 tablespoon Worcestershire
    sauce
2 tablespoons finely chopped fresh
    parsley
1/3 cup (80 g/2¾ oz) sour
    cream
2 tablespoons cream

1 Trim the chicken thigh fillets of any excess fat and sinew. Melt the butter in a heavy-based frying pan over medium heat. Add the garlic and cook for 1 minute.

2 Add the chicken fillets and cook over medium heat for 4 minutes on each side, or until the chicken is cooked through. Remove the chicken fillets from the pan and set aside. Keep warm.

3 Add the Worcestershire sauce, chopped fresh parsley, sour cream and cream to the frying pan and stir over medium heat for 1 minute. Season to taste with salt and freshly ground black pepper. Return the chicken fillets to the pan and spoon the sauce over them. Serve the chicken with the sauce and some steamed green beans.

NUTRITION PER SERVE
Protein 50 g; Fat 18 g; Carbohydrate 2 g;
Dietary Fibre 0.5 g; Cholesterol 150 mg;
1540 kJ (370 cal)

NOTES: This dish is best cooked just before serving.
Do not allow the sauce to boil or the sour cream will separate and the sauce will have an unpleasant, curdled appearance.

VARIATION: Chicken breast fillets may be used in place of the chicken thigh fillets in this recipe.

Using a large sharp knife, finely chop the fresh parsley.

Cook the chicken in the butter and garlic mixture for 4 minutes on each side.

Add the Worcestershire sauce, parsley, sour cream and cream to the frying pan.

CHICKEN CORDON BLEU

Preparation time: 15 minutes
+ 30 minutes refrigeration
Total cooking time: 20 minutes
Serves 4

4 (460 g/14 oz) chicken
 breast fillets
4 thick slices Swiss cheese
4 slices double-smoked ham or
 pastrami
1/3 cup (40 g/1¼ oz) seasoned plain
 flour
1 egg, lightly beaten
1/2 cup (50 g/1¾ oz) dry
 breadcrumbs
1/2 cup (125 ml/4 fl oz) oil

1 Trim the chicken of excess fat and sinew. Using a sharp knife, cut into the thickest section of each fillet without cutting right through. Open the fillet out flat and season with salt and freshly ground black pepper.
2 Place a slice of cheese and ham on one side of each fillet. Fold the remaining half of the fillet over to enclose the filling.
3 Carefully coat each fillet with flour, then shake off the excess. Dip into the egg, then coat with the breadcrumbs. Place on a foil-lined baking tray. Place, covered, in the refrigerator for 30 minutes.
4 Heat the oil in a medium heavy-based pan. Add the chicken and cook in two batches over medium heat for 4 minutes each side, or until the chicken is golden and cooked through. Add more oil between batches if necessary. Serve the chicken immediately.

NUTRITION PER SERVE
Protein 40 g; Fat 40 g; Carbohydrate 16 g;
Dietary Fibre 1 g; Cholesterol 130 mg;
2438 kJ (582 cal)

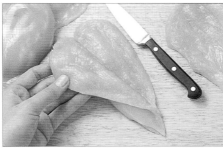

Cut into the thickest section of each chicken fillet without cutting right through.

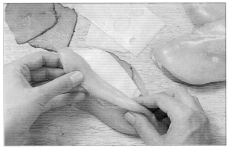

Place a slice of cheese and a slice of ham on one side of each fillet.

Shake the excess flour from the chicken, then dip into the beaten egg.

Cook the chicken in the oil for 4 minutes each side, or until golden and cooked through.

113

CHICKEN WITH MUSHROOMS

Preparation time: 10 minutes
Total cooking time: 20 minutes
Serves 4

4 (460 g/14 oz) chicken breast fillets
30 g (1 oz) butter
2 tablespoons oil
4 small zucchini, thinly sliced
2 leeks, thinly sliced
2 cloves garlic, crushed
2 small red chillies, finely chopped
150 g (5 oz) oyster mushrooms
1 tablespoon lime juice
1/4 cup (60 ml/2 fl oz) cream

1 Trim the chicken of excess fat and sinew. Heat the butter and oil in a heavy-based frying pan. Add the chicken and cook over medium heat for 4 minutes on each side, or until tender. Remove from the pan and drain on paper towels. Keep warm.
2 Add the zucchini, leek, garlic and chopped chilli to the pan. Cook over high heat for 2 minutes. Add the mushrooms and cook for a further 3 minutes, or until the vegetables are tender.
3 Stir in the lime juice and cream. Return the chicken to the pan and cook for 2 minutes, or until heated through. Season to taste. Serve immediately with roasted capsicum and warm crusty rolls, if desired.

NUTRITION PER SERVE
Protein 105 g; Fat 33 g; Carbohydrate 4 g; Dietary Fibre 3.5 g; Cholesterol 265 mg; 3080 kJ (736 cal)

NOTE: If oyster mushrooms are not available, use button or cap mushrooms instead.

HINT: Wear rubber gloves when chopping chillies. Avoid touching your face, because chilli oil can burn eyes and skin.

Cook the chicken fillets over medium heat for 4 minutes on each side.

Add the oyster mushrooms to the zucchini mixture in the pan.

Stir the lime juice and cream into the zucchini mixture before adding the cooked chicken.

ALMOND CHICKEN WITH BRANDY SAUCE

Preparation time: 10 minutes
Total cooking time: 20 minutes
Serves 4

4 (460 g/14 oz) chicken breast
    fillets
1 cup (90 g/3 oz) flaked almonds
2 tablespoons oil
60 g (2 oz) butter
2 leeks, thinly sliced
1/3 cup (80 ml/2³/4 fl oz) brandy or
    cognac
2/3 cup (170 ml/5¹/2 fl oz) cream

1 Trim the chicken of any excess fat and sinew. Place the flaked almonds in a heavy-based frying pan. Stir over medium heat for 3 minutes, or until golden. Remove from the pan and set aside.
2 Heat the oil in the pan and add the chicken. Cook over high heat for 1 minute on each side. Reduce the heat and cook for a further 3 minutes on each side, or until cooked through. Remove from the pan and keep warm. Drain any oil from the pan.
3 Add the butter and leek to the pan. Cook over medium heat for 3 minutes, or until the leek is tender. Add the brandy or cognac and cook until

reduced by half, stirring occasionally. Add the cream and cook for 3 minutes, or until the sauce has thickened slightly. To serve, place the chicken on individual serving plates, pour the sauce over the chicken and sprinkle with the almonds. Serve hot with steamed vegetables.

NUTRITION PER SERVE
Protein 32 g; Fat 40 g; Carbohydrate 3.5 g;
Dietary Fibre 3 g; Cholesterol 115 mg;
2258 kJ (540 cal)

Once the flaked almonds are golden, remove from the pan and set aside.

Reduce the heat and cook the chicken for a further 3 minutes on each side.

Pour the cream into the pan and cook until the sauce has thickened slightly.

Pasta & Rice

CHICKEN AND VEGETABLE LASAGNE

Preparation time: 45 minutes
Total cooking time: 1 hour 20 minutes
Serves 8

500 g (1 lb) chicken breast fillets
cooking oil spray
2 cloves garlic, crushed
1 onion, chopped
2 zucchini, chopped
2 celery sticks, chopped
2 carrots, chopped
300 g (10 oz) pumpkin, diced
2 x 400 g (13 oz) cans tomatoes,
    chopped
2 fresh thyme sprigs
2 bay leaves
1/2 cup (125 ml/4 fl oz) white wine
2 tablespoons tomato paste
2 tablespoons chopped fresh basil
500 g (1 lb) English spinach
500 g (1 lb) reduced-fat cottage
    cheese
450 g (14 oz) ricotta
1/4 cup (60 ml/2 fl oz) skim milk
1/2 teaspoon ground nutmeg
1/3 cup (35 g/1 1/4 oz) grated
    Parmesan
300 g (10 oz) instant or fresh lasagne
    sheets

1 Preheat the oven to moderate 180°C (350°F/Gas 4). Trim excess fat from the chicken breasts, then finely mince in a food processor. Heat a large, deep, non-stick frying pan, spray lightly with oil and cook the chicken mince in batches until browned. Remove and set aside.

2 Add the garlic and onion to the pan and cook until softened. Return the chicken to the pan and add the zucchini, celery, carrot, pumpkin, tomato, thyme, bay leaves, wine and tomato paste. Simmer, covered, for 20 minutes. Remove the bay leaves and thyme, stir in the fresh basil and set aside.

3 Shred the spinach and set aside. Mix the cottage cheese, ricotta, skim milk, nutmeg and half the Parmesan.

4 Spoon a little of the tomato mixture over the base of a casserole dish and top with a single layer of pasta. Top with half the remaining tomato mixture, then the spinach and spoon over half the cottage cheese mixture. Continue with another layer of pasta, the remaining tomato and another layer of pasta. Spread the remaining cottage cheese mixture on top and sprinkle with Parmesan. Bake for 40–50 minutes, or until golden. The top may puff up slightly but will settle on standing.

NUTRITION PER SERVE
Protein 40 g; Fat 10 g; Carbohydrate 35 g;
Dietary Fibre 7 g; Cholesterol 70 mg;
1790 kJ (430 cal)

Finely mince the trimmed chicken breast fillets in a food processor.

Add the vegetables with the thyme, bay leaves, wine and tomato paste to the pan.

TAGLIATELLE WITH CHICKEN LIVERS AND CREAM

Preparation time: 20 minutes
Total cooking time: 15 minutes
Serves 4

1 onion
300 g (10 oz) chicken livers
2 tablespoons olive oil
1 clove garlic, crushed
1 cup (250 ml/8 fl oz) thickened or
   pouring cream
1 tablespoon snipped fresh chives
1 teaspoon wholegrain mustard
2 eggs, beaten

375 g (12 oz) tagliatelle
2 tablespoons grated Parmesan, to
   serve
snipped fresh chives, to serve

1 Peel the onion and chop finely. Trim the chicken livers and chop them into small pieces.
2 Heat the oil in a large frying pan. Add the onion and garlic and stir over low heat until the onion is tender. Add the chicken livers to the pan. Cook gently for 2–3 minutes. Remove from the heat and stir in the cream, chives, mustard and salt and pepper, to taste. Return to the heat and bring to the boil. Add the egg and stir quickly to combine. Remove from the heat.

3 While the sauce is cooking, add the tagliatelle to a large pan of rapidly boiling water and cook until just tender. Drain well and return to the pan. Add the sauce to the hot pasta and toss well to combine. Serve in warmed pasta bowls, sprinkled with the Parmesan and chives.

NUTRITION PER SERVE
Protein 34 g; Fat 38 g; Carbohydrate 69 g;
Dietary Fibre 4 g; Cholesterol 217 mg;
3175 kJ (760 cal)

HINT: Snip the chives with a pair of kitchen scissors.

Trim all of the chicken livers, then cut them into small pieces.

Cook the onion and garlic until tender, then add the chicken livers.

Add the beaten eggs to the sauce mixture, and stir quickly to combine.

CHICKEN RAVIOLI WITH BUTTERED SAGE SAUCE

Preparation time: 15 minutes
Total cooking time: 10 minutes
Serves 4

500 g (1 lb) fresh or dried chicken-filled ravioli or agnolotti
60 g (2 oz) butter
4 spring onions, chopped
2 tablespoons chopped fresh sage

1/2 cup grated Parmesan, to serve
fresh sage leaves, extra, to serve

1 Add the ravioli to a large pan of rapidly boiling water and cook until just tender. Drain the pasta, then return to the pan.
2 While the ravioli is cooking, melt the butter in a heavy-based pan. Add the spring onion and sage, and stir for 2 minutes. Season with salt and ground black pepper.
3 Add the sauce to the pasta and toss

well. Pour onto a warmed serving platter and sprinkle with the Parmesan and sage leaves. Serve immediately.

NUTRITION PER SERVE
Protein 16 g; Fat 24 g; Carbohydrate 18 g; Dietary Fibre 2 g; Cholesterol 74 mg; 1445 kJ (345 cal)

HINT: Bite through a piece of ravioli to test whether it is done.

Cook the ravioli in a large pan of boiling water until just tender.

Add the spring onion and sage to the melted butter, and stir for 2 minutes.

Add the sage sauce to the ravioli and toss until well combined.

CHICKEN AND PUMPKIN CANNELLONI

Preparation time: 1 hour
Total cooking time: 2 hours
Serves 6

500 g (1 lb) butternut pumpkin, with skin and seeds
30 g (1 oz) butter
100 g (3½ oz) pancetta, roughly chopped
2 teaspoons olive oil
2 cloves garlic, crushed
500 g (1 lb) chicken thigh fillets, minced
½ teaspoon garam masala
2 tablespoons chopped fresh flat-leaf parsley
150 g (5 oz) goats cheese
50 g (1¾ oz) ricotta
375 g (12 oz) fresh lasagne sheets
1 cup (100 g/3½ oz) grated Parmesan

TOMATO SAUCE
30 g (1 oz) butter
1 clove garlic, crushed
2 x 425 g (14 oz) cans chopped tomatoes
¼ cup (7 g/¼ oz) chopped fresh flat-leaf parsley
¼ cup (60 ml/2 fl oz) white wine

1 Preheat the oven to hot 220°C (425°F/Gas 7). Brush the pumpkin with 10 g (¼ oz) of the butter and bake on a baking tray for 1 hour, or until tender. When the pumpkin has cooked and while it is still hot, remove the seeds. Scrape out the flesh and mash it with a fork. Set aside to cool.

2 Add another 10 g (¼ oz) of the butter to a heavy-based frying pan and cook the pancetta over medium heat for 2–3 minutes. Remove from the pan and drain on paper towels.

3 In the same pan, heat the remaining butter and the olive oil. Add the garlic and stir for 30 seconds. Add the chicken in small batches and brown, making sure the chicken is cooked through. Remove from the pan and set aside to cool on paper towels. Reduce the oven temperature to moderately hot 200°C (400°F/Gas 6).

4 Combine the pumpkin with the pancetta and chicken in a bowl. Mix in the garam marsala, parsley, goats cheese, ricotta and some salt and black pepper. Cut the lasagne sheets into rough 15 cm (6 inch) squares. Place 3 tablespoons of the filling at one end of each square and roll up. Repeat with the rest of the lasagne sheets and filling.

5 To make the tomato sauce, melt the butter in a heavy-based pan and add the garlic. Cook for 1 minute, then add the tomato and simmer over medium heat for 1 minute. Add the parsley and white wine, and simmer gently for another 5 minutes. Season with salt and pepper, to taste.

6 Spread a little of the tomato sauce over the bottom of a 3 litre capacity ovenproof dish and arrange the cannelloni on top in a single layer. Spoon the remaining tomato sauce over the cannelloni and sprinkle with the Parmesan. Bake for 20–25 minutes, or until the cheese is golden.

NUTRITION PER SERVE
Protein 44 g; Fat 26 g; Carbohydrate 55 g; Dietary Fibre 6.5 g; Cholesterol 113 mg; 2670 kJ (638 cal)

NOTE: You can use instant cannelloni tubes instead of the lasagne sheets. Stand the tubes on end on a chopping board and spoon in the filling.

Roughly chop the pancetta slices with a large cook's knife.

Finely mince the chicken thigh fillets using a food processor.

Scrape out the flesh of the cooked pumpkin and mash with a fork.

Combine the pumpkin, pancetta, chicken and other filling ingredients in a bowl.

Place 3 tablespoons of the filling onto the end of each lasagne sheet and roll up.

Arrange the cannelloni tubes over a little of the tomato sauce in the dish.

CONCHIGLIE WITH CHICKEN AND RICOTTA

Preparation time: 15 minutes
Total cooking time: 1 hour 10 minutes
Serves 4

500 g (1 lb) conchiglie (shell pasta)
2 tablespoons olive oil
1 onion, chopped
1 clove garlic, crushed
60 g (2 oz) prosciutto, sliced
125 g (4 oz) mushrooms, chopped
250 g (8 oz) chicken mince
2 tablespoons tomato paste
425 g (14 oz) can tomatoes
1/2 cup (125 ml/4 fl oz) dry white wine
1 teaspoon dried oregano
250 g (8 oz) ricotta
1 cup (150 g/5 oz) grated mozzarella
1 teaspoon snipped fresh chives
1 tablespoon chopped fresh parsley
1/4 cup (25 g/3/4 oz) grated Parmesan

1 Add the conchiglie to a large pan of rapidly boiling water and cook until just tender. Drain well. Heat the oil in a large frying pan. Add the onion and garlic and stir over low heat until the onion is tender. Add the prosciutto and stir for 1 minute.

2 Add the mushrooms to the pan and cook for 2 minutes. Add the chicken mince and brown well, breaking up any lumps with a fork as it cooks.

3 Stir in the tomato paste, undrained, crushed tomatoes, wine, oregano, salt and pepper. Bring to the boil, then reduce the heat and simmer for 20 minutes.

4 Preheat the oven to moderate 180°C (350°F/Gas 4). Combine the ricotta, mozzarella, chives, parsley and half the Parmesan. Spoon a little of the mixture into each pasta shell. Spoon some of the chicken sauce into the base of a casserole dish. Arrange the conchiglie on top. Spread the remaining sauce over the top. Sprinkle with the remaining Parmesan and bake for 25–30 minutes, or until golden.

NUTRITION PER SERVE
Protein 40 g; Fat 28 g; Carbohydrate 91 g;
Dietary Fibre 8 g; Cholesterol 70 mg;
3339 kJ (800 cal)

Stir the onion and garlic over low heat until the onion is tender before adding the prosciutto.

Brown the chicken mince well, breaking up with a fork as it cooks.

Stir in the tomato paste, tomato, wine and oregano, and season with salt and pepper.

Spoon a little of the cheese mixture into each pasta shell.

SPAGHETTI WITH CHICKEN MEATBALLS

Preparation time: 30 minutes + chilling
Total cooking time: 1 hour 30 minutes
Serves 4–6

500 g (1 lb) chicken mince
60 g (2 oz) grated Parmesan
2 cups (160 g/5¹/₂ oz) fresh white
　breadcrumbs
2 cloves garlic, crushed
1 egg
1 tablespoon chopped fresh
　flat-leaf parsley
1 tablespoon chopped
　fresh sage
¹/₄ cup (60 ml/2 fl oz) oil
500 g (1 lb) spaghetti
2 tablespoons chopped fresh
　oregano, to serve

TOMATO SAUCE
1 tablespoon olive oil
1 onion, finely chopped
2 kg (4 lb) ripe tomatoes, roughly
　chopped
2 bay leaves
1 cup (30 g/1 oz) fresh basil leaves,
　loosely packed
1 teaspoon coarse ground black
　pepper

1 In a large bowl, mix together the mince, Parmesan, breadcrumbs, garlic, egg, parsley, sage and some freshly ground black pepper. Shape tablespoons of the mixture into small balls and chill for 30 minutes to firm. Heat the oil in a shallow pan and fry the balls in batches until golden brown, turning often by shaking the pan. Drain on paper towels.
2 To make the tomato sauce, heat the oil in a large pan, add the onion and fry for 1–2 minutes. Add the tomato and bay leaves, cover and bring to the boil, stirring occasionally. Reduce the heat to low, partially cover and cook for 50–60 minutes.
3 Add the meatballs, basil leaves and pepper, and simmer, uncovered, for 10–15 minutes. Cook the spaghetti in boiling water until just tender. Drain, then return to the pan. Add some sauce to the pasta and toss gently to combine. Serve the pasta in individual bowls with the remaining sauce and the meatballs, sprinkled with fresh oregano.

NUTRITION PER SERVE (6)
Protein 40 g; Fat 20 g; Carbohydrate 83 g;
Dietary Fibre 9.5 g; Cholesterol 80 mg;
2890 kJ (690 cal)

Shape tablespoons of the chicken mixture into small balls.

Partially cover the pan and cook the sauce for 50–60 minutes.

Add the meatballs, basil and pepper to the tomato mixture.

CHICKEN AGNOLOTTI

Preparation time: 45 minutes +
    30 minutes standing
Total cooking time: 2 hours 45 minutes
Serves 4

PASTA
2 cups (250 g/8 oz) plain flour
3 eggs
1 tablespoon olive oil
1 egg yolk, extra

FILLING
125 g (4 oz) chicken mince
75 g (2¹/₂ oz) ricotta or cottage
    cheese
60 g (2 oz) chicken livers, trimmed and
    chopped
30 g (1 oz) prosciutto, chopped
1 slice salami, chopped
2 tablespoons grated Parmesan
1 egg, beaten
1 tablespoon chopped fresh parsley
1 clove garlic, crushed
¹/₄ teaspoon mixed spice

TOMATO SAUCE
2 tablespoons olive oil
1 onion, finely chopped
2 cloves garlic, crushed
2 x 425 g (14 oz) cans tomatoes
¹/₄ cup (15 g/¹/₂ oz) chopped fresh
    basil
¹/₂ teaspoon mixed herbs

1 To make the pasta, sift the flour and a pinch of salt onto a board. Make a well in the centre of the flour. In a bowl, whisk together the eggs, oil and 1 tablespoon water. Add the egg mixture gradually to the flour, working in with your hands until the mixture forms a ball. Knead on a lightly floured surface for 5 minutes, or until smooth and elastic. Place the dough in a lightly oiled bowl and cover with plastic wrap. Allow to stand for 30 minutes.

2 To make the filling, place the chicken, cheese, liver, prosciutto, salami, Parmesan, egg, parsley, garlic, mixed spice and some salt and ground black pepper in a food processor. Process until finely chopped. Set aside.

3 To make the tomato sauce, heat the oil in a medium pan. Add the onion and garlic and stir over low heat until the onion is tender. Increase the heat, add the undrained, crushed tomatoes, basil, herbs, and salt and pepper, to taste. Stir to combine, then bring to the boil. Reduce the heat and simmer for 15 minutes. Remove from the heat.

4 Roll out half the pasta dough until 1 mm (¹/₁₆ inch) thick. Cut with a knife or fluted pastry cutter into 10 cm (4 inch) strips. Place teaspoons of filling at 5 cm (2 inch) intervals down one side of each strip. Whisk together the extra egg yolk and ¹/₄ cup (60 ml/ 2 fl oz) water. Brush along one side of the dough and between the filling. Fold the dough over the filling to meet the other side. Repeat with the remaining filling and dough.

5 Press the edges of the dough together firmly to seal. Cut between the mounds of filling with a knife or a fluted pastry cutter.

6 Cook the ravioli in batches in a large pan of rapidly boiling water for 10 minutes each batch. Reheat the tomato sauce in a large pan. Add the cooked ravioli and toss well until the sauce is evenly distributed. Simmer, stirring, for 5 minutes, then serve.

NUTRITION PER SERVE
Protein 30 g; Fat 25 g; Carbohydrate 60 g;
Dietary Fibre 6 g; Cholesterol 223 mg;
2534 kJ (605 cal)

Knead the pasta mixture on a lightly floured surface until smooth and elastic.

Place the filling ingredients in a food processor and process until finely chopped.

Stir the tomatoes, basil, mixed herbs and salt and pepper into the onion mixture.

Place teaspoons of the filling at 5 cm (2 inch) intervals down one side of each strip.

Use a fluted pastry cutter or knife to cut between the mounds of filling.

Add the cooked ravioli to the tomato sauce, and toss until combined.

CHICKEN RAVIOLI WITH FRESH TOMATO SAUCE

Preparation time: 40 minutes
Total cooking time: 40 minutes
Serves 4

TOMATO SAUCE
1 tablespoon oil
1 large onion, chopped
2 cloves garlic, crushed
1/3 cup (90 g/3 oz) tomato paste
1/4 cup (60 ml/2 fl oz) red wine
2/3 cup (170 ml/51/2 fl oz) chicken
    stock
2 tomatoes, chopped
1 tablespoon chopped fresh basil

RAVIOLI
200 g (61/2 oz) chicken mince
1 tablespoon chopped fresh basil
1/4 cup (25 g/3/4 oz) grated Parmesan
3 spring onions, finely chopped
50 g (13/4 oz) ricotta
250 g (8 oz) packet (48) round
    won ton or gow gee wrappers

1 To make the tomato sauce, heat the oil in a pan and add the onion and garlic. Cook for 2–3 minutes, then stir in the tomato paste, wine, stock and tomato, and simmer for 20 minutes. Stir in the basil, and season with salt and freshly ground black pepper.
2 To make the ravioli, combine the chicken mince, basil, Parmesan, spring onion, ricotta and some salt and black pepper. Lay half of the wrappers on a flat surface and brush with a little water. Place slightly heaped teaspoons of the mixture onto the centre of each wrapper. Place another wrapper on top and press the edges firmly together to seal.
3 Bring a large pan of water to the boil. Add the ravioli, a few at a time, and cook for 2–3 minutes, or until just tender. Drain well and serve with the tomato sauce.

NUTRITION PER SERVE
Protein 24 g; Fat 5.5 g; Carbohydrate 50 g;
Dietary Fibre 6 g; Cholesterol 37 mg;
1520 kJ (363 cal)

For the tomato sauce, add the basil, salt and pepper to the tomato mixture.

For the ravioli, combine the chicken, basil, Parmesan, spring onion and ricotta.

Place the mixture between two wrappers and press together to make the ravioli.

SUCCULENT CHICKEN AND PASTA SALAD

Preparation time: 30 minutes
Total cooking time: 25 minutes
Serves 4

250 g (8 oz) chicken breast fillet
1¹/₂ cups (375 ml/12 fl oz) chicken
   stock
350 g (11 oz) fusilli pasta
155 g (5 oz) asparagus, cut into
   short lengths
150 g (5 oz) Gruyère cheese, grated
2 spring onions, thinly sliced

DRESSING
¹/₄ cup (60 ml/2 fl oz) olive oil
¹/₄ cup (60 ml/2 fl oz) lemon juice
¹/₂ teaspoon sugar

1 Put the chicken and stock in a frying pan. Bring to the boil, then reduce the heat and poach gently, turning regularly, for 8 minutes, or until tender. Remove the chicken, cool and slice thinly.
2 Cook the pasta in a large pan of boiling salted water for 10–12 minutes, or until al dente. Drain and cool.
3 Cook the asparagus in boiling water for 2 minutes. Drain and place in a bowl of iced water. Drain again. Combine with the chicken, pasta and cheese in a large bowl.
4 To make the dressing, whisk the ingredients together. Season with salt and pepper. Add to the salad and toss well. Transfer to a serving bowl and scatter with the spring onion.

NUTRITION PER SERVE
Protein 40 g; Fat 30 g; Carbohydrate 60 g;
Dietary Fibre 5 g; Cholesterol 70 mg;
2785 kJ (665 cal)

Grate the cheese, chop the asparagus and thinly slice the spring onion.

Pour the stock over the chicken and poach over low heat, turning regularly.

Cook the asparagus pieces in a small pan of boiling water.

CHICKEN TORTELLINI WITH TOMATO SAUCE

Preparation time: 30 minutes
+ resting
Total cooking time: 30 minutes
Serves 4

PASTA
2 cups (250 g/8 oz) plain flour
3 eggs
1 tablespoon olive oil

FILLING
20 g (³/₄ oz) butter
80 g (2³/₄ oz) chicken breast fillet, cubed
2 slices pancetta, chopped
1/2 cup (50 g/1³/₄ oz) grated Parmesan
1/2 teaspoon nutmeg
1 egg, lightly beaten

TOMATO SAUCE
1/3 cup (80 ml/2³/₄ fl oz) olive oil
1¹/₂ kg (3 lb) fresh ripe tomatoes, peeled and chopped
1/4 cup (7 g/¹/₄ oz) chopped fresh oregano
1/2 cup (50 g/1³/₄ oz) grated Parmesan

100 g (3¹/₂ oz) fresh bocconcini, thinly sliced, to serve

1 To make the pasta, sift the flour and a pinch of salt into a bowl and make a well in the centre. In a jug, whisk together the eggs, oil and 1 tablespoon water. Add the egg mixture gradually to the flour, mixing to a firm dough. Gather together into a ball, adding a little extra water if necessary.
2 Knead on a lightly floured surface for 5 minutes, or until the dough is smooth and elastic. Place in a lightly oiled bowl, cover with plastic wrap and leave for 30 minutes.

3 To make the filling, heat the butter in a frying pan, add the chicken and cook until golden brown, then drain. Process the chicken and pancetta in a food processor or mincer until finely chopped. Transfer to a bowl and add the cheese, nutmeg, egg and salt and pepper, to taste. Set aside.

4 Roll out the dough very thinly on a lightly floured surface. Using a floured cutter, cut into 5 cm (2 inch) rounds. Spoon about 1/2 teaspoon of filling into the centre of each round. Fold the rounds in half to form semi-circles, pressing the edges together firmly. Wrap each semi-circle around your finger to form a ring and then press the ends of the dough together firmly.

5 To make the tomato sauce, place the oil, tomato and oregano in a frying pan and cook over high heat for 10 minutes. Stir in the Parmesan, then set aside.

6 Cook the tortellini in two batches in a large pan of rapidly boiling water for about 6 minutes each batch, or until just tender. Drain well and return to the pan. Reheat the tomato sauce, add to the tortellini and toss to combine. Divide the tortellini among individual bowls, top with the bocconcini and allow the cheese to melt a little before serving.

NUTRITION PER SERVE
Protein 33 g; Fat 44 g; Carbohydrate 53 g; Dietary Fibre 7 g; Cholesterol 230 mg; 3090 kJ (740 cal)

HINT: To peel fresh tomatoes, score a cross in the base of the tomato, put in a bowl of boiling water for 1 minute, then plunge into cold water. The skin will peel away from the cross.

Gather the dough together into a smooth ball with your hands.

Place the dough in a lightly oiled bowl, cover with plastic wrap and leave.

Add the cheese, nutmeg, egg and seasoning to the processed filling mixture.

Roll out the dough very thinly and cut into rounds with a floured pastry cutter.

Wrap the semi-circles around your finger to make a ring and press the ends together.

Stir the grated Parmesan into the tomato sauce, then set aside.

129

RICE WITH CHICKEN AND SEAFOOD

Preparation time: 40 minutes
Total cooking time: 40 minutes
Serves 4–6

500 g (1 lb) raw medium prawns
500 g (1 lb) mussels
200 g (6¹/2 oz) calamari tubes
¹/4 cup (60 ml/2 fl oz) oil
2 chorizo sausages, thickly sliced
500 g (1 lb) chicken pieces
300 g (10 oz) pork fillet, thickly sliced
4 cloves garlic, crushed
2 red onions, chopped
¹/4 teaspoon saffron threads, soaked
   in hot water
¹/4 teaspoon turmeric
4 large tomatoes, peeled, seeded and
   chopped

2 cups (440 g/14 oz) short-grain rice
1.25 litres hot chicken stock
125 g (4 oz) green beans, cut into
   4 cm (1¹/2 inch) lengths
1 red capsicum, cut into thin strips
1 cup (155 g/5 oz) fresh peas

1 Peel the prawns. Devein, leaving the tails intact. Scrub the mussels and remove the beards. Cut the calamari tubes into 5 mm (¹/4 inch) thin slices. Heat 1 tablespoon of the oil in a large, heavy-based pan and add the chorizo. Cook over medium heat for 5 minutes, or until browned. Drain on paper towels. Add the chicken pieces and cook for 5 minutes, or until golden, turning once. Drain on paper towels.
2 Add the pork to the pan and cook for 3 minutes, or until browned, turning once. Drain on paper towels. Heat the remaining oil in the pan, add

the garlic, onion, drained saffron and turmeric, and cook over medium heat for 3 minutes, or until the onion is soft. Add the tomato and cook for 3 minutes, or until soft.
3 Add the rice and stir for 5 minutes, or until the rice is translucent. Stir in the hot chicken stock, bring to the boil, cover and simmer for 10 minutes. Add the chicken, cover and cook for 20 minutes. Add the pork, prawns, mussels, calamari, chorizo and vegetables. Cover and cook for 10 minutes, or until the liquid has been absorbed.

NUTRITION PER SERVE (6)
Protein 66 g; Fat 12 g; Carbohydrate 66 g;
Dietary Fibre 6 g; Cholesterol 278 mg;
2695 kJ (644 cal)

Drain the cooked chorizo sausage slices on paper towels.

Cook the pork slices until they are browned on both sides.

Add the rice to the pan and stir until the rice is translucent.

CHICKEN PILAF WITH SPICES

Preparation time: 25 minutes
Total cooking time: 40 minutes
Serves 4

1.5 kg (3 lb) chicken pieces
1/3 cup (80 ml/2³/4 fl oz) oil
1/4 cup (40 g/1¹/4 oz) unblanched
    whole almonds
2 onions, thinly sliced
3 cloves garlic, crushed
1 teaspoon whole black peppercorns
1 teaspoon turmeric
1 teaspoon cumin seeds
2 bay leaves
5 whole cloves
1 cinnamon stick
2 cups (440 g/14 oz) long-grain rice
1 litre chicken stock

1/2 cup (80 g/2³/4 oz) fresh or frozen
    peas
1/4 cup (30 g/1 oz) sultanas
3 hard-boiled eggs, peeled and
    quartered
fresh coriander leaves, to serve

1 Trim the chicken of excess fat and sinew. Heat half the oil in a large pan. Add the chicken pieces in batches and cook over medium heat for 5–10 minutes, or until the chicken is brown all over. Drain on paper towels. Heat 1 tablespoon of the oil in a pan. Add the almonds and cook over medium heat for 2 minutes, or until the nuts are brown. Remove from the pan and set aside.

2 Heat the remaining oil in a large pan. Add the onion and garlic and cook gently over low heat for 2 minutes, stirring occasionally. Add the peppercorns, turmeric, cumin, bay leaves, cloves and cinnamon stick. Fry over high heat for 1 minute, or until fragrant. Stir in the rice, making sure it is well coated with the spices.

3 Add the stock, browned chicken pieces and salt to taste. Bring to the boil, then reduce the heat and simmer, covered, for 20 minutes. Add the peas and sultanas and simmer for a further 5 minutes, or until all the liquid is absorbed and the chicken is tender (you may need to add extra stock or water). Remove the bay leaves and cinnamon stick and discard. Serve the pilaf with quartered eggs, topped with almonds and fresh coriander leaves.

NUTRITION PER SERVE
Protein 67 g; Fat 38 g; Carbohydrate 14 g;
Dietary Fibre 4 g; Cholesterol 280 mg;
2755 kJ (658 cal)

Cook the almonds in 1 tablespoon of the oil until they are brown.

Stir the rice into the onion and spice mixture, making sure it is well coated.

Add the peas and sultanas to the pan and simmer for 5 minutes.

CHICKEN BIRYANI

Preparation time: 1 hour 30 minutes
+ 3–4 hours marinating
Total cooking time: about 2 hours
Serves 6

MARINADE
6 cardamom pods
3 onions, peeled
3 cloves garlic
5 cm (2 inch) piece ginger, sliced
8 cloves or 1/4 teaspoon ground
  cloves
1 teaspoon whole black
  peppercorns
1 teaspoon ground cumin
1 teaspoon ground cinnamon
1 1/2 tablespoons poppy seeds
1/4 teaspoon ground nutmeg
1 teaspoon salt
2 tablespoons lemon juice
250 g (8 oz) natural yoghurt

1 kg (2 lb) chicken pieces, cut into
  small pieces
1/3 cup (80 ml/2 3/4 fl oz) oil
3 bay leaves
2 whole cardamom pods, lightly
  crushed
3 onions, very thinly sliced
2 tablespoons raisins
1 1/2 cups (300 g/10 oz) long-grain
  white rice
1/4 cup (60 ml/2 fl oz) milk
1 teaspoon sugar
1 teaspoon saffron threads
plain yoghurt, to serve
1/4 cup (40 g/1 1/4 oz) toasted
  cashews, to serve

1 To make the marinade, crush the cardamom pods with the flat side of a large knife blade to release the seeds; discard the pods. Chop the onions,

garlic and ginger in a food processor. Add the cardamom seeds, cloves, peppercorns, cumin, cinnamon, poppy seeds, nutmeg, salt and lemon juice, and process to a smooth paste. Stir in the yoghurt and set aside.

2 Prick the skin of the chicken with a fork (this helps the flavour infuse into the chicken) and place in a large mixing bowl. Add the marinade and mix well to thoroughly coat the chicken, then refrigerate for 3–4 hours, or overnight.

3 Heat about 3 tablespoons of the oil in a heavy-based frying pan over low heat. Add the bay leaves and whole cardamom pods and toss in the oil. Cook for 2 minutes, being careful not to burn. Remove the bay leaves and set aside; discard the cardamom pods. Add the onion and fry over low heat for 8 minutes, or until a rich golden colour. Remove with a slotted spoon, leaving the oil in the pan. Drain on paper towels. Quickly fry the raisins until plump; set aside with the onions. Reserve the remaining oil.

4 Place the chicken and the marinade in a heavy-based flameproof casserole dish and bring slowly to the boil. Cover and simmer for 15 minutes. Using tongs or a slotted spoon, remove the chicken, leaving as much marinade in the pan as possible. Reduce the marinade down, cooking it over low heat until only about 1 cup (250 ml/8 fl oz) remains. Return the chicken to the pan and toss to coat in the thickened sauce. Cover and set aside while preparing the rice.

5 Add the rice to a large pan of boiling water and cook for 7 minutes. (Do not cook the rice until tender.) Drain the rice into a colander. Meanwhile, heat the milk and sugar, pour into a bowl, add the saffron and

soak for 5 minutes.

6 Preheat the oven to slow 150°C (300°F/Gas 2). Spoon the rice over the spice-coated chicken and pour over the saffron mixture. Streak the orange colour gently through the rice with a

Crush the cardamom pods to release the seeds with the flat side of a knife.

Prick the skin of the chicken with a fork to help the flavour infuse into the meat.

Remove the onion with a slotted spoon, keeping as much oil as possible in the pan.

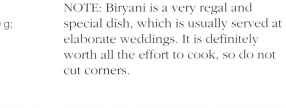

fork. Pour over the reserved flavoured oil, and scatter with bay leaves. Cover the dish tightly with foil and bake for 1 hour, or until the rice and chicken are tender. Serve topped with the onion, raisins, yoghurt and cashews.

NUTRITION PER SERVE
Protein 40 g; Fat 45 g; Carbohydrate 60 g; Dietary Fibre 4 g; Cholesterol 140 mg; 3305 kJ (785 cal)

NOTE: Biryani is a very regal and special dish, which is usually served at elaborate weddings. It is definitely worth all the effort to cook, so do not cut corners.

Cook the marinade over low heat until reduced and thickened.

Add the saffron threads to the heated milk and sugar mixture.

Gently streak the saffron mixture through the rice using a fork.

SPAGHETTI WITH CHICKEN BOLOGNAISE

Preparation time: 10 minutes
Total cooking time: 15 minutes
Serves 4

2 tablespoons olive oil
2 leeks, trimmed, thinly sliced
1 red capsicum, finely chopped
2 cloves garlic, crushed
500 g (1 lb) chicken mince
2 cups (500 g/1 lb) tomato pasta
   sauce
1 tablespoon chopped fresh thyme
1 tablespoon chopped fresh rosemary
2 tablespoons seeded and chopped
   black olives
400 g (13 oz) spaghetti
125 g (4 oz) feta cheese, crumbled

1 Heat the oil in a large, heavy-based pan. Add the leek, capsicum and garlic and cook over medium-high heat for 2 minutes, or until lightly browned.
2 Add the chicken mince and cook over high heat for 3 minutes, or until browned and any liquid has evaporated. Stir occasionally to break up any lumps as the mince cooks.
3 Add the tomato pasta sauce, thyme and rosemary, and bring to the boil. Reduce the heat and simmer, uncovered, for 5 minutes, or until the sauce has reduced and thickened. Add the olives and stir to combine. Season with salt and pepper.
4 Meanwhile, cook the spaghetti in a large pan of rapidly boiling water with a little oil until just tender; drain. Place the spaghetti on individual serving plates or pile into a large deep serving dish and pour the chicken mixture over the top. Sprinkle with the feta and serve immediately.

NUTRITION PER SERVE
Protein 50 g; Fat 23 g; Carbohydrate 88 g;
Dietary Fibre 10 g; Cholesterol 84 mg;
3158 kJ (758 cal)

VARIATION: Any type of pasta, dried or fresh, is suitable to use. Freshly grated Parmesan or Pecorino can be used instead of feta cheese.

Remove the seeds and white membrane from the capsicum, and finely chop the flesh.

Add the chicken mince to the leek, capsicum and garlic in the pan.

Stir in the tomato pasta sauce, chopped thyme and rosemary.

While the sauce is cooking, cook the spaghetti in a large pan of rapidly boiling water.

FETTUCINE WITH CHICKEN AND MUSHROOM SAUCE

Preparation time: 10 minutes
Total cooking time: 25 minutes
Serves 4

2 (330 g/11 oz) chicken breast fillets
1 tablespoon olive oil
30 g (1 oz) butter
2 slices bacon, cut into thin strips
2 cloves garlic, crushed
250 g (8 oz) button mushrooms, sliced
1/3 cup (80 ml/2³/4 fl oz) dry white wine
2/3 cup (170 ml/5¹/2 fl oz) cream
4 spring onions, chopped
1 tablespoon plain flour
400 g (13 oz) fettucine
1/3 cup (35 g/1¹/4 oz) grated
    Parmesan

1 Trim the chicken of excess fat and sinew, and cut into thin strips. Heat the oil and butter in a heavy-based frying pan. Add the chicken and cook over medium heat for 3 minutes, or until browned.
2 Add the bacon, garlic and mushrooms, and cook over medium heat for 2 minutes, stirring occasionally.
3 Add the wine and cook until the liquid has reduced by half. Add the cream and spring onion, and bring to the boil. Blend the flour with 2 tablespoons water until smooth. Add to the pan and stir over the heat until the mixture boils and thickens, then reduce the heat and simmer for 2 minutes. Season to taste.
4 Cook the fettucine in a large pan of rapidly boiling water with a little oil added, then drain. Add the fettucine to the sauce and stir over low heat until combined. Sprinkle with Parmesan and serve immediately with a green salad and herb bread.

NUTRITION PER SERVE
Protein 40 g; Fat 35 g; Carbohydrate 75 g;
Dietary Fibre 7 g; Cholesterol 136 mg;
3380 kJ (808 cal)

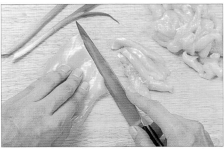

Trim the chicken of excess fat and sinew, and cut into thin strips.

Add the bacon, garlic and mushrooms to the chicken and cook over medium heat.

Add the cream and spring onion to the pan and bring to the boil.

Add the fettucine to the sauce and stir over low heat until combined.

Grills & Barbecues

HONEY-GLAZED CHICKEN BREASTS

Preparation time: 10 minutes
  + 20 minutes marinating
Total cooking time: 10 minutes
Serves 6

6 chicken breast fillets (1 kg/2 lb)
50 g (1³/₄ oz) butter, softened
¹/₄ cup (90 g/3 oz) honey
¹/₄ cup (60 ml/2 fl oz) barbecue sauce
2 teaspoons wholegrain mustard

1 Trim the chicken of any excess fat and sinew. Using a sharp knife, make three or four diagonal cuts across one side of each chicken breast. Preheat a barbecue grill or flatplate to high.
2 Combine the butter, honey, barbecue sauce and mustard in a small bowl. Spread half of the honey mixture thickly over the slashed side of the chicken. Cover with plastic wrap and stand at room temperature for 20 minutes. Set the remaining honey mixture aside.
3 Lightly grease the hot barbecue grill or flatplate. Cook the chicken breasts, slashed-side up, for 2–3 minutes each side, or until the chicken is cooked through and tender. Brush with the reserved honey mixture several times during cooking. Serve with hot buttered pasta, if desired.

NUTRITION PER SERVE
Protein 38 g; Fat 11 g; Carbohydrate 16 g;
Dietary Fibre 0 g; Cholesterol 105 mg;
1297 kJ (310 cal)

HINT: Any leftover cooked chicken can be shredded and served mixed through a green salad or sliced thickly and made into sandwiches.

NOTES: Barbecue the chicken just before serving. The chicken can be marinated overnight in the refrigerator. When honey is cooked, its sugars caramelize and some of its flavour is lost. For a distinctive taste to this dish, use honey with a strong, dark flavour, such as leatherwood, lavender or rosemary. Lighter honeys, such as yellow box, orange blossom or clover, will sweeten and glaze the meat without necessarily affecting its flavour. Usually the paler the honey, the milder its flavour.

Use a sharp knife to cut three or four diagonal cuts on one side of the chicken.

Combine the butter, honey, barbecue sauce and mustard in a small bowl.

CHICKEN BURGER WITH TANGY GARLIC MAYONNAISE

Preparation time: 20 minutes
+ 3 hours marinating
Total cooking time: 15 minutes
Serves 4

4 chicken breast fillets
1/2 cup (125 ml/4 fl oz) lime juice
1 tablespoon sweet chilli sauce
4 slices bacon
4 hamburger buns, halved
4 lettuce leaves
1 large tomato, sliced

GARLIC MAYONNAISE
2 egg yolks
2 cloves garlic, crushed
1 tablespoon Dijon mustard
1 tablespoon lemon juice
1/2 cup (125 ml/4 fl oz) olive oil

1 Place the chicken in a shallow non-metal dish. Prick the chicken breasts with a skewer several times. Combine the lime juice and sweet chilli sauce in a jug. Pour the mixture over the chicken, cover and refrigerate for several hours or overnight.
2 To make the mayonnaise, place the egg yolks, garlic, mustard and lemon juice in a food processor bowl or blender and process until smooth. With the motor running, add the oil in a thin, steady stream. Process until the mixture reaches a thick consistency. Refrigerate, covered, until required.
3 Preheat a barbecue grill or flatplate to high. Remove and discard the rind from the bacon, and cut the bacon in half crossways. Lightly grease the hot barbecue. Cook the chicken and bacon for 5 minutes, or until crisp. Cook the chicken for a further 5–10 minutes, or until well browned and cooked through, turning once.
4 Toast the hamburger buns until lightly browned. Arrange the lettuce, tomato, chicken and bacon on the bases. Top with the garlic mayonnaise and finish with the remaining bun top.

NUTRITION PER SERVE
Protein 70 g; Fat 42 g; Carbohydrate 52 g;
Dietary Fibre 5 g; Cholesterol 211 mg;
3624 kJ (866 cal)

VARIATION: For a tangy mayonnaise, substitute the lemon juice with lime juice and omit the garlic.

Pour the combined lime juice and sweet chilli sauce over the chicken fillets.

Cook the chicken until it is well browned and cooked through, turning once.

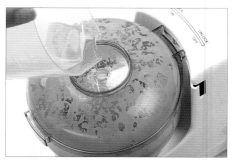

Add the oil to the egg yolk mixture in a thin, steady stream.

KETTLE CHICKEN

Preparation time: 10 minutes
Total cooking time: 1 hour 30 minutes
Serves 4–6

1.8 kg (3 lb 10 oz) chicken
1 whole head of garlic
small bunch fresh oregano
1/4 cup (60 ml/2 fl oz) olive oil

1 Prepare a kettle barbecue for indirect cooking at medium heat. Place a drip tray underneath the top grill.
2 Remove the giblets and any large fat deposits from the chicken. Wipe the chicken and pat dry with paper towels. Season the chicken cavity with salt and cracked black pepper. Using a sharp knife, cut the top off the head of garlic. Push the whole head of garlic, unpeeled, into the cavity, then add the whole bunch of oregano. Close the cavity with several toothpicks or a skewer.
3 Rub the chicken skin with salt and brush with olive oil. Place on the barbecue over the drip tray. Put the lid on the barbecue and cook for 1 hour, brushing occasionally with the olive oil to keep the skin moist. Insert a skewer into the chicken thigh. If the juices run clear, the chicken is cooked through. Stand the chicken away from the heat for 5 minutes before carving.
4 Carefully separate the garlic cloves and serve 1 or 2 cloves with each serving of chicken. (The flesh can be squeezed from the clove and eaten with the chicken.)

NUTRITION PER SERVE
Protein 42 g; Fat 16 g; Carbohydrate 0.5 g; Dietary Fibre 1 g; Cholesterol 138 mg; 1328 kJ (317 cal)

Cut the top off the head of garlic, then push the whole head of garlic into the chicken cavity.

Insert a skewer into the thickest part of the chicken thigh to see if the chicken is cooked.

Carefully separate the garlic cloves and serve with the chicken.

THAI CHICKEN CUTLETS

Preparation time: 20 minutes
   + 1 hour marinating
Total cooking time: 20 minutes
Serves 4–6

12 chicken thigh fillets (1.25 kg/2¹/₂ lb)
6 cloves garlic
1 teaspoon black peppercorns
3 fresh coriander roots and stems,
   roughly chopped
¹/₄ teaspoon salt

CHILLI GARLIC DIP
4–5 dried red chillies
2 large cloves garlic, chopped
¹/₄ cup (60 g/2 oz) sugar
¹/₃ cup (80 ml/2³/₄ fl oz) cider or rice
   vinegar
pinch salt
¹/₄ cup (60 ml/2 fl oz) boiling water

1 Trim the chicken thigh fillets of any excess fat and sinew.
2 Place the garlic, peppercorns, coriander and salt in a food processor bowl. Process for 20–30 seconds, or until the mixture forms a smooth paste. (This can also be done using a mortar and pestle.) Place the chicken in a shallow non-metal dish. Spread the garlic mixture over the chicken. Refrigerate the chicken, covered, for 1 hour.
3 To make the chilli garlic dip, soak the chillies in hot water for 20 minutes. Drain the chillies and chop finely. Place in a mortar with the garlic and sugar, and grind to a smooth paste. Place the mixture in a small pan and add the vinegar, salt and boiling water. Bring to the boil, then reduce the heat and simmer for 2–3 minutes. Set aside to cool.
4 Preheat a barbecue grill or flatplate to high. Grease the barbecue and cook the chicken for 5–10 minutes on each side, turning once. Serve with the chilli garlic dip.

NUTRITION PER SERVE (6)
Protein 47 g; Fat 5 g; Carbohydrate 0.5 g;
Dietary Fibre 1 g; Cholesterol 105 mg;
1005 kJ (240 cal)

Using a sharp knife, trim any excess fat and sinew from the chicken.

Place the garlic, peppercorns, coriander and salt in a food processor bowl.

Grind the chilli, garlic and sugar to a smooth paste using a mortar and pestle.

Cook the chicken on a greased barbecue grill or flat plate.

MIDDLE-EASTERN BAKED CHICKEN

Preparation time: 30 minutes
Total cooking time: 1 hour 15 minutes
Serves 6

1.6 kg (3¼ lb) chicken
½ cup (125 ml/4 fl oz) boiling water
½ cup (95 g/3 oz) instant couscous
4 pitted dates, chopped
4 dried apricots, chopped
1 tablespoon lime juice
20 g (¾ oz) butter
2 tablespoons olive oil
1 onion, chopped
1–2 cloves garlic, chopped
1 teaspoon salt
¼ teaspoon cracked black pepper
1 teaspoon ground coriander
2 tablespoons chopped fresh parsley
1 teaspoon ground cumin

1 Prepare a kettle barbecue for indirect cooking at medium heat. Place a drip tray underneath the top grill.
2 Remove the giblets and any fat from the chicken. Wipe the chicken with paper towels. Pour boiling water over the couscous and leave to soak for 15 minutes. Soak the dates and apricots in the lime juice and set aside.
3 Heat the butter and half the oil in a pan and cook the onion and garlic for 3–4 minutes, or until translucent. Remove from the heat and add the couscous, dates, apricots, coriander, parsley and some salt and pepper. Mix well. Spoon into the chicken cavity and close with a skewer. Tie the legs with string.
4 Rub the chicken with the combined salt, cracked black pepper, cumin and remaining oil. Place the chicken in the centre of a large piece of greased foil. Wrap the chicken securely. Place on the barbecue over the drip tray. Cover the barbecue and cook for 50 minutes. Open the foil, crimping the edges to form a tray. Cook for 20 minutes, or until the chicken is tender and golden. Stand for 5–6 minutes before carving.

NUTRITION PER SERVE
Protein 46 g; Fat 14 g; Carbohydrate 5.5 g; Dietary Fibre 1 g; Cholesterol 110 mg; 1378 kJ (329 cal)

Remove the giblets and any large deposits of fat from the chicken.

Combine the onion, garlic, couscous, dates, apricots, salt, pepper, coriander and parsley.

Rub the chicken skin all over with the combined salt, cracked pepper, cumin and remaining oil.

Open the foil and crimp the edges to form a tray to retain the cooking liquid.

CHICKEN CUTLETS WITH CORN RELISH

Preparation time: 20 minutes
Total cooking time: 25 minutes
Serves 4

8 chicken thigh cutlets, skin on (1 kg)
1 tablespoon olive oil
1 small clove garlic, crushed
1/4 teaspoon ground turmeric
1/2 teaspoon salt

CORN RELISH
1 cup (200 g/6 1/2 oz) frozen corn
    kernels
1 tablespoon olive oil
1 red chilli, seeded and chopped
1 small green capsicum, finely
    chopped
1 onion, finely chopped
1/3 cup (80 ml/2 3/4 fl oz) white vinegar
1/4 cup (60 g/2 oz) sugar
1 teaspoon wholegrain mustard
3 teaspoons cornflour
1 teaspoon paprika
1 teaspoon finely chopped fresh
    coriander leaves
1 tablespoon olive oil, extra

1 Preheat a barbecue grill or flatplate to high. Trim the chicken of excess fat and sinew. Prick the skin of the chicken cutlets with the point of a knife. Place the cutlets in a large frying pan of boiling water. Reduce the heat and simmer for 5 minutes. Remove from the pan, then drain and allow to cool.
2 Place the olive oil, garlic, turmeric and salt in a bowl and whisk to combine. Rub the mixture over the skin side of the chicken cutlets. Set aside.
3 To make the corn relish, cook the corn in a pan of boiling water for 2–3 minutes, or until tender, then drain. Heat the oil in a pan. Add the chilli, capsicum and onion. Cook over medium heat until tender. Add the corn, vinegar, sugar and mustard, and cook, stirring, for a further 5 minutes. Mix the cornflour with 1/2 cup (125 ml/ 4 fl oz) water. Pour into the corn mixture. Bring to the boil, then reduce the heat and stir until thickened. Stir in the paprika, coriander and extra oil. Remove from the heat and cool.
4 Lightly grease the hot barbecue grill or flatplate. Cook the cutlets, skin-side up for 2 minutes, then turn and cook for 4 minutes. Continue cooking for another 5–10 minutes, turning frequently, until the chicken is well browned and cooked through. Serve with the corn relish.

NUTRITION PER SERVE
Protein 47 g; Fat 20 g; Carbohydrate 30 g;
Dietary Fibre 2 g; Cholesterol 100 mg;
2047 kJ (490 cal)

Simmer the chicken cutlets in a large frying pan of boiling water.

Pour the blended cornflour and water into the corn mixture.

Cook the chicken cutlets, turning frequently, until the chicken is well browned and cooked through.

CHICKEN KEBABS WITH CURRY MAYONNAISE

Preparation time: 25 minutes
+ 30 minutes marinating
Total cooking time: 10 minutes
Serves 4

600 g (1¹/₄ lb) chicken breast fillets
4 large spring onions
1 small green capsicum
1 small red capsicum
¹/₄ cup (60 ml/2 fl oz) olive oil
1 teaspoon freshly ground black
    pepper
¹/₂ teaspoon ground turmeric
1¹/₂ teaspoons ground coriander

CURRY MAYONNAISE
³/₄ cup (185 g/6 oz) whole-egg
    mayonnaise
1 tablespoon hot curry powder
¹/₄ cup (60 g/2 oz) sour cream
1 tablespoon sweet fruit or mango
    chutney, mashed
¹/₄ cup (45 g/1¹/₂ oz) peeled, finely
    chopped cucumber
¹/₂ teaspoon toasted cumin seeds
1 tablespoon finely chopped fresh
    mint
1 teaspoon finely chopped fresh mint,
    extra

1 Preheat a barbecue grill or flatplate to high. Trim the chicken of excess fat and sinew. Cut the chicken into 3 cm (1¹/₄ inch) cubes. Cut the spring onions into 3 cm (1¹/₄ inch) lengths. Cut the red and green capsicum into 3 cm (1¹/₄ inch) squares.
2 Thread the chicken, spring onion and capsicum onto skewers. Arrange the kebabs, side by side, in a shallow, non-metal dish. Combine the oil, pepper, turmeric and coriander in a jug. Pour over the kebabs and place in the refrigerator to marinate for 30 minutes.
3 To make the curry mayonnaise, combine the mayonnaise, curry powder, sour cream, chutney, cucumber, cumin seeds and mint in a bowl, and mix well. Spoon the mixture into a dish or jug for serving and sprinkle with the extra chopped mint.
4 Lightly oil the hot barbecue grill or flatplate. Cook the kebabs for 2–3 minutes each side, or until cooked through and tender. Serve with the curry mayonnaise.

NUTRITION PER SERVE
Protein 36 g; Fat 40 g; Carbohydrate 14 g; Dietary Fibre 2 g; Cholesterol 110 mg; 2316 kJ (553 cal)

Cut the chicken, spring onions and capsicums into even-sized pieces.

Pour the oil mixture over the chicken kebabs, and marinate for 30 minutes.

Combine the curry mayonnaise ingredients in a bowl and mix well.

CITRUS CHICKEN DRUMSTICKS

Preparation time: 20 minutes
  + 3 hours marinating
Total cooking time: 20 minutes
Serves 4

8 chicken drumsticks
1/3 cup (80 ml/2³/4 fl oz) orange juice
1/3 cup (80 ml/2³/4 fl oz) lemon juice
1 teaspoon grated orange rind
1 teaspoon grated lemon rind
1 teaspoon sesame oil
1 tablespoon olive oil
1 spring onion, finely chopped

1 Pat the chicken drumsticks dry with paper towels. Trim any excess fat and score the thickest part of the chicken with a knife. Place in a shallow non-metal dish.
2 Combine the juices, rinds, oils and spring onion. Pour over the chicken. Refrigerate, covered, for several hours or overnight, turning occasionally.
3 Preheat a barbecue grill or flatplate to high. Drain the chicken, reserving the marinade. Lightly grease the hot barbecue grill or flatplate. Cook the drumsticks for 15–20 minutes, or until tender. Brush occasionally with the reserved marinade. Serve immediately.

NUTRITION PER SERVE
Protein 43 g; Fat 10 g; Carbohydrate 3.5 g; Dietary Fibre 0 g; Cholesterol 94 mg; 1175 kJ (280 cal)

Score the thickest part of the chicken drumsticks with a knife.

Remove the chicken from the marinade, reserving the marinade.

Cook the drumsticks until tender, brushing with the reserved marinade.

TANDOORI BARBECUE CHICKEN

Preparation time: 15 minutes
  + 4 hours marinating
Total cooking time: 1 hour
Serves 4

4 chicken marylands (drumstick and thigh), skin removed
1 teaspoon salt
2 cloves garlic, crushed
1 tablespoon lemon juice
1 cup (250 g/8 oz) plain yoghurt
1¹/2 teaspoons garam masala
1/2 teaspoon ground black pepper
1/2 teaspoon ground turmeric
2–3 drops red food colouring
20–30 mesquite or hickory chips, for smoking
olive oil, for basting

1 Place the chicken in a large non-metal dish and rub with the salt and garlic. Combine the lemon juice, yoghurt, garam masala, pepper and turmeric in a jug. Add enough food colouring to make the marinade a bright orange-red colour. Pour the marinade over the chicken and coat evenly with the back of a spoon. Refrigerate, covered, for 4 hours, turning the chicken every hour.
2 Prepare a kettle barbecue for indirect cooking. When the barbecue coals are covered with fine white ash, add the mesquite or hickory chips to the coals. Cover the barbecue and leave until the smoke is well established (about 5 minutes).
3 Brush the barbecue grill with oil. Arrange the chicken on the grill and put the lid on the barbecue. Smoke-cook for 45 minutes to 1 hour, or until the chicken is well crisped. Brush the chicken with the oil several times during cooking.

NUTRITION PER SERVE
Protein 45 g; Fat 11 g; Carbohydrate 3 g; Dietary Fibre 0 g; Cholesterol 100 mg; 1255 kJ (300 cal)

Pour the marinade over the chicken and coat evenly with the back of a spoon.

Add the mesquite or hickory chips to the ash-covered coals.

Brush the marinated chicken with the oil several times during cooking.

BUFFALO WINGS WITH RANCH DRESSING

Preparation time: 25 minutes
  + 3 hours marinating
Total cooking time: 10 minutes
Serves 4

8 large chicken wings
2 teaspoons black pepper
2 teaspoons garlic salt
2 teaspoons onion powder
olive oil, for deep-frying
1/2 cup (125 ml/4 fl oz) tomato sauce
2 tablespoons Worcestershire sauce
20 g (3/4 oz) butter, melted
2 teaspoons sugar
Tabasco sauce, to taste

RANCH DRESSING
1/2 cup (125 g/4 oz) whole-egg
    mayonnaise
1/2 cup (125 g/4 oz) sour cream
2 tablespoons lemon juice
2 tablespoons chopped fresh chives

1 Pat the chicken wings dry with paper towels. Cut the tips off each wing and discard. Bend each wing back to snap the joint, and cut through to create two pieces. Combine the pepper, garlic salt and onion powder. Rub into each chicken piece.
2 Heat the oil to moderately hot in a deep heavy-based pan. Cook the chicken in batches for 2 minutes. Remove and drain on paper towels.
3 Transfer the chicken to a non-metal bowl or shallow dish. Combine the sauces, butter, sugar and Tabasco. Pour the mixture over the chicken and stir to coat. Refrigerate, covered, for several hours or overnight.
4 To make the ranch dressing, combine the mayonnaise, sour cream, lemon juice, chives, salt and white pepper in a bowl and mix well.
5 Preheat a barbecue grill or flatplate to high. Lightly oil the hot barbecue. Cook the chicken for 5 minutes, turning and brushing with the marinade. Serve with the dressing.

NUTRITION PER SERVE
Protein 44 g; Fat 40 g; Carbohydrate 18 g;
Dietary Fibre 1 g; Cholesterol 157 mg;
2539 kJ (605 cal)

Bend the wings back to snap the joint, then cut through to make two pieces.

Cook the chicken in batches in the hot oil, then remove and drain on paper towels.

Pour the sauce mixture over the chicken and stir to coat.

Cook the chicken for 5 minutes, turning and brushing with the marinade.

CHICKEN BURGER WITH TARRAGON MAYONNAISE

Preparation time: 25 minutes
Total cooking time: 20 minutes
Serves 6

1 kg (2 lb) chicken mince
1 small onion, finely chopped
2 teaspoons lemon rind
2 tablespoons sour cream
1 cup (80 g/2³/4 oz) fresh
    breadcrumbs
6 onion bread rolls

TARRAGON MAYONNAISE
1 egg yolk
1 tablespoon tarragon vinegar
1/2 teaspoon French mustard
1 cup (250 ml/8 fl oz) olive oil

1 Place the chicken mince in a mixing bowl. Add the onion, lemon rind, sour cream and breadcrumbs. Using your hands, mix until thoroughly combined. Divide the mixture into 6 equal portions and shape into 1.5 cm (⁵/8 inch) thick patties.
2 Preheat a barbecue grill or flatplate to high. Lightly oil the hot barbecue. Cook the patties for 7 minutes each side, turning once. Serve the patties on the onion rolls with the mayonnaise.
3 To make the tarragon mayonnaise, place the egg yolk, half the vinegar and the mustard in a small mixing bowl. Whisk together for 1 minute, or until light and creamy. Add the oil about 1 teaspoon at a time, whisking constantly until the mixture thickens. Increase the flow of oil to a thin stream and continue whisking until all of the oil has been incorporated. Stir in the remaining vinegar and season with salt and white pepper.

NUTRITION PER SERVE
Protein 40 g; Fat 47 g; Carbohydrate 11 g; Dietary Fibre 1 g; Cholesterol 122 mg; 2628 kJ (628 cal)

HINT: The mayonnaise can also be made in a food processor. Add the oil in a thin stream, with the motor constantly running, until the mixture thickens and turns creamy.

Mix the chicken mince, onion, lemon rind, sour cream and breadcrumbs together.

Cook the patties for 7 minutes each side, turning once, or until they are cooked through.

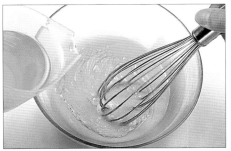
Once the mayonnaise mixture has thickened, add the oil in a steady stream.

CHICKEN BREASTS WITH FRUIT MEDLEY

Preparation time: 25 minutes
+ 3 hours marinating
Total cooking time: 20 minutes
Serves 4

4 chicken breast fillets
3/4 cup (80 ml/2³/4 fl oz) white
  wine
1/4 cup (60 ml/2 fl oz) olive
  oil
2 teaspoons grated fresh
  ginger
1 clove garlic, crushed

FRUIT MEDLEY
225 g (7 oz) can pineapple slices,
  drained
1 small mango
2 small kiwi fruit
150 g (5 oz) watermelon, seeds
  removed
1 tablespoon finely chopped fresh
  mint

1 Trim the chicken breast fillets of
fat and sinew. Place the chicken in a
shallow non-metal dish. Combine
the wine, oil, ginger and garlic in a
jug, and pour over the chicken.
Refrigerate, covered, for several hours
or overnight, turning occasionally.

2 Preheat a barbecue grill or flatplate
to high. Lightly oil the hot barbecue.
Cook the marinated chicken fillets for
5–10 minutes each side, or until well
browned on the outside. Serve
immediately with the fruit medley.
3 To make the fruit medley, finely
chop the pineapple, mango, kiwi fruit
and watermelon. Combine with the
mint in a small serving bowl.

NUTRITION PER SERVE
Protein 50 g; Fat 20 g; Carbohydrate 15 g;
Dietary Fibre 3 g; Cholesterol 110 mg;
2000 kJ (480 cal)

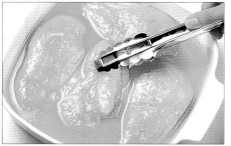

Marinate the chicken in the wine, oil, ginger and
garlic mixture, turning occasionally.

Cook the chicken on a hot barbecue grill until well
browned on the outside.

For the fruit medley, finely chop the pineapple,
mango, kiwi fruit and watermelon.

TANDOORI CHICKEN SKEWERS

Preparation time: 20 minutes
+ 3 hours marinating
Total cooking time: 10 minutes
Serves 4–6

1 kg (2 lb) chicken thigh fillets
1 cup (250 g/8 oz) plain yoghurt
1 teaspoon chilli powder
1 teaspoon turmeric
1 teaspoon ground cumin
1 teaspoon ground coriander

1 teaspoon grated fresh ginger
1 clove garlic, crushed

1 Trim the chicken of excess fat and
sinew. Cut each chicken fillet into thin
strips and weave them onto small
skewers, bunching the chicken along
about three-quarters of the length.
2 Combine the yoghurt, chilli powder,
turmeric, cumin, coriander, ginger and
garlic, and mix well. Place the skewers
in a shallow non-metal dish, cover
with the yoghurt mixture and
refrigerate, covered, for several hours
or overnight, turning occasionally.

3 Preheat a barbecue grill or flatplate
to high. Lightly oil the hot barbecue.
Cook the marinated chicken skewers
for 8–10 minutes or until tender.

NUTRITION PER SERVE (6)
Protein 40 g; Fat 5 g; Carbohydrate 1.5 g;
Dietary Fibre 0 g; Cholesterol 90 mg;
885 kJ (212 cal)

HINT: Serve the chicken with a sauce
of plain yoghurt, chopped cucumber
and a pinch of cumin, or accompany
with a selection of sweet chutneys.

Thread the chicken strips onto the skewers,
bunching them along the length.

Combine the yoghurt, chilli powder, turmeric,
cumin, coriander, ginger and garlic.

Cook the marinated chicken skewers on a hot
barbecue grill until tender.

TERIYAKI CHICKEN WINGS

Preparation time: 15 minutes
  + 3 hours marinating
Total cooking time: 15 minutes
Serves 4

8 chicken wings
1/4 cup (60 ml/2 fl oz) soy sauce
2 tablespoons sherry
2 teaspoons grated fresh ginger
1 clove garlic, crushed
1 tablespoon honey

1 Pat the chicken wings dry with paper towels. Trim any excess fat from the wings, and tuck the tips under to form a triangle.

2 Place the wings in a shallow non-metal dish. Combine the soy sauce, sherry, ginger, garlic and honey in a jug, and mix well. Pour the mixture over the chicken wings. Refrigerate, covered, for several hours or overnight. Lightly brush two sheets of aluminium foil with oil. Place 4 wings in a single layer on each piece of foil and wrap completely.

3 Preheat a barbecue grill or flatplate to high. Cook the parcels on the hot barbecue for 10 minutes. Remove the parcels from the heat and unwrap. Place the wings directly on a lightly greased grill for 3 minutes, or until brown. Turn the wings frequently and brush with any remaining marinade.

NUTRITION PER SERVE
Protein 43 g; Fat 4.5 g; Carbohydrate 6 g;
Dietary Fibre 0 g; Cholesterol 95 mg;
998 kJ (238 cal)

Tuck the tips of the chicken wings under to form a triangle.

Place four chicken wings on each piece of foil and wrap completely.

Place the wings directly on a lightly greased grill and cook until brown.

CHICKEN FAJITAS

Preparation time: 35 minutes
  + 3 hours marinating
Total cooking time: 10 minutes
Serves 4

4 chicken breast fillets
2 tablespoons olive oil
1/4 cup (60 ml) lime juice
2 cloves garlic, crushed
1 teaspoon ground cumin
1/4 cup (15 g/1/2 oz) chopped fresh
    coriander leaves
8 flour tortillas
1 tablespoon olive oil, extra
2 onions, sliced

2 green capsicums, cut into thin strips
1 cup (125 g/4 oz) grated Cheddar
1 large avocado, sliced
1 cup (250 g/8 oz) bottled tomato
    salsa

1 Trim the chicken of fat and sinew, and cut into thin strips. Place the chicken strips in a shallow non-metal dish. Combine the oil, lime juice, garlic, cumin and coriander in a jug, and mix well. Pour the mixture over the chicken. Refrigerate, covered, for several hours or overnight.
2 Preheat a barbecue grill or flatplate to high. Wrap the tortillas in foil and place on a cool part of the barbecue grill to warm through for 10 minutes.

Heat the oil on a flatplate. Cook the onion and capsicum for 5 minutes, or until soft. Move the vegetables to a cooler part of the plate to keep warm.
3 Place the chicken and marinade on the flatplate and cook for 5 minutes, or until just tender. Transfer the chicken, vegetables and wrapped tortillas to a serving platter. Make up individual fajitas by placing the chicken, onion and capsicum, cheese and avocado over the tortillas. Top with the salsa and roll up to enclose the filling.

NUTRITION PER SERVE
Protein 88 g; Fat 59 g; Carbohydrate 116 g; Dietary Fibre 9.5 g; Cholesterol 173 mg; 5660 kJ (1352 cal)

Combine the oil, lime juice, garlic, cumin and coriander, and pour over the chicken.

Cook the onion and capsicum on the flatplate until soft.

Cook the chicken and marinade on the flatplate until just tender.

SMOKED CHICKEN FILLETS

Preparation time: 5 minutes
Total cooking time: 25 minutes
Serves 4

4 chicken breast fillets
1 tablespoon olive oil
seasoned pepper, to taste

hickory or mesquite chips,
    for smoking

1 Prepare a kettle barbecue for indirect cooking at medium heat. Trim the chicken of excess fat and sinew. Brush the chicken with the oil and sprinkle with the seasoned pepper.
2 Spoon a pile of hickory or mesquite chips (about 25) over the coals in each charcoal rail.

3 Cover the barbecue and cook the chicken for 15 minutes. Test with a sharp knife. If the juices do not run clear, cook for another 5–10 minutes, or until cooked through. Serve with chilli noodles.

NUTRITION PER SERVE
Protein 50 g; Fat 10 g; Carbohydrate 0 g;
Dietary Fibre 0 g; Cholesterol 116 mg;
1208 kJ (288 cal)

Brush the chicken fillets with the oil and sprinkle with the seasoned pepper.

Spoon some hickory or mesquite chips over the coals in each charcoal rail.

Test the chicken with a sharp knife to check that the juices run clear.

CHARGRILLED CHICKEN

Preparation time: 20 minutes
  + 2 hours marinating
Total cooking time: 1 hour
Serves 4

4 chicken breast fillets
2 tablespoons honey
1 tablespoon wholegrain mustard
1 tablespoon soy sauce
2 red onions, cut into wedges
8 Roma tomatoes, halved lengthways
2 tablespoons soft brown sugar

2 tablespoons balsamic vinegar
cooking oil spray
snow pea sprouts, for serving

1 Preheat the oven to moderate 180°C (350°F/Gas 4). Trim the chicken of any excess fat and place in a shallow dish. Combine the honey, mustard and soy sauce and pour over the chicken, tossing to coat. Cover and refrigerate for 2 hours, turning once.
2 Place the onion wedges and tomato halves on a baking tray covered with baking paper. Sprinkle with the sugar and drizzle with the balsamic vinegar.

Bake for 40 minutes.
3 Heat a chargrill pan and lightly spray with oil. Remove the chicken from the marinade and cook for 4–5 minutes on each side, or until cooked through. Slice the chicken and serve with the snow pea sprouts, tomato halves and onion wedges.

NUTRITION PER SERVE
Protein 25 g; Fat 2.5 g; Carbohydrate 30 g; Dietary Fibre 3 g; Cholesterol 50 mg; 990 kJ (235 cal)

Pour the marinade over the chicken and toss to coat thoroughly.

Drizzle the balsamic vinegar over the onion wedges and tomato halves.

Cook the marinated chicken in a hot, lightly oiled chargrill pan.

SWEET CHILLI CHICKEN

Preparation time: 15 minutes +
  2 hours marinating
Total cooking time: 20 minutes
Serves 6

1 kg (2 lb) chicken thigh fillets
2 tablespoons lime juice
1/2 cup (125 ml/4 fl oz) sweet chilli
  sauce
1/4 cup (60 ml/2 fl oz) kecap manis
  (see Note)

1 Trim any excess fat from the chicken thigh fillets and cut them in half. Transfer to a shallow non-metal dish.
2 Place the lime juice, sweet chilli sauce and kecap manis in a bowl and whisk to combine.
3 Pour the marinade over the chicken, cover and refrigerate for 2 hours.
4 Chargrill for 10–15 minutes, turning once, or until the chicken is tender and cooked through and the marinade has caramelized.

NUTRITION PER SERVE
Protein 35 g; Fat 4.5 g; Carbohydrate 4 g;
Dietary Fibre 1 g; Cholesterol 85 mg;
880 kJ (210 cal)

NOTE: Kecap manis (ketjap manis) is a thick Indonesian sauce, similar to—but sweeter than—soy sauce, and is generally flavoured with garlic and star anise. Store in a cool, dry place and refrigerate after opening. If not available, use soy sauce sweetened with a little soft brown sugar.

Trim the excess fat from the thigh fillets, and cut them in half.

To make the marinade, whisk together the lime juice, sweet chilli sauce and kecap manis.

Pour the marinade over the chicken, then cover and refrigerate.

BARBECUED GARLIC CHICKEN

Preparation time: 20 minutes +
  marinating
Total cooking time: 10 minutes
Serves 4

6 cloves garlic, crushed
1¹/₂ tablespoons cracked black
    peppercorns
¹/₂ cup (25 g/³/₄ oz) chopped fresh
    coriander leaves and stems
4 coriander roots, chopped
¹/₃ cup (80 ml/2³/₄ fl oz) lime juice
1 teaspoon soft brown sugar
1 teaspoon ground turmeric
2 teaspoons light soy sauce
4 chicken breast fillets

CUCUMBER AND TOMATO SALAD
1 small green cucumber, unpeeled
1 large Roma tomato
¹/₄ small red onion, thinly sliced
1 small red chilli, finely chopped
2 tablespoons fresh coriander leaves
2 tablespoons lime juice
1 teaspoon soft brown sugar
1 tablespoon fish sauce

1 Blend the garlic, peppercorns, coriander, lime juice, sugar, turmeric and soy sauce in a food processor until smooth. Transfer to a bowl.
2 Remove the tenderloins from the chicken fillets. Score the top of each fillet three times. Add the fillets and tenderloins to the marinade, cover and refrigerate for 2 hours or overnight, turning the chicken occasionally.
3 To make the salad, halve the cucumber and scoop out the seeds with a teaspoon. Cut into slices. Halve the tomato lengthways and slice. Combine the cucumber, tomato, onion, chilli and coriander in a small bowl. Drizzle with the combined lime juice, sugar and fish sauce.
4 Cook the chicken on a lightly greased barbecue hotplate for 3 minutes on each side, or until tender. Serve the chicken immediately with the salad.

NUTRITION PER SERVE
Protein 52 g; Fat 5.5 g; Carbohydrate 6 g;
Dietary Fibre 2 g; Cholesterol 110 mg;
1195 kJ (285 cal)

Add the chopped coriander roots to the other ingredients and blend until smooth.

Separate the tenderloins from the chicken fillets by pulling them away.

Use a teaspoon to scoop the seeds out of the halved cucumber.

Drizzle the combined lime juice, sugar and fish sauce over the salad ingredients.

Marinades & Glazes

LIME AND GINGER GLAZE

In a small pan combine 1/2 cup (160 g/51/2 oz) lime marmalade, 1/4 cup (60 ml/2 fl oz) lime juice, 2 tablespoons sherry, 2 tablespoons soft brown sugar and 2 teaspoons finely grated fresh ginger. Stir over low heat until it reaches a liquid consistency. Pour over 1 kg (2 lb) chicken wings and toss well to combine. Cover and refrigerate for 2 hours or overnight. Cook in a moderately hot 190°C (375°F/Gas 5) oven for 40 minutes, or until cooked through. Makes 1 cup (250 ml/8 fl oz).

HONEY SOY MARINADE

Combine 1/4 cup (90 g/3 oz) honey, 1/4 cup (60 ml/2 fl oz) soy sauce, 1 crushed garlic clove, 2 tablespoons sake and 1/2 teaspoon Chinese five-spice powder. Remove excess fat from 500 g (1 lb) chicken thigh fillets. Pour on the marinade and toss well. Cover and refrigerate for 2 hours or overnight. Cook on a hot barbecue for 10 minutes, turning once, or until cooked through. Makes 2/3 cup (170 ml/51/2 fl oz).

REDCURRANT GLAZE

In a small saucepan combine a 340 g (11 oz) jar redcurrant jelly, 2 tablespoons lemon juice, 2 tablespoons brandy and 1 teaspoon chopped fresh thyme, and stir over low heat until it reaches a liquid consistency. Pour the marinade over 500 g (1 lb) chicken breast fillets and toss well to combine. Cover and refrigerate for 2 hours or overnight. Cook in a moderately hot 190°C (375°F/Gas 5) oven for 20 minutes, or until cooked through. Makes 1 cup (250 ml/8 fl oz).

TANDOORI MARINADE

Soak 8 bamboo skewers in water for 30 minutes to prevent burning. Combine 2 tablespoons tandoori paste, 1 cup (250 g/8 oz) plain yoghurt and 1 tablespoon lime juice. Cut 500 g (1 lb) tenderloins in half lengthwise and thread onto skewers. Pour over the marinade and toss well to combine. Cover and refrigerate for 1–2 hours. Place under a hot grill and cook, basting with the marinade, until cooked through. Makes 11/4 cups (315 ml/10 fl oz).

MEXICAN MARINADE

Combine 440 g (14 oz) bottled taco sauce, 2 tablespoons lime juice and 2 tablespoons chopped fresh coriander leaves. Pour the marinade over 1 kg (2 lb) scored chicken drumsticks and toss well to combine. Cover and refrigerate for 2 hours or overnight. Cook in a moderately hot 190°C (375°F/Gas 5) oven for 30 minutes, or until cooked through. Makes 11/4 cups (315 ml/10 fl oz).

THAI MARINADE

Combine 2 tablespoons fish sauce, 2 tablespoons lime juice, 1 crushed garlic clove, 1 finely chopped lemon grass stem, 2 teaspoons soft brown sugar, 1/2 cup (125 g/4 oz) coconut cream and 2 tablespoons chopped fresh coriander leaves. Pour the marinade over 1 kg (2 lb) chicken drumettes and toss well to combine. Cover and refrigerate for 2 hours or overnight. Cook in a moderately hot 190°C (375°F/Gas 5) oven for 30 minutes, or until cooked through. Makes 3/4 cup (185 ml/6 fl oz).

Clockwise from top left: Lime and ginger glaze; Tandoori marinade; Mexican marinade; Thai marinade; Redcurrant glaze; Honey soy marinade.

Roasts & Bakes

ROAST CHICKEN WITH COUNTRY SAGE STUFFING

Preparation time: 25 minutes
Total cooking time: 1 hour 40 minutes
Serves 4

1.5 kg (3 lb) chicken
45 g (1¹/₂ oz) butter
1 onion, finely chopped
1 celery stick, thinly sliced
2 cups (160 g/5¹/₂ oz) fresh white
    breadcrumbs
1 teaspoon salt
¹/₂ teaspoon white pepper
10 large, fresh, shredded sage leaves,
    or 1¹/₂ teaspoons dried sage
¹/₃ cup (20 g/³/₄ oz) finely chopped
    fresh parsley
2 egg whites, lightly beaten
30 g (1 oz) butter, melted
1 tablespoon plain flour

1 Preheat the oven to moderate 180°C (350°F/Gas 4). Remove the giblets and any large fat deposits from the chicken. Wipe the chicken and pat dry with paper towels. Tuck the wing tips under the chicken. Grease a large shallow baking dish.
2 Heat the butter in a small pan. Add the onion and celery and cook over medium heat for 3–4 minutes, or until the onion has softened. Transfer the mixture to a large mixing bowl and add the breadcrumbs, salt, pepper, sage, parsley and egg whites. The stuffing should be very moist.
3 Spoon the stuffing into the chicken cavity and close the cavity with a skewer or toothpick. Tie the wings and drumsticks securely with string. Brush the chicken all over with the melted butter. Place the chicken in the baking dish. Bake for 1¹/₂ hours, or until the juices run clear, basting occasionally. Transfer the chicken to a serving dish, cover and allow to stand for 10 minutes before carving.
4 Meanwhile, to make the gravy, transfer the baking dish to the stove top. Add the flour to the pan juices and blend to a smooth paste. Stir constantly over low heat for 5 minutes, or until the gravy boils and thickens. If the gravy is too thick, add a little water or chicken stock. Season to taste. Serve the chicken with the gravy and the sage stuffing.

NUTRITION PER SERVE
Protein 70 g; Fat 30 g; Carbohydrate 33 g;
Dietary Fibre 2.5 g; Cholesterol 255 mg;
2865 kJ (684 cal)

Close and secure the chicken cavity, and tie the wings and drumsticks securely with string.

Transfer the baking dish to the stove top and sprinkle with the flour.

BEGGARS' CHICKEN

Preparation time: 40 minutes +
   30 minutes refrigerating
Total cooking time: 1 hour 35 minutes
Serves 4

4 x 400 g (13 oz) baby chickens
2 tablespoons olive oil
1 tablespoon soy sauce
2 tablespoons orange juice
1 tablespoon soft brown sugar
6 cups (750 g/1^1/$_2$ lb) plain flour
1 kg (2 lb) cooking salt
4 thin strips orange rind
4 star anise

1 Remove the giblets and any large fat deposits from the chickens. Pat the chickens dry with paper towels. Place the chickens in a shallow, non-metal dish. Whisk the oil, soy sauce, orange juice and sugar in a bowl until combined. Brush the mixture all over the chickens, inside and out. Cover and refrigerate for 30 minutes. Preheat the oven to very hot 240°C (475°F/Gas 9).
2 Sift the flour into a large mixing bowl and add the salt. Make a well in the centre and add 2^1/$_2$ cups (600 ml/20 fl oz) water all at once. Mix the water into the flour and salt gradually, using your hands to make a firm dough. Turn onto a floured surface and press the dough together until smooth.
3 Divide the dough into four portions. Roll each portion out large enough to cover one of the chickens. Place a strip of orange rind and a star anise into the cavity of each chicken. Wrap each chicken securely with a greased sheet of foil then place, breast-side down, in the centre of a sheet of dough.
4 Wrap the dough over the chickens to enclose. Press firmly, ensuring there are no gaps or openings. Place breast-side up in a large, shallow baking dish. Bake for 1 hour 35 minutes, or until the casing is crisp and well browned. Crack the casing with a hammer or meat mallet and discard. Serve the chicken with baked vegetables.

NUTRITION PER SERVE
Protein 52 g; Fat 15 g; Carbohydrate 280 g;
Dietary Fibre 14 g; Cholesterol 25 mg;
6205 kJ (1482 cal)

Brush the soy sauce mixture all over the chickens, inside and out.

Turn the dough out onto a floured surface and press together until smooth.

Place a strip of orange rind and a star anise into the cavity of each chicken.

Wrap the dough over the chicken to enclose it fully, ensuring there are no gaps or openings.

ROAST CHICKEN WITH BREADCRUMB STUFFING

Preparation time: 40 minutes
Total cooking time: 1 hour 30 minutes
Serves 6

3 slices bacon, finely chopped
6 slices wholegrain bread, crusts
   removed
3 spring onions, chopped
2 tablespoons chopped pecans
2 teaspoons currants
1/4 cup (15 g/1/2 oz) finely chopped
   fresh parsley
1 egg, lightly beaten
1/4 cup (60 ml/2 fl oz) milk
1.4 kg (2 lb 13 oz) chicken
40 g (11/4 oz) butter, melted
1 tablespoon oil
1 tablespoon soy sauce
1 clove garlic, crushed
11/2 cups (375 ml/12 fl oz) chicken
   stock
1 tablespoon plain flour

1 Preheat the oven to moderate
180°C (350°F/Gas 4). Cook the bacon
in a dry frying pan over high heat for
5 minutes, or until crisp. Cut the bread
into 1 cm (1/2 inch) cubes and place in
a bowl. Mix in the bacon, spring
onion, pecans, currants, parsley and
combined egg and milk. Season.
2 Remove the giblets and any large
amounts of fat from the cavity of the
chicken. Pat the chicken dry with
paper towels. Spoon the bacon
mixture into the chicken cavity. Tuck
the wings under the chicken and tie
the legs securely with string.
3 Place the chicken on a rack in a
deep baking dish. Brush with the
combined butter, oil and soy sauce.
Pour any remaining mixture into the
baking dish with the garlic and half
the stock. Roast the chicken for
1–11/4 hours, or until brown and
tender, basting occasionally with the
pan juices. Pierce between the thigh
and body to the bone and check that
any juices running out are clear. If they
are pink, continue cooking. Put the
chicken on a serving dish. Cover
loosely with foil and leave in a warm
place for 5 minutes before carving.
4 Discard all but 1 tablespoon of the

pan juices from the baking dish.
Transfer the baking dish to the stove.
Add the flour to the pan juices and
blend to a smooth paste. Stir
constantly over low heat for 5 minutes,
or until the mixture browns. Gradually
add the remaining stock and stir until
the mixture boils and thickens. Add a
little extra stock or water if the gravy is

too thick. Season with salt and cracked
black pepper and strain into a jug.
Serve the chicken and gravy with
snow peas and roast potatoes.

NUTRITION PER SERVE
Protein 33 g; Fat 20 g; Carbohydrate 15 g;
Dietary Fibre 3 g; Cholesterol 110 mg;
1530 kJ (365 cal)

Pat the chicken dry and spoon the stuffing into
the chicken cavity.

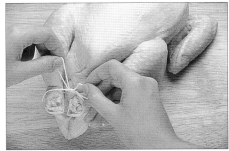

Tuck the wings under the chicken and tie the legs
securely with string.

CHICKEN MARYLANDS WITH REDCURRANT SAUCE

Preparation time: 25 minutes
  + 2 hours marinating
Total cooking time: 30 minutes
Serves 4

4 chicken marylands (drumstick and
    thigh)
1/2 cup (125 ml/4 fl oz) red wine
1 tablespoon finely chopped fresh
    thyme
1 tablespoon finely chopped fresh
    rosemary
1 tablespoon olive oil
1/2 cup (160 g/51/2 oz) redcurrant jelly

1 Trim the chicken of excess fat and sinew. Place the chicken in a shallow non-metal dish. Combine the wine, thyme and rosemary in a small jug and pour over the chicken. Refrigerate, covered, for 2 hours or overnight, turning the chicken occasionally.
2 Preheat the oven to moderately hot 200°C (400°F/Gas 6). Drain the chicken and reserve the marinade. Place the chicken in a baking dish and brush with the oil. Bake for 30 minutes, or until tender, turning occasionally.
3 Combine the reserved marinade and redcurrant jelly in a small pan. Stir over medium heat until smooth, then bring to the boil. Reduce the heat and simmer, uncovered, for 15 minutes. Pour over the chicken and serve with rosemary and some berries.

NUTRITION PER SERVE
Protein 37 g; Fat 8.5 g; Carbohydrate 5 g;
Dietary Fibre 0 g; Cholesterol 90 mg;
1112 kJ (266 cal)

Pour the wine, thyme and rosemary mixture over the chicken marylands.

Place the marinated chicken in a baking dish and brush with the oil.

Combine the reserved marinade and redcurrant jelly in a small pan and stir until smooth.

CHICKEN WITH FIGS AND LEMON

Preparation time: 20 minutes
Total cooking time: 35 minutes
Serves 4

4 large chicken thigh cutlets
1 lemon
1/2 teaspoon ground ginger
1/2 teaspoon garam masala
1 tablespoon soy sauce
2 tablespoons olive oil
1/2 cup (125 ml/4 fl oz) sweet white
    wine
1 tablespoon ginger wine
1/4 cup (60 ml/2 fl oz) lemon juice
2 chicken stock cubes, crumbled
6 plump dried figs, halved
2 teaspoons thinly sliced glacé ginger

1 Trim the chicken of fat and sinew. Preheat the oven to moderate 180°C (350°F/Gas 4). Remove the lemon rind with a vegetable peeler and slice the rind into long thin strips. Place the rind in a small pan with a little water. Boil for 2 minutes, then drain and set aside.
2 Combine the ginger, garam masala and soy sauce. Rub the mixture all over the chicken pieces.
3 Heat the oil in a heavy-based pan. Cook the chicken over medium heat for 5 minutes on each side, or until well browned but not cooked through. Drain the chicken on paper towels. Transfer to a shallow ovenproof dish.
4 Add the white wine, ginger wine, juice, stock cubes and any remaining marinade to the same pan. Bring to the boil. Add the figs and glacé ginger. Remove from the heat and spoon over the chicken. Bake for 20 minutes, or until the chicken is tender, turning once. Serve with the lemon rind.

NUTRITION PER SERVE
Protein 20 g; Fat 12 g; Carbohydrate 7 g;
Dietary Fibre 2 g; Cholesterol 44 mg;
1018 kJ (245 cal)

Remove the rind from the lemon and cut it into long thin strips.

Place the grilled chicken cutlets in a shallow ovenproof dish.

Add the fig halves and glacé ginger to the boiling wine mixture.

TANDOORI CHICKEN

Preparation time: 30 minutes
    + 4 hours 30 minutes marinating
Total cooking time: 45 minutes
Serves 4–6

6 chicken thigh fillets
1/4 cup (60 ml/2 fl oz) lemon juice
3 teaspoons ground coriander
1 tablespoon ground cumin
1/2 small onion, chopped
4 cloves garlic
1 tablespoon grated fresh ginger
1 tablespoon lemon juice, extra
1 teaspoon salt
1/4 teaspoon paprika
pinch chilli powder
1 cup (250 g/8 oz) plain yoghurt
red food colouring
lime wedges, to serve

1 Trim any excess fat from the chicken. Place in a large shallow dish. Brush with the lemon juice, cover, and refrigerate for 30 minutes.
2 Process the coriander, cumin, onion, garlic, ginger, extra lemon juice and salt in a food processor to a smooth paste. Mix in the paprika, chilli, yoghurt and a few drops of food colouring until smooth and pink.
3 Coat the chicken with the tandoori mixture. Cover and refrigerate for at least 4 hours.
4 Preheat the oven to moderate 180°C (350°F/Gas 4). Place the chicken on a wire rack in a large baking dish. Bake for 45 minutes, without turning, until the chicken is cooked through.

NUTRITION PER SERVE (6)
Protein 20 g; Fat 6 g; Carbohydrate 3 g; Dietary Fibre 0 g; Cholesterol 70 mg; 645 kJ (155 cal)

NOTE: You can add extra food colouring to the yoghurt mixture if you prefer the traditional deep-red tandoori colour.

Brush the chicken with lemon juice and marinate for 30 minutes.

Process the tandoori mixture until it becomes smooth and pinkish in colour.

Thoroughly coat the chicken pieces with the yoghurt mixture.

Place the chicken on a wire rack in a large baking dish.

CHICKEN AND BROCCOLI BAKE

Preparation time: 20 minutes
Total cooking time: 1 hour
Serves 6

30 g (1 oz) butter
4 chicken breast fillets, cut into cubes
6 spring onions, sliced
2 cloves garlic, crushed
2 tablespoons plain flour
1¹/₂ cups (375 ml/12 fl oz) chicken
	stock
2 teaspoons Dijon mustard
280 g (9 oz) broccoli, cut into florets
1 kg (2 lb) potatoes, cut into quarters
2 tablespoons milk
60 g (2 oz) butter, extra
2 eggs
¹/₃ cup (30 g/1 oz) flaked toasted
	almonds
snipped fresh chives, to garnish

1 Preheat the oven to moderate 180°C (350°F/Gas 4). Heat half the butter in a large frying pan, and cook the chicken in batches until browned and cooked through. Remove from the pan. In the same pan melt the remaining butter and cook the spring onion and garlic for 2 minutes. Stir in the flour and mix well. Pour in the stock and cook, stirring, until the mixture boils and thickens. Add the mustard and then stir in the chicken. Season well.
2 Meanwhile, steam or microwave the broccoli until just tender, taking care not to overcook it. Refresh the broccoli in iced water and drain well.
3 Boil the potato in plenty of salted water for 15–20 minutes, or until tender. Drain and mash well with the milk, extra butter and eggs. Put the broccoli in a 2.5 litre ovenproof dish and pour in the chicken mixture. Pipe or spoon the mashed potato over the top. Sprinkle with the almonds and bake for 25 minutes, or until the top is browned and cooked through. Scatter the chives over the top before serving.

NUTRITION PER SERVE
Protein 25 g; Fat 20 g; Carbohydrate 25 g; Dietary Fibre 5.5 g; Cholesterol 135 mg; 1610 kJ (385 cal)

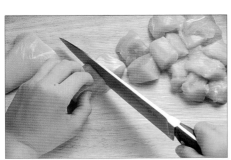

Use a large sharp knife to cut the chicken breasts into cubes.

Add the chicken to the pan and cook in batches until browned.

Pour in the stock and stir over heat until the mixture thickens.

165

SPICY SPATCHCOCKED CHICKEN

Preparation time: 15 minutes
  + 4 hours marinating
Total cooking time: 20 minutes
Serves 4

2 small chickens (750 g/1¹/₂ lb each)
    or 1 kg (2 lb) chicken drumsticks
2 tablespoons malt vinegar or lemon
    juice
1¹/₂ teaspoons chilli powder
1¹/₂ teaspoons ground sweet paprika
2 teaspoons ground coriander
2 teaspoons ground cumin
1 teaspoon garam masala
1 tablespoon finely grated fresh ginger
1 tablespoon crushed garlic
1 teaspoon salt
¹/₃ cup (80 g/2³/₄ oz) plain yoghurt
3 tablespoons ghee, melted, or oil

1 Pat the chickens dry with paper towels. Combine the vinegar, chilli, paprika, coriander, cumin, garam masala, ginger, garlic, salt and yoghurt in a large glass or ceramic bowl.
2 Using scissors, remove the backbones from the chickens. Turn the chickens over and flatten. Make several slashes in the skin. Place the chickens on a tray and coat well with the marinade, working it into the flesh. Cover and refrigerate for 4 hours.
3 Place the chickens on a cold, lightly oiled grill. Brush with the melted ghee. Cook the chickens under a moderately hot grill for 20 minutes, turning halfway through cooking and brushing occasionally with any remaining marinade. Serve the chickens with breads such as naan or chapatis, and lemon wedges.

NUTRITION PER SERVE
Protein 72 g; Fat 20 g; Carbohydrate 1.5 g;
Dietary Fibre 0 g; Cholesterol 196 mg;
2009 kJ (480 cal)

VARIATION: Grilling produces a good flavour, but for a delicious, smoky taste, prepare and marinate the chicken in the same way, then cook on a barbecue.

HINT: If you remove the chicken skin, the flavour of the marinade spices are able to penetrate the flesh much more effectively. Also, the finished dish will contain far less fat than if the skin were left on.

Mix the vinegar, chilli, paprika, coriander, cumin, garam masala, ginger, garlic, salt and yoghurt.

Using a pair of poultry scissors, remove the backbones from the chickens.

Cook the chickens under a moderately hot grill, brushing occasionally with the marinade.

CHICKEN WITH BAKED EGGPLANT AND TOMATO

Preparation time: 30 minutes
Total cooking time: 1 hour 30 minutes
Serves 4

1 red capsicum
1 eggplant
3 tomatoes, cut into quarters
200 g (6½ oz) large button
    mushrooms, halved
1 onion, cut into thin wedges
cooking oil spray
1½ tablespoons tomato paste
½ cup (125 ml/4 fl oz) chicken stock
¼ cup (60 ml/2 fl oz) white wine

2 lean slices bacon
4 chicken breast fillets
4 small fresh rosemary sprigs

1 Preheat the oven to moderately hot 200°C (400°F/Gas 6). Cut the capsicum and eggplant into bite-sized pieces and combine with the tomato, mushrooms and onion in a baking dish. Spray with oil and bake for 1 hour, or until starting to brown and soften, stirring once.
2 Pour the combined tomato paste, stock and wine into the dish and bake for 10 minutes, or until thickened.
3 Meanwhile, discard the fat and rind from the bacon and cut in half. Wrap a strip of bacon around each chicken breast and secure it underneath with a toothpick. Poke a sprig of fresh rosemary underneath the bacon. Pan-fry in a lightly oiled, non-stick frying pan over medium heat until golden on both sides. Cover and cook for 10–15 minutes, or until the chicken is tender and cooked through. Remove the toothpicks. Serve the chicken on the vegetable mixture, surrounded with the sauce.

NUTRITION PER SERVE
Protein 35 g; Fat 4.5 g; Carbohydrate 8 g; Dietary Fibre 5 g; Cholesterol 70 mg; 965 kJ (230 cal)

Spray the vegetables lightly with the cooking oil before baking.

When the vegetables have softened, add the combined tomato paste, stock and wine.

Wrap a strip of bacon around the chicken and secure underneath with a toothpick.

CHICKEN BALLOTINE

Preparation time: 40 minutes
Total cooking time: 1 hour 45 minutes
Serves 8

1.6 kg (3¹/₄ lb) chicken
2 red capsicums
1 bunch (1 kg /2 lb) silverbeet
30 g (1 oz) butter
1 onion, finely chopped
1 clove garlic, crushed
¹/₂ cup (50 g/1³/₄ oz) grated
   Parmesan
1 cup (80 g/2³/₄ oz) fresh
   breadcrumbs
1 tablespoon chopped fresh oregano
200 g (6¹/₂ oz) ricotta

1 To bone the chicken, cut through the skin on the centre back with a sharp knife. Separate the flesh from the bone down one side to the breast, being careful not to pierce the skin. Follow along the bones closely with the knife, gradually easing the meat from the thigh, drumstick and wing. Cut through the thigh bone where it meets the drumstick and cut off the wing tip. Repeat on the other side, then lift the rib cage away, leaving the flesh in one piece and the drumsticks still attached to the flesh. Scrape all the meat from the drumsticks and wings, discarding the bones. Turn the wing and drumstick flesh inside the chicken and lay the chicken out flat, skin-side down. Refrigerate.

2 Preheat the oven to moderate 180°C (350°F/Gas 4). Quarter the capsicums and remove the membranes and seeds. Place skin-side up under a hot grill until the skin blisters and blackens. Place in a plastic bag and allow to cool, then peel off the skin.

3 Remove the stalks from the silverbeet and finely shred the leaves. Melt the butter in a large frying pan and add the onion and garlic. Cook over medium heat for about 5 minutes, or until soft. Add the silverbeet leaves and stir until wilted and all the moisture has evaporated. In a food processor, process the silverbeet and onion mixture with the Parmesan, breadcrumbs, oregano and half the ricotta. Season to taste with salt and cracked pepper.

4 Spread the silverbeet mixture over the chicken and lay the capsicum over the silverbeet. Form the remaining ricotta into a roll and place across the width of the chicken. Fold the sides of the chicken in over the filling so they overlap slightly, and tuck the ends in neatly. Secure with toothpicks and tie with string at 3 cm (1¹/₄ inch) intervals.

5 Lightly grease a large piece of aluminium foil and place the chicken in the centre. Roll the chicken up securely in the foil, sealing the ends well. Place on a baking tray and bake for 1¹/₄–1¹/₂ hours, or until the juices run clear when a skewer is inserted into the centre. Allow to cool, then refrigerate until cold before removing the foil, toothpicks and string. Cut into 1 cm (¹/₂ inch) slices to serve.

NUTRITION PER SERVE
Protein 40 g; Fat 12 g; Carbohydrate 9 g; Dietary Fibre 1.5 g; Cholesterol 105 mg; 1290 kJ (310 cal)

NOTE: If you are not confident about boning a chicken, ask your butcher to do it for you. To be on the safe side, it might be worth ordering your boned chicken a day in advance.

Using a sharp knife, cut through the skin on the centre back.

Separate the flesh from the bone down one side to the breast.

With your knife, gradually ease the meat from the thigh, drumstick and wing.

Use a sharp knife to cut off the wing tips through the joint.

Lay the chicken out flat and cover with the silverbeet mixture and capsicum quarters.

Roll the chicken up to enclose the filling and secure with toothpicks.

SPRING CHICKEN WITH HONEY GLAZE

Preparation time: 15 minutes
Total cooking time: 55 minutes
Serves 6–8

2 small (1.5 kg/3 lb) chickens
1 tablespoon light olive oil

HONEY GLAZE
1/4 cup (90 g/3 oz) honey
juice and finely grated rind of
    1 lemon

1 tablespoon finely chopped fresh
    rosemary
1 tablespoon dry white wine
1 tablespoon white wine vinegar
2 teaspoons Dijon mustard
1 1/2 tablespoons olive oil

1 Preheat the oven to moderate 180°C (350°F/Gas 4). Halve the chickens by cutting down either side of the backbone. Discard the backbones. Cut the chickens into quarters, then brush with the oil and season lightly. Place on a rack in a roasting pan, skin-side down, and roast for 20 minutes.

2 To make the honey glaze, combine the honey, juice, rind, rosemary, wine, vinegar, mustard and oil in a small pan. Bring to the boil, then reduce the heat and simmer for 5 minutes.
3 After cooking one side, turn the chickens over and baste well with the warm glaze. Return to the oven and roast for 20 minutes. Baste once more and cook for a further 15 minutes.

NUTRITION PER SERVE (8)
Protein 70 g; Fat 10 g; Carbohydrate 8.5 g;
Dietary Fibre 0.5 g; Cholesterol 150 mg;
1693 kJ (405 cal)

Halve each chicken by cutting down either side of the backbone.

Cut the chickens into quarters—you will find kitchen scissors easier than a knife.

Cook one side of the chicken, then turn over and baste with the warm glaze.

ROAST GARLIC CHICKEN WITH VEGETABLES

Preparation time: 20 minutes
Total cooking time: 1 hour 20 minutes
Serves 4

315 g (10 oz) orange sweet potatoes, peeled and cut into wedges
315 g (10 oz) pontiac potatoes, peeled and cut into wedges
315 g (10 oz) pumpkin, peeled and cut into wedges
1 chicken, cut into 8 pieces, or 1.5 kg (3 lb) chicken pieces

1/4 cup (60 ml/2 fl oz) olive oil
1 tablespoon fresh thyme leaves
20 large garlic cloves, unpeeled (see Note)
1/2 teaspoon sea salt

1 Preheat the oven to hot 220°C (425°F/Gas 7). Bring a large pan of salted water to the boil and cook the sweet potato, potato and pumpkin for 5 minutes. Drain well.
2 Put the chicken and vegetables in a baking dish, drizzle with the olive oil and scatter with the thyme leaves and garlic cloves. Sprinkle with the sea salt.
3 Roast for 1 hour 15 minutes, turning every 20 minutes, or until the chicken, sweet potato, potato and pumpkin are well browned and crisp at the edges. Serve immediately.

NUTRITION PER SERVE
Protein 35 g; Fat 20 g; Carbohydrate 28 g; Dietary Fibre 6 g; Cholesterol 97 mg; 1848 kJ (440 cal)

NOTE: This may seem an awful lot of garlic, but it loses its pungency when roasted, becoming sweet and mild. To eat the garlic, squeeze the creamy roasted flesh from the skins and over the chicken and vegetables.

Boil the sweet potato, potato and pumpkin for 5 minutes, then drain.

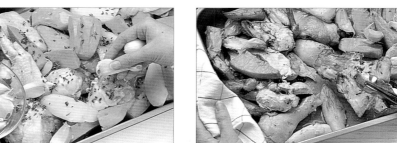
Drizzle the chicken and vegetables with oil, then sprinkle with garlic and thyme.

Turn the chicken pieces and vegetables every 20 minutes, until browned and crisp.

171

BAKED CHICKEN AND ARTICHOKE PANCAKES

Preparation time: 30 minutes
Total cooking time: 1 hour
Serves 4

1 teaspoon baking powder
1¹/₃ cups (165 g/5¹/₂ oz) plain flour
¹/₄ teaspoon salt
2 eggs
300 ml (10 fl oz) milk
90 g (3 oz) butter
2¹/₂ cups (600 ml/20 fl oz) chicken
    stock
2 egg yolks
1 cup (250 ml/8 fl oz) cream
1 teaspoon lemon juice
300 g (10 oz) cooked chicken,
    chopped roughly
350 g (11 oz) artichoke hearts, drained
    and sliced
2 teaspoons chopped fresh thyme
2 teaspoons chopped fresh parsley
100 g (3¹/₂ oz) grated Parmesan

1 Sift the baking powder, 1 cup (125 g/4 oz) flour and salt into a large bowl and make a well in the centre. Whisk the eggs and milk in a jug and pour into the well, whisking until just smooth. Heat a frying pan and brush lightly with melted butter. Add ¹/₄ cup (60 ml/2 fl oz) batter and cook over medium heat until the underside is brown. Turn over and cook the other side. Transfer to a plate and cover with a tea towel while cooking the remaining batter.

2 Melt the butter in a pan and stir in the remaining flour. Cook for 2 minutes, then remove from the heat. Slowly whisk in the chicken stock until smooth. Whisk in the combined egg yolks and cream. Return to the heat

and bring slowly to the boil, stirring constantly. Boil for 30 seconds to thicken the sauce, then remove from the heat and stir in the lemon juice. Season with salt and freshly ground black pepper.

3 Preheat the oven to moderately hot 200°C (400°F/Gas 6). Grease a 3 litre ovenproof dish with melted butter. Line the base with 2 pancakes, slightly overlapping. Spoon half of the chicken, artichokes and herbs evenly over the pancakes. Pour a third of the

sauce over the top and layer with another two pancakes. Repeat, finishing with a layer of 3 pancakes. Spread the remaining sauce over the top, sprinkle with the Parmesan and bake for 30–35 minutes, or until golden brown.

NUTRITION PER SERVE
Protein 40 g; Fat 60 g; Carbohydrate 37 g; Dietary Fibre 4 g; Cholesterol 305 mg; 3568 kJ (850 cal)

Heat a frying pan, add the batter and cook until the underside is brown.

Slowly whisk in the combined yolks and cream, away from the heat.

Line the dish with pancakes, then spoon in half the chicken and artichoke filling.

ORANGE ROASTED CHICKENS

Preparation time: 15 minutes +
  overnight marinating
Total cooking time: 40 minutes
Serves 8

2 x 800 g (1 lb 10 oz) chickens
100 g (3¹/₂ oz) butter, softened
2 cloves garlic, crushed
1 tablespoon finely grated orange
  rind
¹/₂ cup (60 ml/2 fl oz) orange
  juice

1 Preheat the oven to hot 220°C (425°F/Gas 7). Using kitchen scissors, cut the chickens in half through the backbone and breastbone. Pat dry with paper towels and wipe the inside.
2 Combine the butter, garlic and orange rind and beat well. Gently loosen the skin of the chickens by sliding your fingers between the flesh and the skin. Push the orange butter under the skin as evenly as possible. Put the chickens onto a ceramic dish and pour on the orange juice. Cover and refrigerate for 3 hours, or preferably overnight.
3 Drain the chicken pieces well and

arrange cut-side down on roasting racks inside two baking dishes. Pour 2 tablespoons of water into each baking dish.
4 Roast for 30–40 minutes, or until the chickens are golden brown. Cover with foil and allow to rest for 15 minutes. Cut into quarters to serve.

NUTRITION PER SERVE
Protein 30 g; Fat 15 g; Carbohydrate 1 g;
Dietary Fibre 0 g; Cholesterol 95 mg;
990 kJ (235 cal)

NOTE: If you can, use freshly squeezed orange juice.

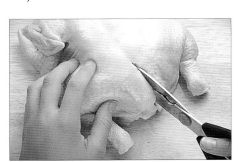
Cut the chickens in half through the backbone and breastbone.

Loosen the skin of the chickens and spread the orange butter underneath.

Put the chicken pieces cut-side down on roasting racks inside the baking dishes.

SMOKED FIVE-SPICE CHICKEN

Preparation time: 30 minutes
  + overnight marinating
Total cooking time: 35 minutes
Serves 6

1 x 1.7 kg (3½ lb) chicken
¼ cup (60 ml/2 fl oz) soy sauce
1 tablespoon finely grated fresh ginger
2 pieces dried mandarin or tangerine
   peel (see Note page 85)
1 star anise
¼ teaspoon five-spice powder
¼ cup (45 g/1½ oz) soft brown sugar

1 Wash the chicken in cold water. Pat dry with paper towels. Discard any large deposits of fat from inside the chicken. Place the chicken in a large bowl with the soy sauce and grated ginger. Cover and refrigerate for several hours or overnight, turning occasionally.

2 Place a small rack in the base of a pan large enough to hold the chicken. Add water to this level. Place the chicken on the rack and bring the water to the boil. Cover tightly, reduce the heat and steam for 15 minutes. Turn off the heat and allow to stand, covered, for another 15 minutes.

Transfer the chicken to a bowl.

3 Wash the pan and line with three or four large pieces of aluminium foil. Pound the dried peel and star anise in a mortar and pestle or crush with a rolling pin until the pieces are the size of coarse breadcrumbs. Add the five-spice powder and sugar, and spread over the foil.

4 Replace the rack in the pan and place the chicken on it. Place the pan over medium heat and, when the spice mixture starts smoking, cover tightly. Reduce the heat to low and smoke the chicken for 20 minutes. Test for doneness by piercing the thigh with a skewer. The juices should run clear. Remove chicken from pan and allow to cool before jointing it or chopping it Chinese-style.

NUTRITION PER SERVE
Protein 46 g; Fat 4.5 g; Carbohydrate 10 g; Dietary Fibre 0 g; Cholesterol 100 mg; 1126 kJ (270 cal)

VARIATION: If you wish to save on cooking time, try the same method using half chicken-breast fillets. Six fillets will take 7 minutes to steam; smoking will take 8 minutes each side. Overnight marinating is not necessary in this instance.

Place the chicken in a large bowl with the soy sauce and grated ginger.

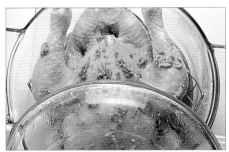
Steam the chicken on a rack in a pan with water in the base.

Pound the dried peel with the star anise in a mortar and pestle.

Line the pan with foil and add the combined peel, star anise, five-spice powder and sugar.

175

AYAM PANGGANG

Preparation time: 20 minutes
Total cooking time: 1 hour
Serves 4–6

1.5 kg (3 lb) chicken
3 teaspoons chopped red and green
   chilli
3 cloves garlic, peeled
2 teaspoons dried green peppercorns,
   crushed
2 teaspoons soft brown sugar
2 tablespoons soy sauce
2 teaspoons ground turmeric

1 tablespoon lime juice
30 g (1 oz) butter, chopped

1 Preheat the oven to moderate 180°C (350°F/Gas 4). Using a large cleaver, cut the chicken in half by cutting down the backbone and along the breastbone. Tuck the wings underneath the chicken to prevent them from burning. Place the chicken, skin-side up, on a rack in a baking dish and bake for 30 minutes.
2 Meanwhile, combine the chilli, garlic, peppercorns and sugar in a small food processor or mortar and pestle and process briefly, or pound,

until smooth. Add the soy sauce, turmeric and lime juice, and process in short bursts until combined.
3 Brush the spice mixture all over the chicken, dot with the butter pieces and bake for another 25–30 minutes, or until thoroughly cooked. Serve warm or at room temperature, garnished with lime wedges and fresh herbs.

NUTRITION PER SERVE (6)
Protein 38 g; Fat 8 g; Carbohydrate 1.5 g;
Dietary Fibre 0 g; Cholesterol 95 mg;
970 kJ (232 cal)

Cut the chicken in half by cutting down the backbone and along the breastbone.

Combine the chilli, garlic, peppercorns and brown sugar in a food processor.

Brush the spice mixture all over the chicken and bake until cooked through.

SPICY ROAST CHICKEN

Preparation time: 30 minutes
Total cooking time: 1 hour 20 minutes
Serves 6

3 small dried red chillies
1 teaspoon fennel seeds
1 teaspoon cumin seeds
1 teaspoon coriander seeds
1/8 teaspoon salt
1.5 kg (3 lb) chicken
2 cloves garlic, crushed
1 tablespoon peanut oil
2 onions, chopped
250 g (8 oz) pork mince
1/2 cup (80 g/2 3/4 oz) peanuts, roasted
    and roughly chopped
1/4 cup (60 ml/2 fl oz) lime juice
1 tablespoon chopped fresh mint
2 tablespoons chopped fresh
    coriander leaves
1 teaspoon oil, extra
1/2 cup (125 ml/4 fl oz) coconut milk

1 Preheat the oven to moderate 180°C (350°F/Gas 4). Place the chillies, fennel, cumin, coriander seeds and salt in a small food processor or mortar and pestle and process or grind until the spices are blended to a powder.
2 Remove any fat from the chicken and rub the skin and cavity with garlic.
3 Heat the oil in a wok and cook the onion over medium heat for 3 minutes, or until golden. Add the pork and cook for 10 minutes, or until brown. Remove from the heat, stir in the peanuts, juice, mint and coriander. Allow the mixture to cool slightly before stuffing the chicken. Tightly secure the opening with a wooden skewer and tie the legs together.
4 Brush the chicken lightly with oil and then rub the skin with the spice mixture. Place the chicken on a rack in a baking dish and bake for 30 minutes. Remove from the oven and baste with the coconut milk and pan juices. Bake for 40 minutes, basting frequently, or until the chicken is tender. Remove the skewer and string before serving.

NUTRITION PER SERVE
Protein 52 g; Fat 20 g; Carbohydrate 5 g;
Dietary Fibre 2 g; Cholesterol 105 mg;
1695 kJ (405 cal)

Grind the chillies, fennel, cumin, coriander and salt until they form a powder.

Cook the chopped onion in the wok until soft and golden.

Spoon the prepared cooled filling into the cavity of the chicken.

Rub the spice mixture all over the surface of the chicken, using your fingers.

Pies & Pastries

CHICKEN AND LEEK PIE

Preparation time: 20 minutes
Total cooking time: 40 minutes
Serves 4

50 g (1³/₄ oz) butter
2 large leeks, washed and thinly sliced
4 spring onions, sliced
1 clove garlic, crushed
¹/₄ cup (30 g/1 oz) plain flour
1¹/₂ cups (375 ml/12 fl oz) chicken
   stock
¹/₂ cup (125 ml/4 fl oz) cream
1 medium barbecued chicken,
   chopped
2 sheets puff pastry, thawed
¹/₄ cup (60 ml/2 fl oz) milk

1 Preheat the oven to moderately hot 200°C (400°F/Gas 6). In a pan, melt the butter and add the leek, spring onion and garlic. Cook over low heat for 6 minutes, or until the leek is soft but not browned. Sprinkle in the flour and mix well. Pour in the stock gradually and cook, stirring well, until the mixture is thick and smooth.
2 Stir in the cream and the chicken. Put the mixture in a shallow 20 cm (8 inch) pie dish and set aside to cool.

3 Cut a circle out of one of the sheets of pastry to cover the top of the pie. Brush around the rim of the pie dish with a little milk. Put the pastry on top and seal around the edge firmly. Trim off any overhanging pastry and decorate the edge with the back of a fork. Cut the other sheet into 1 cm (¹/₂ inch) strips and roll each strip up loosely into a spiral. Arrange the spirals on top of the pie, starting from the middle and leaving a gap between each one. The spirals may not cover the whole surface of the pie. Make a few small holes between the spirals to let out any steam, and brush the top of the pie lightly with milk. Bake for 25–30 minutes, or until the top is brown and crispy. Make sure the spirals look well cooked and are not raw in the middle.

NUTRITION PER SERVE
Protein 25 g; Fat 55 g; Carbohydrate 40 g;
Dietary Fibre 3 g; Cholesterol 185 mg;
3105 kJ (740 cal)

NOTE: Make small pies by placing the mixture into 4 greased 1¹/₄ cup (315 ml/10 fl oz) round ovenproof dishes. Cut the pastry into 4 rounds to fit. Bake for 15 minutes, or until crisp.

Seal the edge firmly and trim off any overhanging pastry with a sharp knife.

Roll up the strips of pastry into spirals and arrange them on top of the pie.

CHICKEN POT PIES WITH HERB SCONES

Preparation time: 25 minutes
Total cooking time: 35 minutes
Serves 6

60 g (2 oz) butter
1 onion, chopped
1/3 cup (40 g/1 1/4 oz) plain flour
2 2/3 cups (670 ml/22 fl oz) milk
1 cup (125 g/4 oz) grated Cheddar
2 teaspoons wholegrain mustard
2 1/2 cups (450 g/14 oz) chopped
    cooked chicken
2 cups (200 g/6 1/2 oz) frozen mixed
    vegetables

TOPPING
2 cups (250 g/8 oz) self-raising flour
15 g (1/2 oz) butter

1 cup (250 ml/8 fl oz) milk
2 tablespoons chopped fresh parsley
1 tablespoon milk, extra

1 Preheat the oven to hot 210°C (415°F/Gas 6–7). Lightly grease six 1 cup (250 ml/8 fl oz) individual dishes with oil or melted butter. Heat the butter in a large heavy-based pan. Add the onion and cook over medium heat until soft. Add the flour and stir over the heat for 1 minute, or until lightly golden and bubbling. Gradually add the milk, stirring constantly over the heat until the sauce boils and thickens. Remove from the heat. Stir in the Cheddar, mustard, chicken and vegetables. Spoon the mixture evenly into the prepared dishes.

2 To make the topping, place the flour in a bowl. Using your fingertips, rub the butter into the flour for 2 minutes,

or until the mixture is fine and crumbly. Make a well in the centre. Stir in the milk and parsley with a flat-bladed knife. Using a cutting action, stir until the mixture is soft and sticky. Turn onto a floured surface.

3 Gather the dough into a smooth ball and pat out to a 2.5 cm (1 inch) thickness. Cut rounds from the pastry with a 4.5 cm (1 3/4 inch) cutter. Re-roll the pastry cuttings to cut more rounds. Place three rounds on top of each chicken pot. Brush the tops with the extra milk. Bake for 25 minutes, or until the scones are browned and cooked and the chicken mixture is heated through.

NUTRITION PER SERVE
Protein 17 g; Fat 30 g; Carbohydrate 14 g; Dietary Fibre 0.5 g; Cholesterol 95 mg; 1656 kJ (396 cal)

Stir the cheese, mustard, chicken and vegetables into the milk mixture.

Stir the milk and parsley into the flour mixture using a flat-bladed knife.

Place three scone rounds on top of each of the chicken pots.

CHICKEN AND SUGAR PEA PARCELS

Preparation time: 40 minutes
Total cooking time: 30 minutes
Makes 8

200 g (6¹/₂ oz) sugar snap peas
1 tablespoon oil
6 chicken thigh fillets, cut into 1 cm
    (¹/₂ inch) thick strips
40 g (1¹/₄ oz) butter
2 tablespoons plain flour
³/₄ cup (185 ml/6 fl oz) chicken stock
²/₃ cup (170 ml/5¹/₂ fl oz) dry white
    wine
1 tablespoon wholegrain mustard
150 g (5 oz) feta cheese, cut into 1 cm
    (¹/₂ inch) cubes
¹/₃ cup (50 g/1³/₄ oz) sliced sun-dried
    tomatoes, finely chopped

24 sheets filo pastry
60 g (2 oz) butter, extra, melted
sesame and sunflower seeds

1 Preheat the oven to hot 210°C (415°F/Gas 6–7). Top and tail the sugar snap peas, then plunge into boiling water for 1 minute, or until bright in colour but still crunchy. Drain well.
2 Heat the oil in a heavy-based pan. Cook the chicken quickly, in small batches, over medium heat until well browned. Drain on paper towels.
3 Melt the butter in a pan and add the flour. Stir over low heat for 2 minutes, or until the flour mixture is light golden and bubbling. Add the stock, wine and mustard, stirring until the mixture is smooth. Stir constantly over medium heat until the mixture boils and thickens. Stir in the chicken, sugar snap peas, feta and tomato and mix gently. Remove from the heat and allow to cool. Divide the mixture evenly into eight portions.
4 Brush three sheets of the pastry with the melted butter. Place the sheets on top of each other. Place one portion of the mixture at one short end of the pastry. Roll and fold the pastry, enclosing the filling to form a parcel. Brush with a little more butter and place seam-side down on a greased baking tray. Repeat with the remaining pastry, butter and filling. Brush the tops with butter. Sprinkle with the sesame and sunflower seeds. Bake for 20 minutes, or until golden brown and heated through.

NUTRITION PER SERVE
Protein 34 g; Fat 20 g; Carbohydrate 20 g;
Dietary Fibre 2 g; Cholesterol 100 mg;
1720 kJ (410 cal)

Cook the chicken strips quickly in the hot oil until they are well browned.

Stir the chicken, sugar snap peas, feta and sun-dried tomato into the stock mixture.

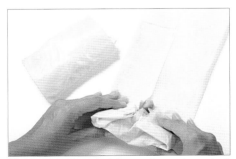
Place one portion of mixture on the pastry and roll up, enclosing the filling to form a parcel.

181

CHICKEN AND HAM PIE

Preparation time: 40 minutes
Total cooking time: 1 hour
Serves 6

PASTRY

3 cups (375 g/12 oz) plain flour
180 g (6 oz) butter, chopped
1/3 cup (80 ml/2³/4 fl oz) iced water

FILLING

1 kg (2 lb) chicken mince
1/2 teaspoon dried thyme
1/2 teaspoon dried sage
2 eggs, lightly beaten
3 spring onions, finely chopped
2 teaspoons finely grated lemon rind
1 teaspoon French mustard
1/3 cup (80 ml/2³/4 fl oz) cream
100 g (3¹/2 oz) sliced leg ham, finely
    chopped
1 egg, lightly beaten, extra

1 Preheat the oven to moderate 180°C (350°F/Gas 4). Process the flour and butter in a food processor for 20 seconds, or until the mixture is fine and crumbly. Add almost all the water and process for 20 seconds, or until mixture comes together. Add more water if needed. Turn onto a lightly floured surface and press together until smooth. Roll out two-thirds of the pastry and line a 20 cm (8 inch) springform tin, bringing the pastry up 2 cm (³/4 inch) higher than the sides. Cover with plastic wrap. Set the pastry trimmings aside.

2 To make the filling, place the chicken, thyme, sage, eggs, spring onion, lemon rind, mustard and cream in a large bowl and stir with a wooden spoon until well combined. Place half the chicken mixture into the pastry-lined tin and smooth the surface. Top with the chopped ham, then the remaining chicken mixture.

3 Brush around the inside edge of the pastry with the egg. Roll out the remaining pastry and lay over the top of the mixture. Press the edges of the pastry together. Trim the pastry edges with a sharp knife.

4 Turn the pastry edges down. Use your index finger to make indentations around the inside edge. Decorate the top of the pie with pastry trimmings. Brush the top of the pie with beaten egg and bake for 1 hour, or until golden brown. Serve the pie warm or at room temperature.

NUTRITION PER SERVE
Protein 52 g; Fat 38 g; Carbohydrate 52 g; Dietary Fibre 3 g; Cholesterol 277 mg; 3180 kJ (759 cal)

Process the flour and butter until the mixture is fine and crumbly.

Stir the chicken, thyme, sage, eggs, spring onion, lemon rind, mustard and cream until combined.

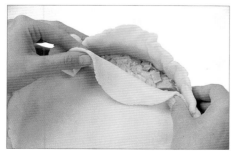

Lay the pastry over the top of the mixture and press the edges together.

Turn the pastry down and make indentations around the inside edge.

MUSTARD CHICKEN AND ASPARAGUS QUICHE

Preparation time: 25 minutes
+ 40 minutes refrigeration
Total cooking time: 1 hour 20 minutes
Serves 8

2 cups (250 g/8 oz) plain flour
100 g (3¹/₂ oz) cold butter, chopped
1 egg yolk

FILLING
150 g (5 oz) asparagus, chopped
25 g (³/₄ oz) butter
1 onion, chopped
¹/₄ cup (60 g/2 oz) wholegrain
    mustard
200 g (6¹/₂ oz) soft cream cheese
¹/₂ cup (125 ml/4 fl oz) cream
3 eggs, lightly beaten
200 g (6¹/₂ oz) cooked chicken,
    chopped
¹/₂ teaspoon black pepper

1 Process the flour and butter until crumbly. Add the egg yolk and ¹/₄ cup (60 ml/2 fl oz) of water. Process in short bursts until the mixture comes together. Add a little extra water if needed. Turn onto a floured surface and gather into a ball. Cover with plastic wrap and chill for 30 minutes. Grease a deep loose-based flan tin measuring 19 cm (7¹/₂ inches) across the base.
2 Roll out the pastry and line the tin. Trim off any excess with a sharp knife. Place the flan tin on a baking tray and chill for 10 minutes. Preheat the oven to moderately hot 200°C (400°F/Gas 6). Cover the pastry with baking paper and fill evenly with baking beads. Bake for 10 minutes. Remove the paper and beads and bake for about

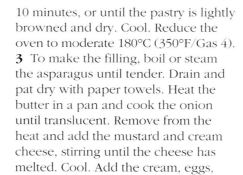

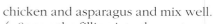

10 minutes, or until the pastry is lightly browned and dry. Cool. Reduce the oven to moderate 180°C (350°F/Gas 4).
3 To make the filling, boil or steam the asparagus until tender. Drain and pat dry with paper towels. Heat the butter in a pan and cook the onion until translucent. Remove from the heat and add the mustard and cream cheese, stirring until the cheese has melted. Cool. Add the cream, eggs,

chicken and asparagus and mix well.
4 Spoon the filling into the pastry shell and sprinkle with the pepper. Bake for 50 minutes to 1 hour, or until puffed and set. Cool for at least 15 minutes before cutting.

NUTRITION PER SERVE
Protein 15 g; Fat 30 g; Carbohydrate 25 g;
Dietary Fibre 2 g; Cholesterol 190 mg;
1860 kJ (440 cal)

When the flour and butter mixture is crumbly, add the egg yolk.

Dry the asparagus well to prevent excess moisture from softening the quiche.

Add the mustard and cream cheese and stir until the cheese has melted.

CHICKEN CORIANDER PIE

Preparation time: 40 minutes
Total cooking time: 45 minutes
Serves 4

50 g (1³/₄ oz) butter
2 onions, chopped
100 g (3¹/₂ oz) button mushrooms,
    sliced
250 g (8 oz) cooked chicken, roughly
    chopped
4 hard-boiled eggs
1 tablespoon plain flour
280 ml (9 fl oz) chicken stock
1 egg yolk
¹/₄ cup (15 g/¹/₂ oz) chopped fresh
    coriander
250 g (8 oz) block or packet puff
    pastry
1 egg, lightly beaten, to glaze

1 Melt half of the butter in a large pan. Add the onion and mushrooms and sauté for about 5 minutes, or until soft, then stir in the chicken. Spoon half of the mixture into a 20 cm (8 inch) round, straight-sided pie dish. Slice the eggs and lay over the chicken. Top with the remaining mixture.

2 Preheat the oven to moderately hot 200°C (400°F/Gas 6). Melt the remaining butter in a pan, add the flour and cook for 1 minute. Gradually add the stock and cook for 4 minutes, stirring constantly, then remove from the heat. Stir in the egg yolk and coriander, and season with salt and ground black pepper. Allow the mixture to cool before pouring over the chicken filling.

3 Roll out the pastry into a square larger than the pie dish. Dampen the dish rim with water and lay the pastry over, pressing down firmly to seal. Trim the edges and roll out the leftover pastry into a long strip. Slice it into 3 equal lengths and make a plait. Brush the top of the pie with beaten egg and place the plait around the edge. Brush again with beaten egg. Make a few slits in the centre and bake for 35 minutes, or until golden.

NUTRITION PER SERVE
Protein 25 g; Fat 35 g; Carbohydrate 30 g;
Dietary Fibre 3 g; Cholesterol 385 mg;
2220 kJ (530 cal)

Add the chicken to the cooked onion and mushrooms in the pan.

Slice the hard-boiled eggs and arrange them over the chicken filling.

Stir the egg yolk and coriander into the heated stock and flour.

Brush the top of the pie with egg, then lay the decorative plait around the edge of the pie.

CURRIED CHICKEN PIE

Preparation time: 40 minutes
Total cooking time: 1 hour
Serves 6

PASTRY
2 cups (250 g/8 oz) plain flour
1 teaspoon ground turmeric
1 teaspoon ground cumin
125 g (4 oz) butter, cubed
1 egg, lightly beaten
2–3 tablespoons cold water

1 cooked chicken (barbecued or
    poached)
40 g (1³/₄ oz) butter, extra
1 onion, chopped
2 tablespoons curry powder
1 teaspoon cumin seeds
1 tablespoon plain flour
1¹/₂ cups (375 ml/12 fl oz) chicken
    stock
¹/₂ cup (125 ml/4 fl oz) cream
1 tablespoon mango chutney
200 g (6¹/₂ oz) sweet potato, cubed
    and cooked
milk, for glazing

1 To make the pastry, place the
flour, turmeric, cumin and butter in a
food processor. Process the mixture
for about 15 seconds, or until fine
and crumbly. Add the egg and
2–3 tablespoons cold water to bring
the mixture together. Turn out onto
a lightly floured surface and press
together until smooth. Cover with
plastic wrap and refrigerate for
20 minutes while making the filling.
2 Remove the skin and bones from
the chicken and chop the meat into
bite-sized pieces. Heat the butter in a
large pan or deep frying pan and cook
the onion until soft and transparent.

Add the curry powder and cumin
seeds and cook for 1 minute longer.
3 Add the flour and cook for another
30 seconds. Remove from the heat and
stir in the stock gradually, making sure
the mixture is smooth between each
addition. Return to the heat and cook,
stirring, until the sauce bubbles and
thickens. Add the cream, mango
chutney, sweet potato and chicken
meat. Simmer for 5 minutes, then
season to taste with salt and black
pepper. Remove from the heat and
cool completely. Preheat the oven to
moderately hot 190°C (375°F/Gas 5).
4 Divide the pastry into two portions.
Roll out one half on a lightly floured
surface until it is large enough to
cover the base and side of a 23 cm
(9 inch) pie dish. Line the dish with
the pastry and spoon the chicken
mixture into the base.
5 Roll out the remaining pastry to
cover the top of the pie. Brush the
adjoining edges with water and press
together. Trim the edges with a sharp
knife. Roll out the trimmings and cut
into decorative shapes. Brush the
underneath of the shapes with milk
and press gently on to the pie.
6 Brush the top of the pie with milk
and bake for 40 minutes, or until the
top is golden brown. Serve hot or at
room temperature.

NUTRITION PER SERVE
Protein 30 g; Fat 50 g; Carbohydrate 40 g;
Dietary Fibre 5 g; Cholesterol 240 mg;
2795 kJ (710 cal)

NOTE: It is very important that the
filling is cold when added to the
pastry, otherwise it will cause the
pastry to become soggy.

Add the egg and enough water to bring the
mixture together.

After removing the skin and bones, chop the
chicken meat into bite-sized pieces.

Stir in the stock, making sure the mixture is
smooth after each addition.

Spoon the chicken mixture into the pastry in the pie dish.

Seal the adjoining edges of the pie and trim with a sharp knife.

Brush the top of the pie with milk before placing in the oven.

MOROCCAN CHICKEN FILO PIE

Preparation time: 40 minutes
Total cooking time: 40 minutes
Serves 4–6

1 tablespoon olive oil
1 red onion, chopped
2–3 cloves garlic, crushed
2 teaspoons grated fresh ginger
1 teaspoon ground turmeric
1 teaspoon ground cumin
1 teaspoon ground coriander
500 g (1 lb) cooked chicken, shredded
60 g (2 oz) slivered almonds, toasted
1 cup (50 g/1¾ oz) chopped fresh
    coriander
⅓ cup (20 g/¾ oz) chopped fresh
    parsley
1 teaspoon grated lemon rind
2 tablespoons stock or water
1 egg, lightly beaten
9 sheets filo pastry
50 g (1¾ oz) butter, melted
1 teaspoon caster sugar
¼ teaspoon ground cinnamon

1 Heat the oil in a large heavy-based frying pan and cook the onion, garlic and ginger, stirring, for 5 minutes, or until the onion is soft. Stir in the turmeric, cumin and coriander and cook, stirring, for 1–2 minutes. Remove from the heat and stir in the chicken, almonds, coriander, parsley and lemon rind. Leave to cool for 5 minutes, then stir in the stock or water and the beaten egg.
2 Preheat the oven to moderate 180°C (350°F/Gas 4). Grease a baking tray. Cut 6 sheets of filo into approximately 30 cm (12 inch) squares, retaining the extra strips. Cut each of the remaining sheets into 3 equal strips. Cover with a damp cloth. Brush 1 square with the melted butter and place on the baking tray. Lay another square at an angle on top and brush with melted butter. Repeat with the other squares to form a rough 8-pointed star. Spoon the chicken mixture into the centre, leaving a 5 cm (2 inch) border.
3 Turn the pastry edge in over the filling, leaving the centre open. Brush the pastry strips with melted butter and lightly scrunch and lay them over the top of the pie. Sprinkle with the combined caster sugar and cinnamon. Bake for 25 minutes, or until the pastry is cooked and golden brown.

NUTRITION PER SERVE (6)
Protein 30 g; Fat 20 g; Carbohydrate 15 g;
Dietary Fibre 2 g; Cholesterol 130 mg;
1510 kJ (360 cal)

Gently shred the cooked chicken into pieces with your fingers.

Gather the edges of the pastry squares up over the chicken mixture.

Lightly scrunch the remaining pastry strips and arrange them around the pie top.

CHICKEN AND BACON GOUGERE

Preparation time: 40 minutes
Total cooking time: 50 minutes
Serves 6

60 g (2 oz) butter
1–2 cloves garlic, crushed
1 red onion, chopped
3 slices bacon, chopped
1/4 cup (30 g/1 oz) plain flour
1 1/2 cups (375 ml/12 fl oz) milk
1/2 cup (125 ml/4 fl oz) cream
2 teaspoons wholegrain mustard
250 g (8 oz) cooked chicken, chopped
1/2 cup (30 g/1 oz) chopped fresh
　　parsley

CHOUX PASTRY
60 g (2 oz) butter, chopped
1/2 cup (60 g/2 oz) plain flour
2 eggs, lightly beaten
1/3 cup (35 g/1 1/4 oz) grated Parmesan

1 Melt the butter in a frying pan and cook the garlic, onion and bacon for 5–7 minutes, stirring occasionally, until cooked but not browned. Stir in the flour and cook for 1 minute. Gradually add the milk and stir until thickened. Simmer for 2 minutes, then add the cream and mustard. Remove from the heat and fold in the chopped chicken and parsley. Season with pepper.
2 To make the pastry, place the butter and 1/2 cup (125 ml/4 fl oz) water in a pan. Stir until melted. Bring to the boil. Add the flour and beat for 2 minutes, or until the mixture leaves the side of the pan. Cool for 5 minutes. Gradually mix in the egg with an electric beater, until thick and glossy. Add the Parmesan.
3 Preheat the oven to hot 210°C (415°F/ Gas 6–7). Grease a deep 23 cm (9 inch) ovenproof dish, pour in the filling and spoon heaped tablespoons of choux around the outside. Bake for 10 minutes, then reduce the oven to 180°C (350°F/ Gas 4) and bake for 20 minutes, or until the choux is puffed and golden. Sprinkle with grated Parmesan.

NUTRITION PER SERVE
Protein 25 g; Fat 35 g; Carbohydrate 15 g;
Dietary Fibre 1 g; Cholesterol 215 mg;
2010 kJ (480 cal)

Stir the garlic, onion and bacon until cooked but not browned.

Bring the butter and water to the boil, then add the flour all at once.

Beat with a wooden spoon until the choux leaves the side of the pan.

Pour the filling into the ovenproof dish, then spoon the choux around the outside.

CHICKEN AND LEEK COBBLER

Preparation time: 1 hour
Total cooking time: 1 hour
Serves 4–6

50 g (1³/4 oz) butter
1 kg (2 lb) chicken breast fillets, cut into thick strips
1 large (225 g/7 oz) leek, trimmed and thinly sliced
1 celery stick, thinly sliced
1 tablespoon plain flour
1 cup (250 ml/8 fl oz) chicken stock
1 cup (250 ml/8 fl oz) cream
3 teaspoons Dijon mustard
3 teaspoons drained and rinsed green peppercorns

TOPPING
400 g (13 oz) potatoes, quartered
1¹/3 cups (165 g/5¹/2 oz) self-raising flour
¹/2 teaspoon salt
¹/4 cup (30 g/1 oz) grated mature Cheddar
100 g (3¹/2 oz) cold butter, chopped
1 egg yolk, lightly beaten, to glaze

1 Melt half the butter in a pan. When it begins to foam, add the chicken and cook until golden. Remove from the pan. Add the remaining butter and cook the leek and celery over medium heat until soft. Return the chicken to the pan.

2 Sprinkle the flour over the chicken and stir for about 1 minute. Remove from the heat and stir in the stock and cream. Mix well, making sure that there are no lumps. Return to the heat. Bring to the boil, then reduce the heat and simmer for about 20 minutes. Add the mustard and peppercorns and season to taste with salt and freshly ground black pepper. Transfer the mixture to a 1.25–1.5 litre capacity casserole dish and allow to cool. Preheat the oven to moderately hot 200°C (400°F/Gas 6).

3 To make the topping, cook the potato in a pan of boiling water until tender. Drain and mash until smooth. Place the flour and salt in a food processor and add the cheese and butter. Process in short bursts until the mixture forms crumbs. Add this mixture to the mashed potato and bring together with your hands to form a dough.

4 Roll out the dough on a floured surface, until it is 1 cm (¹/2 inch) thick. Cut into circles with a 6 cm (2¹/2 inch) diameter pastry cutter. Keep re-rolling the pastry scraps until all the dough is used. Carefully lift the circles up with your fingers, and arrange them so that they overlap on top of the cooled chicken and leek filling.

5 Brush the dough circles with the egg yolk and add a little milk if more glaze is needed. Bake for 30 minutes, or until the filling is heated through and the pastry is golden.

NUTRITION PER SERVE (6)
Protein 45 g; Fat 30 g; Carbohydrate 30 g; Dietary Fibre 4 g; Cholesterol 185 mg; 2405 kJ (570 cal)

NOTE: For a lower-fat variation, you can use a non-stick frying pan to cook the chicken in Step 1. You can also replace the mature Cheddar with low-fat Cheddar and reduce the amount of butter used in the filling.

Rinse the leeks thoroughly before cooking, and slice very thinly.

Remove the pan from the heat and stir in the chicken stock and cream.

Add the mustard and peppercorns to the simmering chicken and leek mixture.

Bring together the crumb mixture and mashed potato with your hands.

Roll out the dough and cut circles from it with a pastry cutter.

Arrange the circles, overlapping, on top of the cooled filling mixture.

CHICKEN AND WATERCRESS STRUDEL

Preparation time: 30 minutes
Total cooking time: 50 minutes
Serves 6

3/4 cup (60 g/2 oz) fresh white
    breadcrumbs
1–2 teaspoons sesame seeds
1 bunch (60 g/2 oz) watercress
4 chicken breast fillets
25 g (3/4 oz) butter
3 tablespoons Dijon mustard
1 cup (250 ml/8 fl oz) thick cream
15 sheets filo pastry
100 g (31/2 oz) butter, melted

1 Preheat the oven to moderately hot 190°C (375°F/Gas 5) and bake the breadcrumbs and sesame seeds, on separate trays, until golden. Steam the watercress for 3–5 minutes, or until just wilted, and squeeze out any water.
2 Slice the chicken into thin strips. Heat the butter in a pan and stir-fry the chicken until just cooked. Remove from the pan and season to taste. Stir the mustard and cream into the pan and simmer gently until reduced to about 1/2 cup (125 ml/4 fl oz). Remove from the heat and stir in the chicken and watercress.
3 Brush a sheet of filo with melted butter and sprinkle with toasted breadcrumbs. Lay another filo sheet on top, brush with butter and sprinkle with breadcrumbs. Repeat with the remaining filo and breadcrumbs and place on a baking tray.
4 Place the chicken filling along the centre of the filo pastry. Fold the sides over and roll into a parcel, with the join underneath. Brush with the remaining butter and sprinkle with the toasted sesame seeds. Bake for 30 minutes, or until golden. Cool slightly before serving.

NUTRITION PER SERVE
Protein 25 g; Fat 65 g; Carbohydrate 30 g; Dietary Fibre 2 g; Cholesterol 235 mg; 3350 kJ (795 cal)

Steam the watercress until just wilted, then drain and squeeze out the water.

Layer the buttered sheets of filo pastry and place on a baking tray.

Fold in the pastry sides to enclose the filling, then roll up into a parcel.

CHILLI CHICKEN PIE

Preparation time: 45 minutes
Total cooking time: 1 hour 20 minutes
Serves 4–6

2 tablespoons olive oil
1 onion, chopped
750 g (1¹/₂ lb) chicken breast fillets,
    chopped
3 cloves garlic, crushed
1 teaspoon chilli powder
2 teaspoons cumin seeds
1 tablespoon plain flour
2 x 410 g (13 oz) cans chopped
    tomatoes
1 tablespoon soft brown sugar

1 red capsicum, thinly sliced
375 g (12 oz) can red kidney beans,
    rinsed and drained
15 sheets filo pastry
100 g (3¹/₂ oz) butter, melted

1 Heat half the oil in a large frying pan and cook the onion until softened and golden. Remove from the pan, add the remaining oil and brown the chicken over high heat.
2 Stir in the garlic, chilli powder and cumin seeds and cook for 1 minute. Return the onion to the pan, stir in the flour and cook for 30 seconds. Stir in the chopped tomatoes.
3 Add the sugar and capsicum and simmer over low heat for 40 minutes,

or until reduced and thickened. Increase the heat and, stirring constantly to prevent burning, add the kidney beans. Allow to cool, then spoon into a 20 x 28 cm (8 x 11 inch) casserole dish. Preheat the oven to moderate 180°C (350°F/Gas 4).
4 Cut the filo sheets in half, brush with the melted butter and scrunch up. Place on top of the filling, to cover it completely. Brush with the remaining butter and bake for 25–30 minutes, or until golden.

NUTRITION PER SERVE (6)
Protein 40 g; Fat 25 g; Carbohydrate 35 g;
Dietary Fibre 7 g; Cholesterol 105 mg;
2175 kJ (515 cal)

Stir the garlic, chilli powder and cumin seeds into the browned chicken.

Add the kidney beans to the filling mixture, stirring constantly to prevent the mixture from burning.

Scrunch up the sheets of filo pastry and arrange them on top of the filling.

LOW-FAT CHICKEN PIES

Preparation time: 50 minutes
+ 30 minutes refrigeration
Total cooking time: 1 hour
Serves 4

300 g (10 oz) chicken breast fillets
1 bay leaf
2 cups (500 ml/16 fl oz) chicken stock
2 large potatoes, chopped
250 g (8 oz) orange sweet potato,
   chopped
2 celery sticks, chopped
2 carrots, chopped
1 onion, chopped
1 parsnip, chopped
1 clove garlic, crushed
1 tablespoon cornflour
1 cup (250 ml/8 fl oz) skim milk
1 cup (155 g/5 oz) frozen peas,
   thawed
1 tablespoon chopped fresh chives
1 tablespoon chopped fresh parsley
1 1/2 cups (185 g/6 oz) self-raising flour
20 g (3/4 oz) butter
1/3 cup (80 ml/2 3/4 fl oz) milk
1 egg, lightly beaten
1/2 teaspoon sesame seeds

1 Combine the chicken, bay leaf and stock in a large, deep non-stick frying pan and simmer over low heat for about 10 minutes, until the chicken is cooked through. Remove the chicken, set aside and, when cool, cut into small pieces. Add the chopped potato, orange sweet potato, celery and carrot to the pan and simmer, covered, for about 10 minutes, or until just tender. Remove the vegetables from the pan with a slotted spoon.

2 Add the onion, parsnip and garlic to the pan and simmer, uncovered, for about 10 minutes, or until very soft.

Discard the bay leaf. Purée the mixture in a food processor until smooth.

3 Stir the cornflour into 2 tablespoons of the skim milk until it forms a smooth paste. Stir the cornflour mixture into the puréed mixture with the remaining milk and then return to the pan. Stir over low heat until the mixture boils and thickens. Preheat the oven to moderately hot 200°C (400°F/Gas 6).

4 Combine the puréed mixture with the remaining vegetables, chicken, chives and parsley. Season with salt and pepper. Spoon into four 1 3/4 cup (440 ml/14 fl oz) ovenproof dishes.

5 To make the pastry, sift the flour into a large bowl, rub in the butter with your fingertips, then make a well in the centre. Combine the milk with 1/3 cup (80 ml/2 3/4 fl oz) water and add enough to the dry ingredients to make a soft dough. Turn out onto a lightly floured surface and knead until just smooth. Cut the dough into four portions and roll each out so that it is 1 cm (1/2 inch) larger than the top of the dish. Brush the edge of the dough with some of the egg and fit it over the top of each dish, pressing the edge firmly to seal.

6 Brush the pastry lightly with beaten egg and sprinkle with the sesame seeds. Bake for about 30 minutes, or until the tops are golden and the filling is heated through.

NUTRITION PER SERVE
Protein 30 g; Fat 10 g; Carbohydrate 65 g;
Dietary Fibre 9.5 g; Cholesterol 100 mg;
2045 kJ (490 cal)

Cut the vegetables into even-sized pieces so that they cook at the same rate.

Simmer the chicken with the bay leaf and stock until cooked through.

Purée the cooked onion, parsnip and garlic together until smooth.

Stir the sauce constantly until the mixture boils and thickens.

Add enough liquid to the dry ingredients to make a soft dough.

Brush the edge of the dough with egg, then press it over the top of each dish.

CHICKEN AND MUSHROOM PITHIVIER

Preparation time: 45 minutes
  + 30 minutes refrigeration
Total cooking time: 40 minutes
Serves 4

50 g (1³/₄ oz) butter
2 slices bacon, chopped
4 spring onions, chopped
100 g (3¹/₂ oz) button mushrooms,
    sliced
1 tablespoon plain flour
³/₄ cup (185 ml/6 fl oz) milk
1 tablespoon cream
1 cup (180 g/6 oz) chopped cooked
    chicken breast
¹/₃ cup (20 g/³/₄ oz) chopped fresh
    parsley
2 sheets ready-rolled puff pastry
1 egg yolk, lightly beaten, to glaze

1 Melt the butter in a pan and cook the bacon and spring onion, stirring, for 2–3 minutes. Add the mushrooms and cook, stirring, for 3 minutes. Stir in the flour and cook for 1 minute. Add the milk all at once and stir for 2–3 minutes, or until thickened. Simmer for 1 minute, then remove from the heat. Stir in the cream, chicken and parsley. Set aside to cool.
2 Cut two 23 cm (9 inch) circles from the pastry sheets, using a dinner plate or cake tin as a guide. Place 1 circle on a greased baking tray. Pile the chicken filling into the centre of the pastry, mounding slightly in the centre and leaving a 2 cm (³/₄ inch) border. Combine the egg yolk with 1 teaspoon of water, and brush the pastry border.
3 Using a small pointed knife, and starting from the centre of the second circle, mark curved lines at regular

intervals. Take care not to cut through the pastry. Place this sheet over the other and stretch a little to fit evenly. Press the edges together to seal. Using the back of a knife, push up the outside edge at 1 cm (¹/₂ inch) intervals. Cover and refrigerate for at least 30 minutes. Preheat the oven to moderately hot 190°C (375°F/Gas 5).

Brush the pastry with the egg mixture and make a small hole in the centre for steam to escape. Bake for 25 minutes, or until golden.

NUTRITION PER SERVE
Protein 25 g; Fat 40 g; Carbohydrate 35 g; Dietary Fibre 2 g; Cholesterol 160 mg; 2395 kJ (570 cal)

Stir the cream, chicken and chopped parsley into the filling mixture.

Draw curved lines from the centre to the edge of the pastry.

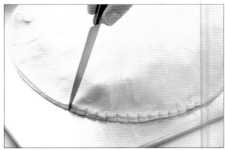
Use the back of a knife to push up the edge of the pastry.

SPICY CHICKEN TARTS

Preparation time: 50 minutes
Total cooking time: 45 minutes
Makes 8

2 large onions, finely chopped
400 g (13 oz) eggplant, cubed
2 cloves garlic, crushed
2 x 410 g (13 oz) cans chopped
    tomatoes
1 tablespoon tomato paste
3 teaspoons soft brown sugar
1 tablespoon red wine vinegar
1/4 cup (15 g/1/2 oz) chopped fresh
    parsley
4 sheets ready-rolled shortcrust pastry

2 teaspoons ground cumin seeds
2 teaspoons ground coriander
1 teaspoon paprika
400 g (13 oz) chicken breast fillets
oil, for cooking
sour cream, to serve
fresh coriander leaves, to serve

1 Fry the onion in a little oil until
golden. Add the eggplant and garlic
and cook for a few minutes. Stir in
the tomato, tomato paste, sugar and
vinegar. Bring to the boil, then reduce
the heat, cover and simmer for
20 minutes. Uncover and simmer for
10 minutes, or until thick. Add the
parsley and season. Preheat the oven
to moderately hot 190°C (375°F/Gas 5).

2 Grease 8 small pie tins measuring
7.5 cm (3 inches) across the base, line
with the pastry and decorate the
edges. Prick the bases using a fork.
Bake for 15 minutes, or until golden.
3 Mix the cumin, coriander and
paprika together. Coat the chicken
pieces in the spices. Heat some oil in a
frying pan and cook the chicken until
brown and cooked through. Cut
diagonally. Fill the pie shells with the
eggplant mixture and add the chicken,
sour cream and coriander leaves.

NUTRITION PER SERVE
Protein 20 g; Fat 35 g; Carbohydrate 45 g;
Dietary Fibre 5 g; Cholesterol 65 mg;
2315 kJ (550 cal)

Simmer the tomato mixture to reduce the liquid,
then add the parsley.

Use a spoon to decorate the edge of the
uncooked pastry cases.

Coat the chicken fillets in the combined cumin,
coriander and papriika.

THAI GREEN CURRY CHICKEN PIES

Preparation time: 45 minutes
  + 30 minutes refrigeration
Total cooking time: 45 minutes
Serves 4

1 cup (125 g/4 oz) plain flour
65 g (2¼ oz) cold butter, chopped

FILLING
200 g (6½ oz) green beans
1 tablespoon oil
1 tablespoon Thai green curry paste
½ cup (125 ml/4 fl oz) coconut milk
500 g (1 lb) chicken thigh fillets, cut
    into bite-sized pieces
2 kaffir lime leaves
2 teaspoons fish sauce
1 tablespoon lime juice
2 teaspoons soft brown sugar
1 tablespoon cornflour
1 egg, lightly beaten, to glaze

1 Process the flour and butter in a food processor until the mixture resembles fine breadcrumbs. Add 1–2 tablespoons of cold water. Process in short bursts until the mixture just comes together, adding a little extra water if necessary. Turn out onto a lightly floured surface and quickly bring together into a ball. Cover with plastic wrap and refrigerate for at least 30 minutes.

2 Cut the beans into short lengths. Heat the oil in a wok or heavy-based frying pan. Add the curry paste and cook for 1 minute, stirring constantly. Add the coconut milk and ¼ cup (60 ml/2 fl oz) of water and bring to the boil. Add the chicken, beans and kaffir lime leaves and stir through. Simmer gently for 15 minutes, or until the chicken is cooked. Add the fish sauce, lime juice and sugar. In a small bowl, mix together the cornflour and 1 tablespoon of water to a smooth consistency. Add to the curry and stir constantly until the sauce thickens and begins to bubble. Remove the kaffir lime leaves, and divide the mixture between four ½ cup (125 ml/4 fl oz) capacity ramekins.

3 Divide the pastry into 4 equal pieces. Roll each piece between two sheets of baking paper until it is slightly larger than the top of the ramekins. Brush the edges of the ramekins with the beaten egg and cover with the pastry. Press the edges around the rim to seal. Trim off any excess pastry with a sharp knife. Decorate the edges of the pastry with the end of a teaspoon. Cut a small air hole in the top of each pie to allow the steam to escape during cooking. Brush with the beaten egg. Place the ramekins on a baking tray and bake for 20–25 minutes, or until the pastry is golden brown. Serve immediately.

NUTRITION PER SERVE
Protein 35 g; Fat 30 g; Carbohydrate 30 g;
Dietary Fibre 3 g; Cholesterol 175 mg;
2225 kJ (530 cal)

NOTE: Coconut milk varies greatly in quality. You may get a 'curdled' or 'split' appearance, however this will not affect the flavour.

HINT: Dried kaffir lime leaves can be stored for up to 1 year if kept in a sealed plastic bag.

Cook the curry paste for 1 minute, then add the coconut milk.

Add the chicken, beans and kaffir lime leaves to the wok or pan.

Add the cornflour mixture to the curry and stir until it thickens and bubbles.

Remove the kaffir lime leaves before spooning the mixture into the ramekins.

Roll out each piece of pastry and place over the top of the ramekins.

Glaze the pastry crusts with a little beaten egg to give a golden finish.

FAMILY CHICKEN PIE

Preparation time: 40 minutes
  + 20 minutes chilling
Total cooking time: 1 hour
Serves 6

PASTRY
2 cups (250 g/8 oz) self-raising flour
125 g (4 oz) butter, chopped
1 egg

FILLING
1 barbecued chicken
30 g (1 oz) butter
1 onion, finely chopped
310 g (10 oz) can creamed corn
1¼ cups (315 ml/10 fl oz) cream

1 To make the pastry, process the flour and butter in a food processor for 15 seconds, or until the mixture is fine and crumbly. Add the egg and 2–3 tablespoons water and process for 30 seconds, or until the mixture just comes together. Turn onto a lightly floured surface and gather together into a smooth ball. Cover with plastic wrap and refrigerate for 20 minutes.
2 Meanwhile, to make the filling, remove the meat from the chicken carcass and shred finely. Heat the butter in a pan and cook the onion over medium heat for 3 minutes. Add the chicken, corn and cream. Bring to the boil, then reduce the heat and simmer for 10 minutes. Remove from the heat and allow to cool slightly.
3 Preheat the oven to moderate 180°C (350°F/Gas 4). Roll half the pastry between two sheets of plastic wrap to cover the base and side of a 23 cm (9 inch) pie dish. Spoon the chicken mixture into the pastry-lined dish.
4 Roll the remaining pastry to cover the top of the pie. Brush with milk. Press the edges together to seal. Trim the edges with a sharp knife. Roll the excess pastry into two long ropes and twist together. Brush the pie edge with a little milk and place the pastry rope around the rim. Bake for 45 minutes.

NUTRITION PER SERVE
Protein 18 g; Fat 48 g; Carbohydrate 44 g; Dietary Fibre 4 g; Cholesterol 212 mg; 2832 kJ (676 cal)

Add the egg and water to the flour and butter mixture and process.

Add the chicken, corn and cream to the onion and bring to the boil.

Roll half the pastry out between two sheets of plastic wrap.

Brush the pie edge with a little milk, then place the pastry rope around the rim of the pie.

CREAMY CHICKEN, SAGE AND TARRAGON PIE

Preparation time: 25 minutes
Total cooking time: 1 hour 10 minutes
Serves 4–6

1.5 kg (3 lb) chicken thigh fillets
2 tablespoons olive oil
2 slices bacon, finely chopped
1 onion, roughly chopped
4 fresh sage leaves, chopped
1 tablespoon chopped fresh tarragon
45 g (1 1/2 oz) butter, melted
2 tablespoons plain flour
1/2 cup (125 ml/4 fl oz) milk
220 g (7 oz) can creamed corn
2 sheets ready-rolled puff pastry
1 egg, lightly beaten

1 Preheat the oven to hot 210°C (415°F/Gas 6–7). Brush a 23 cm (9 inch) pie dish with butter. Cut the chicken into bite-sized pieces. Heat the oil in a large frying pan. Add the chicken, bacon and onion, and cook over medium heat for 5 minutes, or until browned. Add the sage, tarragon, 1 cup (250 ml/8 fl oz) water, salt and pepper. Bring to the boil, then reduce the heat and simmer, covered, for 25 minutes, or until the chicken is tender. Drain, reserving the juices.

2 Melt the butter in a heavy-based pan. Add the flour and stir over low heat for 1 minute. Remove from the heat and gradually add the milk and reserved juice, stirring until smooth. Return to the heat and stir over medium heat until thickenened. Stir in the chicken mixture and corn. Spoon into the dish.

3 Brush a sheet of pastry with egg and top with a second sheet. Brush the rim of the pie dish with egg and place the pastry over the filling. Trim any excess.

4 Decorate the pie with pastry. Brush with egg and make a few slits in the top. Bake for 15 minutes, then reduce the heat to 180°C (350°F/Gas 4) and bake for 10–15 minutes, or until crisp and golden. Leave for 5 minutes.

NUTRITION PER SERVE
Protein 66 g; Fat 40 g; Carbohydrate 34 g; Dietary Fibre 2.5 g; Cholesterol 217 mg; 3150 kJ (753 cal)

Add the salt, pepper, tarragon, sage and water to the chicken mixture.

Add the chicken mixture and corn to the sauce, and stir to combine.

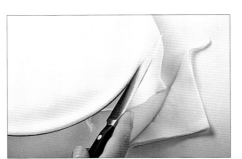

Place the pastry over the filling, then trim the excess with a sharp knife.

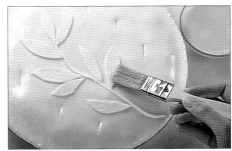

Brush the pie with the beaten egg and make a few slits to allow the steam to escape.

Stews & Casseroles

MEDITERRANEAN CHICKEN

Preparation time: 30 minutes
Total cooking time: 1 hour 10 minutes
Serves 4

8 chicken thigh cutlets
2 tablespoons olive oil
150 g (5 oz) French shallots
4 cloves garlic
1/2 cup (125 ml/4 fl oz) white wine
425 g (14 oz) can chopped tomatoes
12 Kalamata olives
1 tablespoon red wine vinegar
2 teaspoons tomato paste
1 tablespoon fresh oregano leaves
1 tablespoon chopped fresh basil
1 teaspoon sugar
4 slices prosciutto
1 teaspoon grated lemon rind
1/2 cup (30 g/1 oz) chopped fresh
   parsley
1 tablespoon capers, rinsed

1 Preheat the oven to moderate 180°C (350°F/Gas 4). Remove the skin and fat from the chicken thighs. Heat half the oil in a large pan and brown the chicken over high heat for 3–4 minutes on each side. Arrange the chicken in a large flameproof casserole dish.
2 Heat the remaining oil in the same pan. Add the shallots and garlic and cook over medium heat for 4 minutes, or until soft but not brown. Add the wine and bring to the boil.
3 Add the tomatoes, olives, vinegar, tomato paste, oregano, basil and sugar. Season with salt and black pepper. Boil, stirring, for 2 minutes, then pour over the chicken and cover with a tight-fitting lid. Bake for 45 minutes, or until the chicken is tender.
4 Meanwhile, place the prosciutto in a single layer in a frying pan. Dry-fry for 3 minutes, or until crisp, turning once. Break into large chunks and set aside.
5 Arrange the chicken on a serving dish, cover and keep warm. Transfer the casserole to the stove top and boil the pan juices for 5 minutes, or until thickened, stirring occasionally. Spoon the juices over the chicken and sprinkle with the lemon rind, parsley and capers. Top with the prosciutto.

NUTRITION PER SERVE
Protein 75 g; Fat 25 g; Carbohydrate 15 g; Dietary Fibre 8 g; Cholesterol 155 mg; 2390 kJ (570 cal)

Cook the shallots and garlic until soft, then add the wine.

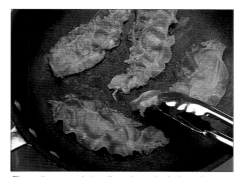

Place the prosciutto slices in a single layer in a dry frying pan and fry until crisp.

PERSIAN CHICKEN

Preparation time: 20 minutes
Total cooking time: 1 hour
Serves 6

1.5 kg (3 lb) small chicken thighs
1/2 cup (60 g/2 oz) plain flour
2 tablespoons olive oil
1 large onion, chopped
2 cloves garlic, chopped
1/2 teaspoon ground cinnamon
4 ripe tomatoes, chopped
6 fresh dates, stones removed, halved
2 tablespoons currants
2 cups (500 ml/16 fl oz) rich chicken
　　stock
2 teaspoons finely grated lemon rind

1/2 cup (80 g/2¾ oz) almonds,
　　toasted and roughly chopped
2 tablespoons chopped fresh parsley

1 Coat the chicken pieces with flour and shake off any excess. Heat the oil in a large heavy-based pan over medium heat. Brown the chicken on all sides, turning regularly, and then remove from the pan. Drain any excess oil from the pan.
2 Add the onion, garlic and ground cinnamon to the pan and cook, stirring regularly, for 5 minutes, or until the onion is soft.
3 Add the tomato, dates, currants and stock, and bring to the boil. Return the chicken to the pan, cover with the sauce, reduce the heat and simmer,

uncovered, for 30 minutes. Add the lemon rind and season to taste. Bring back to the boil and boil for 5 minutes, or until thickened. Sprinkle with the almonds and parsley, and serve with buttered rice.

NUTRITION PER SERVE
Protein 42 g; Fat 16 g; Carbohydrate 17 g;
Dietary Fibre 3.5 g; Cholesterol 83 mg;
1597 kJ (382 cal)

VARIATION: Chicken drumsticks can be used instead of thighs.

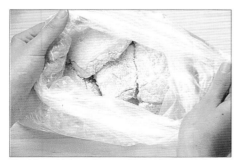
Coat the chicken pieces with the flour and shake off any excess.

Brown the chicken on all sides, turning regularly to prevent it from sticking.

Add the tomato, dates, currants and stock to the softened onion.

SPICY GARLIC CHICKEN

Preparation time: 30 minutes
Total cooking time: 1 hour
Serves 4–6

1.4 kg (2 lb 13 oz) chicken
1 small bunch coriander
2 tablespoons olive oil
4 cloves garlic, crushed
2 red onions, thinly sliced
1 large red capsicum, cut into squares
1 teaspoon ground ginger
1 teaspoon chilli powder
1 teaspoon caraway seeds, crushed
1 teaspoon ground turmeric
2 teaspoons ground coriander
2 teaspoons ground cumin
1/2 cup (60 g/2 oz) raisins
1/2 cup (90 g/3 oz) black olives
1 teaspoon finely grated lemon rind

1 Trim the chicken of excess fat and sinew. Cut the chicken into 12 serving pieces. Finely chop the coriander roots, reserving the leaves.
2 Heat the oil in a large heavy-based pan. Add the garlic, onion, capsicum, ginger, chilli powder, caraway seeds, turmeric, coriander, cumin and coriander roots. Cook over medium heat for 10 minutes.
3 Add the chicken pieces and stir until combined. Add 1 1/2 cups (375 ml/12 fl oz) water and bring to the boil. Reduce the heat and simmer for 45 minutes, or until the chicken is tender and cooked through.
4 Add the raisins, black olives and lemon rind and simmer for a further 5 minutes. Serve with pasta or rice. May be served sprinkled with the reserved coriander leaves.

NUTRITION PER SERVE
Protein 33 g; Fat 13 g; Carbohydrate 13 g;
Dietary Fibre 2 g; Cholesterol 105 mg;
1236 kJ (295 cal)

VARIATION: Chicken pieces may be used instead of whole chicken.

Wash the coriander and finely chop the roots, reserving the leaves.

Heat the oil in a large pan and add the garlic, onion, capsicum and spices.

Add the chicken pieces to the mixture and stir until combined.

Add the raisins, olives and lemon rind to the chicken mixture.

CHICKEN CACCIATORE

Preparation time: 45 minutes
Total cooking time: 1 hour 20 minutes
Serves 4

4 tomatoes
1.5 kg (3 lb) chicken pieces
20 g (³⁄₄ oz) butter
1 tablespoon oil
20 g (³⁄₄ oz) butter, extra
1 large onion, chopped
2 cloves garlic, chopped
1 small green capsicum, chopped
150 g (5 oz) mushrooms, thickly sliced
1 tablespoon plain flour
1 cup (250 ml/8 fl oz) white wine
1 tablespoon white wine vinegar
2 tablespoons tomato paste
¹⁄₂ cup (90 g/3 oz) small black olives
¹⁄₃ cup (20 g/³⁄₄ oz) chopped fresh
    parsley

1 Score a cross in the base of each tomato. Put the tomatoes in a bowl of boiling water for 30 seconds, then transfer to a bowl of cold water. Drain and peel the skin away from the cross. Halve the tomatoes and remove the seeds with a teaspoon. Chop the flesh. Preheat the oven to moderate 180°C (350°F/Gas 4).

2 Remove excess fat from the chicken pieces and pat dry with paper towels. Heat half the butter and oil in a large flameproof casserole. Cook half the chicken over high heat until browned all over, then set aside. Heat the remaining butter and oil and cook the remaining chicken. Set aside.

3 Heat the extra butter in the casserole and cook the onion and garlic for 2–3 minutes. Add the capsicum and mushrooms, and cook, stirring, for 3 minutes. Stir in the flour and cook for 1 minute. Add the wine,

vinegar, tomato and tomato paste and cook, stirring, for 2 minutes, or until slightly thickened.

4 Return the chicken to the casserole and make sure it is covered by the tomato and onion mixture. Place in the oven and cook, covered, for 1 hour, or until the chicken is tender. Stir in the olives and parsley. Season with salt and cracked black pepper and serve with pasta.

NUTRITION PER SERVE
Protein 55 g; Fat 15 g; Carbohydrate 9.5 g;
Dietary Fibre 5 g; Cholesterol 125 mg;
1675 kJ (401 cal)

NOTE: If you prefer a thicker sauce, remove the cooked chicken from the casserole and reduce the sauce over high heat until slightly thickened. Return all the chicken to the casserole and add the olives and parsley.

Drain the tomatoes, then peel away the skin from the cross.

Cut the tomatoes in half and remove the seeds with a teaspoon.

Cook the chicken in batches over high heat until browned all over.

APRICOT CHICKEN

Preparation time: 10 minutes
Total cooking time: 1 hour
Serves 6

6 chicken thigh cutlets
425 ml (14 fl oz) can apricot nectar
40 g (1¹⁄₄ oz) packet French onion
    soup mix
425 g (14 oz) can apricot halves in
    natural juice, drained
¹⁄₄ cup (60 g/2 oz) sour cream

1 Preheat the oven to moderate 180°C (350°F/Gas 4). Remove the skin from the chicken thigh cutlets. Put the chicken in an ovenproof dish. Mix the apricot nectar with the French onion

soup mix until well combined, and pour over the chicken.

2 Bake, covered, for 50 minutes, then add the apricot halves and bake for a further 5 minutes. Stir in the sour cream just before serving. Delicious served with creamy mashed potato or rice to soak up the juices.

NUTRITION PER SERVE
Protein 23 g; Fat 6 g; Carbohydrate 10 g;
Dietary Fibre 0 g; Cholesterol 63 mg;
780 kJ (187 cal)

NOTE: If you are looking for a healthy alternative, you can use low-fat sour cream in place of the full-fat version.

Pour in the apricot nectar and stir to combine with the soup mix.

Add the apricot halves to the chicken and bake for 5 minutes more.

CREAMY CHICKEN WITH MUSHROOMS

Preparation time: 20 minutes
Total cooking time: 40 minutes
Serves 6

2 tablespoons olive oil
200 g (6¹/₂ oz) button mushrooms, halved
200 g (6¹/₂ oz) field mushrooms, chopped
1 small red capsicum, sliced
4 chicken breast fillets, cut into bite-sized pieces
2 tablespoons plain flour
1 cup (250 ml/8 fl oz) chicken stock

¹/₂ cup (125 ml/4 fl oz) red wine
3 spring onions, finely chopped
1¹/₄ cups (315 ml/10 fl oz) cream
1 tablespoon chopped fresh chives
1 tablespoon finely chopped fresh parsley
¹/₄ teaspoon turmeric

1 Heat the oil in a large heavy-based pan and add the button and field mushrooms and capsicum. Cook over medium heat for 4 minutes, or until soft. Remove and set aside.
2 Add the chicken to the pan in batches and brown quickly over medium-high heat. Sprinkle with the flour and cook for a further 2 minutes, or until the flour is golden. Add the

stock and wine and bring to the boil. Cover and simmer for 10 minutes, or until the chicken is tender.
3 Add the spring onion and cream, return to the boil and simmer for 10–15 minutes, or until the cream has reduced and thickened. Return the mushrooms and capsicum to the pan and add the chives, parsley and turmeric. Stir, season to taste and simmer for a further 5 minutes to heat through.

NUTRITION PER SERVE
Protein 40 g; Fat 33 g; Carbohydrate 6.5 g; Dietary Fibre 2 g; Cholesterol 150 mg; 2060 kJ (493 cal)

Choose large field mushrooms and wipe them with a damp cloth before chopping.

Add the spring onion and cream to the pan and return to the boil.

Add the mushrooms, capsicum, chives, parsley and turmeric.

CHICKEN IN MUSHROOM AND PAPRIKA SAUCE

Preparation time: 25 minutes
Total cooking time: 20 minutes
Serves 4

4 chicken breast fillets
1/4 cup (30 g/1 oz) plain flour
30 g (1 oz) butter
1 tablespoon oil
1 onion, finely chopped
2 cloves garlic, crushed
250 g (8 oz) button mushrooms, thinly
　　sliced
1 tablespoon sweet paprika
1 tablespoon tomato paste
1/2 cup (125 ml/4 fl oz) chicken stock
1/3 cup (80 g/2 3/4 oz) sour cream
2 tablespoons finely chopped fresh
　　parsley

1 Trim the chicken of excess fat and sinew, and cut into bite-sized pieces. Coat the chicken pieces with the flour by shaking together in a plastic bag. Heat half the butter and oil in a large frying pan, add the chicken in small batches and cook over medium heat for 5 minutes, or until browned. Drain on paper towels.
2 Heat the remaining butter and oil in the same pan. Add the onion and garlic and cook over medium heat for 2 minutes, or until the onion has softened. Add the mushrooms and cook for 1–2 minutes, or until tender.

Remove from the heat. Add the paprika and cooked chicken, and stir to combine.
3 Combine the tomato paste with the stock in a small bowl. Add to the pan and stir until well combined with the chicken mixture. Season to taste. Return to the heat and bring to the boil. Reduce the heat and simmer, covered, for 5 minutes, or until the chicken is cooked through. Stir in the sour cream and warm through, but do not boil. Serve sprinkled with the parsley.

NUTRITION PER SERVE
Protein 54 g; Fat 25 g; Carbohydrate 10 g;
Dietary Fibre 3 g; Cholesterol 156 mg;
2007 kJ (480 cal)

Place the chicken pieces and flour into a plastic bag and shake to coat.

Remove from the heat, add the chicken and paprika, and stir to combine.

Stir the sour cream into the chicken mixture and warm through, but do not boil.

CHICKEN AND ORANGE CASSEROLE

Preparation time: 50 minutes
Total cooking time: 1 hour 30 minutes
Serves 4–6

2 small chickens
1 tablespoon olive oil
2 thick slices bacon, rind removed and thinly sliced
50 g (1³/₄ oz) butter
16 small pickling onions, peeled, ends left intact
2–3 cloves garlic, crushed
3 teaspoons grated fresh ginger
2 teaspoons grated orange rind
2 teaspoons ground cumin
2 teaspoons ground coriander
2 tablespoons honey
1 cup (250 ml/8 fl oz) fresh orange juice
1 cup (250 ml/8 fl oz) white wine
¹/₂ cup (125 ml/4 fl oz) chicken or vegetable stock
1 bunch baby carrots
1 large parsnip, peeled
fresh coriander and orange zest, to serve

1 Using a sharp knife or a pair of kitchen scissors, cut each chicken into 8 pieces, discarding the backbone. Remove any excess fat and discard (remove the skin as well, if preferred).
2 Heat about a teaspoon of the oil in a large, deep, heavy-based pan. Add the bacon and cook over medium heat for 2–3 minutes or until just crisp. Remove from the pan and set aside to drain on paper towels. Add the remaining oil and half the butter to the pan. Cook the onions over medium heat until dark golden brown. Shake the pan occasionally to ensure even cooking and browning. Remove from the pan and set aside.

3 Add the chicken pieces to the pan and brown in small batches over medium heat. Remove from the pan and drain on paper towels.
4 Add the remaining butter to the pan. Stir in the garlic, ginger, orange rind, cumin, coriander and honey, and cook, stirring, for 1 minute. Add the orange juice, wine and stock to the pan. Bring to the boil, then reduce the heat and simmer for 1 minute. Return the chicken pieces to the pan, cover and leave to simmer over low heat for 40 minutes.
5 Return the onions and bacon to the pan and simmer, covered, for a further 15 minutes. Remove the lid and leave to simmer for a further 15 minutes.
6 Trim the carrots, leaving a little green stalk, and wash well or peel if necessary. Cut the parsnip into small batons. Add the carrots and parsnip to the pan. Cover and cook for 5–10 minutes, or until the carrots and parsnip are just tender. Do not overcook the carrots or they will lose their bright colouring. When you are ready to serve, arrange 2–3 chicken pieces on each plate. Arrange a couple of carrots and a few parsnip batons with the chicken and spoon a little sauce over the top. Garnish with the coriander leaves and orange zest.

NUTRITION PER SERVE
Protein 42 g; Fat 12 g; Carbohydrate 22 g; Dietary Fibre 2 g; Cholesterol 135 mg; 1635 kJ (395 cal)

Cut each chicken into 8 pieces using a knife or pair of scissors.

Cook the pickling onions in the oil and butter until they are dark golden brown.

Brown the chicken pieces in batches and drain on paper towels.

Add the orange juice, white wine and stock to the pan, and bring to the boil.

Return the browned pickling onions and cooked bacon to the pan.

Cut the parsnip into batons and leave the stalks on the carrots to provide colour.

CHICKEN CHASSEUR

Preparation time: 20 minutes
Total cooking time: 1 hour 30 minutes
Serves 4

1 kg (2 lb) chicken thigh fillets
2 tablespoons oil
1 clove garlic, crushed
1 large onion, sliced
100 g (3¹/₂ oz) button mushrooms,
    sliced
1 teaspoon fresh thyme leaves
400 g (13 oz) can chopped tomatoes

¹/₄ cup (60 ml/2 fl oz) chicken stock
¹/₄ cup (60 ml/2 fl oz) white wine
1 tablespoon tomato paste

1 Preheat the oven to moderate 180°C (350°F/Gas 4). Trim the chicken of excess fat and sinew. Heat the oil in a heavy-based frying pan and brown the chicken in batches over medium heat. Drain on paper towels, then transfer to a casserole dish.
2 Add the garlic, onion and sliced mushrooms to the pan and cook over medium heat for 5 minutes, or until soft. Add to the chicken with the

thyme and tomatoes.
3 Combine the stock, wine and tomato paste and pour over the chicken. Bake, covered, for 1¹/₄ hours, or until the chicken is tender.

NUTRITION PER SERVE
Protein 60 g; Fat 15 g; Carbohydrate 6 g;
Dietary Fibre 2 g; Cholesterol 125 mg;
1710 kJ (410 cal)

NOTE: Don't be tempted to use poor-quality wine for cooking, as the taste will affect the flavour of the dish.

Brown the chicken in the hot oil over medium heat and drain on paper towels.

Add the garlic, onion and mushrooms to the pan and cook until soft.

Pour the combined stock, wine and tomato paste over the chicken mixture.

VIETNAMESE CHICKEN AND NOODLE CASSEROLE

Preparation time: 40 minutes
Total cooking time: 25 minutes
Serves 4

1 stem lemon grass
4 kaffir lime leaves
1 litre chicken stock
400 ml (13 fl oz) coconut cream
1/4 cup (30 g/1 oz) coconut milk
    powder
2 tablespoons peanut oil
400 g (13 oz) chicken breast fillets, cut
    into strips
12 raw king prawns, peeled and
    deveined, tails intact
8 spring onions, sliced
2 teaspoons finely chopped fresh
    ginger
4 cloves garlic, finely chopped
2 small red chillies, seeded and finely
    chopped
500 g (1 lb) Hokkien noodles
1 teaspoon dried shrimp paste
2 tablespoons lime juice
1 cup (90 g/3 oz) bean sprouts
fresh mint leaves, to garnish
fresh coriander leaves, to garnish

1 Finely chop the white stem of the lemon grass. Remove the centre stem from the kaffir lime leaves, then finely shred the leaves.

2 Place the lemon grass and lime leaves in a large, heavy-based pan with the stock, coconut cream and coconut milk powder. Bring to the boil, stirring constantly to dissolve the coconut milk powder. Reduce the heat and simmer, covered, for 15 minutes.

3 Heat a wok over high heat and add the peanut oil. Add the chicken, prawns, spring onion, ginger, garlic and chilli. Stir-fry for 5–10 minutes, or until the chicken and prawns are cooked through.

4 Place the noodles in the simmering coconut cream, then add the chicken and prawn mixture from the wok. Add the shrimp paste and lime juice. Allow the noodles to heat through.

5 Divide the sprouts among warmed deep bowls and place the noodles, chicken and prawns on top. Ladle the sauce over, scatter with mint and coriander and serve at once.

NUTRITION PER SERVE
Protein 40 g; Fat 35 g; Carbohydrate 10 g;
Dietary Fibre 4 g; Cholesterol 135 mg;
2150 kJ (515 cal)

Using a sharp knife, finely chop the white stem of the lemon grass.

Stir-fry the chicken, prawns, spring onion, ginger, garlic and chilli.

Add the Hokkien noodles to the simmering coconut cream mixture.

CHICKEN AND MUSHROOM CASSEROLE

Preparation time: 20 minutes
Total cooking time: 1 hour
Serves 4

20 g (³/₄ oz) dried porcini mushrooms
¹/₄ cup (30 g/1 oz) plain flour
1.5 kg (3 lb) chicken pieces
2 tablespoons oil
1 large onion, chopped
2 cloves garlic, crushed
¹/₄ cup (60 ml/2 fl oz) chicken stock
¹/₃ cup (80 ml/2³/₄ fl oz) white wine
425 g (14 oz) can peeled whole
    tomatoes

1 tablespoon balsamic vinegar
3 fresh thyme sprigs
1 bay leaf
300 g (10 oz) field mushrooms, thickly
    sliced

1 Preheat the oven to moderate 180°C (350°F/Gas 4). Put the porcini mushrooms in a bowl and cover with ¹/₄ cup (60 ml/2 fl oz) boiling water. Leave for 5 minutes, or until the mushrooms are rehydrated.
2 Season the flour with salt and pepper. Lightly toss the chicken in flour to coat and shake off any excess.
3 Heat the oil in a flameproof casserole and cook the chicken in batches until well browned all over. Set aside. Add

the onion and garlic to the casserole and cook for 3–5 minutes, or until the onion softens. Stir in the stock.
4 Return the chicken to the casserole with the porcini mushrooms and any remaining liquid, wine, tomatoes, vinegar, thyme and bay leaf. Cover and cook in the oven for 30 minutes.
5 After 30 minutes, remove the lid and add the field mushrooms. Return to the oven and cook, uncovered, for 15–20 minutes, or until the sauce thickens slightly. Serve immediately.

NUTRITION PER SERVE
Protein 55 g; Fat 10 g; Carbohydrate 7 g;
Dietary Fibre 4 g; Cholesterol 115 mg;
1515 kJ (360 cal)

Cover the porcini mushrooms with boiling water and soak until rehydrated.

Lightly toss the chicken pieces in the flour and shake off any excess.

Add the chicken to the casserole and cook in batches until browned.

CHICKEN MOLE

Preparation time: 25 minutes
Total cooking time: 1 hour
Serves 4

8 chicken drumsticks
plain flour, for dusting
cooking oil spray
1 large onion, finely chopped
2 cloves garlic, finely chopped
1 teaspoon ground cumin
1 teaspoon chilli powder
2 teaspoons cocoa powder
440 g (14 oz) can tomatoes, roughly
    chopped
440 ml (14 fl oz) tomato purée

1 cup (250 ml/8 fl oz) chicken stock
toasted almonds, to garnish
chopped fresh parsley, to garnish

1 Remove and discard the chicken skin. Wipe the chicken with paper towels and lightly dust with flour. Spray a large, deep, non-stick pan with oil. Cook the chicken for 8 minutes over high heat, turning until golden brown. Remove and set aside.
2 Add the onion, garlic, cumin, chilli powder, cocoa, 1 teaspoon salt, 1/2 teaspoon black pepper and 1/4 cup (60 ml/2 fl oz) water to the pan and cook for 5 minutes, or until softened.
3 Stir in the tomato, tomato purée and chicken stock. Bring to the boil, then

add the chicken drumsticks, cover and simmer for 45 minutes, or until tender. Uncover and simmer for 5 minutes, until the mixture is thick. Garnish with the almonds and parsley. Delicious with kidney beans.

NUTRITION PER SERVE
Protein 25 g; Fat 7 g; Carbohydrate 10 g;
Dietary Fibre 4 g; Cholesterol 100 mg;
910 kJ (220 cal)

NOTE: This is a traditional Mexican dish, usually flavoured with a special type of dark chocolate rather than cocoa powder.

Pull the skin off the chicken drumsticks, then wipe the chicken with paper towels.

Turn the chicken until brown on all sides, then remove from the pan.

Stir in the onion, garlic, cumin, chilli powder, cocoa, salt, pepper and water.

MOROCCAN CHICKEN

Preparation time: 20 minutes +
  2 hours marinating
Total cooking time: 1 hour 25 minutes
Serves 4

8 large chicken drumsticks
3 cloves garlic, crushed
1 teaspoon grated fresh ginger
1 teaspoon ground turmeric
2 teaspoons ground cumin
1 teaspoon ground cardamom
1 teaspoon finely grated lemon rind
2 tablespoons oil
1 onion, sliced
2 cups (500 ml/16 fl oz) chicken stock

6 pitted dates, chopped
1/3 cup (20 g/3/4 oz) shredded coconut

1 Trim the chicken of excess fat and sinew. Place the chicken in a large bowl. Combine the garlic, ginger, turmeric, cumin, cardamom and rind in a small bowl. Add to the chicken and stir to completely coat. Cover and marinate for 2 hours.
2 Preheat the oven to moderate 180°C (350°F/Gas 4). Heat the oil in a large heavy-based frying pan. Cook the chicken quickly over medium heat until well browned. Drain on paper towels. Place the chicken in an ovenproof casserole dish.
3 Add the onion to the pan and cook,

stirring, for 5 minutes, or until soft. Add the cooked onion, chicken stock, dates and shredded coconut to the casserole dish. Cover and bake for 1 hour 15 minutes, or until the chicken is tender, stirring occasionally.

NUTRITION PER SERVE
Protein 47 g; Fat 18 g; Carbohydrate 9 g; Dietary Fibre 2.8 g; Cholesterol 100 mg; 1622 kJ (388 cal)

NOTE: The chicken may be left to marinate overnight in the refrigerator.

VARIATION: Dried apricots or prunes are great alteratives to dates.

Drain the chicken on paper towels, then place in an ovenproof casserole dish.

Add the combined garlic, ginger, turmeric, cumin, cardamom and lemon rind to the chicken.

Add the onion, stock, dates and coconut to the casserole dish.

CHICKEN IN RICH MUSHROOM SAUCE

Preparation time: 40 minutes
Total cooking time: 1 hour 10 minutes
Serves 4

1.4 kg (2 lb 13 oz) chicken
1 onion, sliced
2 whole cloves
8–10 peppercorns
1 teaspoon salt
90 g (3 oz) butter
500 g (1 lb) mushrooms, sliced
2 cloves garlic, crushed
2 tablespoons plain flour
1/2 cup (125 ml/4 fl oz) cream
1 tablespoon French mustard
1 cup (125 g/4 oz) grated Cheddar
1/2 cup (80 g/2³/4 oz) stale
    breadcrumbs
1/4 cup (15 g/¹/2 oz) finely chopped
    fresh parsley

1 Preheat the oven to moderate 180°C (350°F/Gas 4). Trim the chicken of excess fat and sinew. Cut the chicken into 10 portions. Place the chicken, onion, cloves, peppercorns and salt into a 2 litre ovenproof dish with 3 cups (750 ml/24 fl oz) water. Bake for 30 minutes. Remove the chicken from the dish and strain the liquid into a bowl, reserving 2 cups (500 ml/ 16 fl oz). Melt half the butter in a frying pan. Add the mushrooms and cook until soft. Add the garlic and cook for 2 minutes. Transfer the mixture to a bowl.
2 Melt the remaining butter in the pan. Add the flour and cook for 2 minutes. Gradually add the reserved liquid and stir until smooth. Bring to the boil. Remove from the heat and stir in the cream, mustard and mushrooms.

3 Return the chicken and sauce to the dish. Sprinkle with the combined Cheddar, breadcrumbs and parsley. Bake for 30 minutes.

NUTRITION PER SERVE
Protein 75 g; Fat 60 g; Carbohydrate 16 g; Dietary Fibre 4.5 g; Cholesterol 275 mg; 3727 kJ (890 cal)

Place the chicken, onion, cloves, peppercorns and salt into an ovenproof dish.

Remove the sauce from the heat and stir in the cream, mustard and mushrooms.

Sprinkle the chicken and sauce with the combined cheese, breadcrumbs and parsley.

SPICY CHICKEN AND BEANS

Preparation time: 30 minutes
Total cooking time: 45–50 minutes
Serves 4

1 tablespoon olive oil
4 spring onions, finely chopped
1 celery stick, finely chopped
1 jalapeño chilli, seeded and chopped
500 g (1 lb) chicken mince
3 cloves garlic, crushed
1/4 teaspoon ground cinnamon
1/4 teaspoon chilli powder
1 teaspoon ground cumin

2 teaspoons plain flour
425 g (14 oz) can tomatoes, chopped
1/2 cup (125 ml/4 fl oz) chicken stock
2 x 300 g (10 oz) cans butter beans, drained
2 teaspoons soft brown sugar
1/4 cup (15 g/1/2 oz) finely chopped fresh coriander

1 Heat the oil in a large frying pan, add the spring onion and cook until softened. Add the celery and chilli and cook for 1–2 minutes. Increase the heat, add the mince and brown, breaking up lumps with a fork or wooden spoon. Stir in the crushed garlic, cinnamon, chilli powder and cumin. Cook for 1 minute. Add the flour to the pan and stir well.

2 Stir in the chopped tomato and stock. Bring the mixture to the boil, reduce the heat and simmer, covered, for 10–15 minutes.

3 Add the butter beans to the pan and simmer for another 15 minutes, or until the liquid is reduced to a thick sauce. Add the sugar and season, to taste. Just before serving, scatter the coriander over the top.

NUTRITION PER SERVE
Protein 35 g; Fat 8.5 g; Carbohydrate 12 g;
Dietary Fibre 6.5 g; Cholesterol 63 mg;
1113 kJ (266 cal)

Add the mince to the pan and stir until brown, breaking up any lumps.

Add the tomato and chicken stock to the pan and bring to the boil.

Add the drained butter beans to the pan and simmer for another 15 minutes.

BASIL AND COCONUT CHICKEN

Preparation time: 30 minutes
Total cooking time: 15–20 minutes
Serves 4

1 tablespoon peanut oil
1 red onion, finely chopped
1 teaspoon finely chopped red chilli
1 teaspoon finely chopped green chilli
2 cloves garlic, crushed
1 teaspoon chopped lemon grass, white part only

1 teaspoon grated fresh ginger
500 g (1 lb) chicken mince
2 tablespoons fish sauce
1 tablespoon palm sugar or soft brown sugar
1 cup (250 g/8 oz) coconut cream
1/3 cup (20 g/3/4 oz) shredded fresh basil leaves
fresh red chilli, to garnish

1 Heat the oil in a frying pan, add the onion and cook over low heat for 2 minutes, or until soft. Add the red and green chilli, garlic, lemon grass and ginger, and cook for 1 minute.

2 Stir in the chicken mince, breaking up any large lumps of meat with a fork or wooden spoon, then add the fish sauce and sugar.

3 Pour in the coconut cream and gently cook, without boiling, for about 10 minutes. Just before serving, stir in the basil, garnish with some red chilli and serve with jasmine rice.

NUTRITION PER SERVE
Protein 30 g; Fat 20 g; Carbohydrate 4.5 g;
Dietary Fibre 2 g; Cholesterol 62 mg;
1352 kJ (323 cal)

Add the chilli, garlic, lemon grass and ginger to the softened onion.

Add the fish sauce and sugar to the pan and stir to combine.

Pour in the coconut cream and cook, without boiling, for about 10 minutes.

CHICKEN, LEEK AND WHITE WINE CASSEROLE

Preparation time: 30 minutes
Total cooking time: 1 hour
Serves 6

2 kg (4 lb) chicken thigh cutlets
1/2 cup (60 g/2 oz) plain flour,
    seasoned
2 tablespoons oil
30 g (1 oz) butter
4 slices bacon, roughly chopped
2 leeks
2 celery sticks
2 cloves garlic, crushed

2 carrots, cut into thin strips
1 bay leaf
1 1/2 cups (375 ml/12 fl oz) chicken
    stock
1 cup (250 ml/8 fl oz) good-quality
    white wine

1 Trim the chicken of excess fat and sinew. Toss the chicken cutlets lightly in seasoned flour and shake off the excess. Heat the oil and butter in a heavy-based pan. Cook the chicken pieces quickly, in batches, until well browned. Drain on paper towels. Cook the bacon for 3 minutes, or until brown. Drain on paper towels. Drain the excess fat from the frying pan,

leaving approximately 2 tablespoons.
2 Cut the leek and celery into strips. Add to the pan with the garlic. Cook, stirring, until the leek is soft.
3 Add the chicken, bacon, carrot, bay leaf, stock and wine. Bring to the boil, reduce the heat and simmer, covered, for 30 minutes. Simmer, uncovered, for 15 minutes, or until thickened slightly.

NUTRITION PER SERVE
Protein 75 g; Fat 20 g; Carbohydrate 89 g;
Dietary Fibre 6.5 g; Cholesterol 150 mg;
3595 kJ (860 cal)

HINT: A whole large chicken can be jointed and used in this recipe.

Toss the chicken cutlets lightly in the seasoned flour, and shake off the excess.

Cook the leek, celery and garlic in the pan, stirring until soft.

Add the chicken, bacon, carrot, bay leaf, stock and wine to the pan and bring to the boil.

CHICKEN PAPRIKA

Preparation time: 25 minutes
Total cooking time: 45 minutes
Serves 4–6

800 g (1 lb 10 oz) chicken thigh fillets
1/2 cup (60 g/2 oz) plain flour
2 tablespoons oil
2 onions, chopped
1–2 cloves garlic, crushed
2 tablespoons sweet paprika
1/2 cup (125 ml/4 fl oz) good-quality
    red wine
1 tablespoon tomato paste
425 g (14 oz) can tomatoes
200 g (6 1/2 oz) button mushrooms

1/2 cup (125 ml/4 fl oz) chicken stock
2/3 cup (80 g/2 3/4 oz) sour cream

1 Rinse the chicken and dry well. Trim the chicken of excess fat and sinew. Cut the chicken into 3 cm (1 1/4 inch) pieces. Season the flour with salt and pepper. Toss the chicken pieces lightly in the seasoned flour, shake off the excess and reserve the flour. Heat half the oil in a large heavy-based pan. Cook the chicken pieces quickly in small batches over medium-high heat. Remove from the pan and drain on paper towels.

2 Heat the remaining oil in the pan and add the onion and garlic. Cook, stirring, until the onion is soft. Add the paprika and reserved flour, and stir for 1 minute. Add the chicken, wine, tomato paste and undrained crushed tomatoes. Bring to the boil, then reduce the heat and simmer, covered, for 15 minutes.

3 Add the mushrooms and chicken stock. Simmer, covered, for a further 10 minutes. Add the sour cream and stir until heated through, but do not allow to boil.

NUTRITION PER SERVE
Protein 35 g; Fat 20 g; Carbohydrate 14 g; Dietary Fibre 3 g; Cholesterol 105 mg; 1668 kJ (399 cal)

Trim the chicken thigh fillets of excess fat and sinew, and cut into pieces.

Add the chicken, red wine, tomato paste and undrained crushed tomatoes.

Stir in the sour cream until heated through, but do not allow to boil.

CLAY-POT CHICKEN AND VEGETABLES

Preparation time: 20 minutes
 + 30 minutes marinating
Total cooking time: 25 minutes
Serves 4

500 g (1 lb) chicken thigh fillets
1 tablespoon soy sauce
1 tablespoon dry sherry
6 dried Chinese mushrooms
2 small leeks
250 g (8 oz) orange sweet potato
2 tablespoons peanut oil
5 cm (2 inch) piece ginger, shredded
1/2 cup (125 ml/4 fl oz) chicken stock
1 teaspoon sesame oil
3 teaspoons cornflour

1 Pat the chicken dry with paper towels. Cut into small pieces. Place in a dish with the soy sauce and sherry, cover and marinate for 30 minutes in the refrigerator.
2 Soak the mushrooms in hot water to cover for 30 minutes. Drain and squeeze to remove the excess liquid. Remove the stems and shred the caps.
3 Wash the leeks thoroughly to remove all the grit, then cut into thin slices. Cut the sweet potato into thin slices.
4 Drain the chicken, reserving the marinade. Heat half the peanut oil in a wok or heavy-based frying pan, swirling it gently to coat the base and side. Carefully add half the chicken pieces and stir-fry briefly until seared on all sides. Transfer to a flameproof clay pot or casserole. Stir-fry the remaining chicken and add to the clay pot.
5 Heat the remaining oil in a wok, add the leek and ginger and stir-fry for

1 minute. Add the mushrooms, the remaining marinade, the stock and sesame oil. Transfer to the clay pot, add the sweet potato and cook, covered, on the stove top over very low heat for about 20 minutes. Dissolve the cornflour with a little water and add to the pot. Cook, stirring, until the mixture boils and thickens. Serve the chicken and

vegetables at once with steamed brown or white rice or with noodles.

NUTRITION PER SERVE
Protein 30 g; Fat 15 g; Carbohydrate 13 g; Dietary Fibre 2.5 g; Cholesterol 60 mg; 1277 kJ (305 cal)

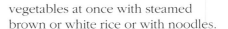

Wash the leeks to remove all the grit, then cut into thin slices.

Stir-fry the marinated chicken pieces until seared on all sides.

Add the mushrooms, marinade, stock and sesame oil to the leek mixture.

WHITE-COOKED CHICKEN WITH SPRING ONION SAUCE

Preparation time: 5 minutes
Total cooking time: 1 hour
   + 1 hour chilling
Serves 6

1.8 kg (3 lb 10 oz) chicken
3 slices fresh ginger
1½ teaspoons salt
iced water (see Hint)

SPRING ONION SAUCE
2 tablespoons oil
3 spring onions, thinly sliced
1 tablespoon soy sauce

1 Remove any pockets of fat from the chicken, then remove and discard the tail. Place the chicken in a large pan and add enough water to cover. Add the ginger and salt and bring to the boil. Cover and simmer for 20 minutes.
2 Turn off the heat, keeping the pan covered tightly. Set aside for 35 minutes. Remove the chicken carefully from the pan, draining off any of the stock that has lodged inside. Plunge the chicken into a large bowl of iced water. This process stops the chicken cooking and tightens the skin, sealing in the juices.
3 Leave the cooled chicken in the bowl of iced water and chill in the refrigerator for 1 hour. Just before serving, drain the chicken from the water and chop, Chinese-style.
4 To make the spring onion sauce, heat the oil in a wok, add the spring onion and cook briefly just to heat through. Stir in the soy sauce. Serve the chicken with the spring onion sauce poured over.

NUTRITION PER SERVE
Protein 50 g; Fat 11 g; Carbohydrate 0.5 g;
Dietary Fibre 0 g; Cholesterol 110 mg;
1265 kJ (302 cal)

HINT: Use this recipe whenever cold, boiled chicken is called for. Because the chicken never boils and is chilled very rapidly, the juices are sealed in and the result is very succulent, moist and tender. To achieve the result required, it is essential that the water into which the chicken is plunged is very well chilled. Add 2 or 3 trays of ice cubes to ensure that it is as cold as possible.

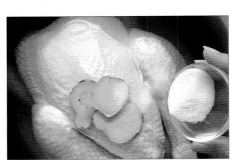

Cover the chicken with water and add the ginger slices and salt.

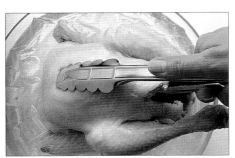

Plunge the chicken into a large bowl filled with iced water to stop the cooking process.

Just before serving, drain the chicken from the water and chop Chinese-style.

CHICKEN ADOBO

Preparation time: 20 minutes
 + 2 hours marinating
Total cooking time: 1 hour
Serves 6

1.5 kg (3 lb) chicken pieces
6 cloves garlic, crushed
1 cup (250 ml/8 fl oz) cider
 vinegar
1¹/₂ cups (375 ml/12 fl oz) chicken
 stock
1 bay leaf
1 teaspoon coriander seeds
1 teaspoon black peppercorns
¹/₄ cup (60 ml/2 fl oz) soy sauce

1 teaspoon annatto seeds or
 ¹/₄ teaspoon paprika and
 ¹/₈ teaspoon turmeric
2 tablespoons oil

1 Combine all the ingredients, except the oil, in a large bowl. Cover and refrigerate for 2 hours.
2 Transfer the mixture to a large heavy-based pan and bring to the boil over high heat. Reduce the heat and simmer, covered, for 30 minutes. Uncover the pan and continue cooking for 10 minutes, or until the chicken is tender. Remove the chicken from the pan and set aside. Bring the liquid back to the boil and cook over high heat for 10 minutes,

or until reduced by half.
3 Heat the oil in a wok or large non-stick frying pan and add the chicken in batches, cooking over medium heat for 5 minutes, or until crisp and golden. Serve the reduced sauce mixture over the chicken pieces and accompany with rice.

NUTRITION PER SERVE
Protein 38 g; Fat 10 g; Carbohydrate 0.5 g; Dietary Fibre 0.5 g; Cholesterol 83 mg; 1070 kJ (256 cal)

NOTE: Annatto seeds are available at speciality stores.

Mix the chicken with the marinade and refrigerate, covered, for 2 hours.

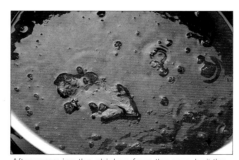

After removing the chicken from the pan, boil the liquid until it has reduced by half.

Cook the chicken pieces, in batches, until they are crisp and golden.

COUNTRY-STYLE CHICKEN WITH BABY VEGETABLES

Preparation time: 45 minutes
Total cooking time: 2 hours
Serves 4

1.5 kg (3 lb) chicken pieces (about
   8 portions)
60 g (2 oz) clarified butter
12 baby pickling onions
1 cup (250 ml/8 fl oz) dry white wine
1 cup (250 ml/8 fl oz) chicken stock
1 cup (250 ml/8 fl oz) cream
12 baby carrots
16 snow peas
16 asparagus spears
12 button mushrooms
1 tablespoon chopped fresh
   chives

1 Season the chicken portions with a little salt and pepper. Heat half the butter in a frying pan, then brown the chicken in batches for 2–3 minutes on each side to seal the flavours. Place in a casserole dish and add the onions. Preheat the oven to moderately hot 200°C (400°F/Gas 6).

2 Pour the wine into the frying pan and stir over medium heat, scraping down the side and base of the pan. Add the stock and whisk in the cream. Bring to the boil, then reduce the heat and simmer for 20 minutes. Pour the sauce over the chicken. Cover and bake for 1 hour 10 minutes.

3 Meanwhile, bring a pan of salted water to the boil. In separate batches, boil or steam the carrots, snow peas and asparagus until just cooked, but still slightly crunchy. Plunge in iced water, then drain and set aside.

4 Heat the remaining butter in a frying pan. Sauté the mushrooms for 2–3 minutes, stirring constantly.

5 Place the mushrooms on top of the stew with the blanched vegetables and cook for another 20 minutes, or until the chicken is tender. Skim off any fat, stir carefully to mix all the vegetables through and sprinkle with the chives to serve.

NUTRITION PER SERVE
Protein 95 g; Fat 50 g; Carbohydrate 15 g;
Dietary Fibre 4 g; Cholesterol 350 mg;
4040 kJ (965 cal)

Lightly brown the seasoned chicken in half the melted butter.

Plunge the blanched vegetables into a bowl of iced water to stop them cooking.

Place the drained blanched vegetables on top of the stew and cook for 20 minutes.

225

CREAMY TOMATO AND CHICKEN STEW

Preparation time: 35 minutes
Total cooking time: 50 minutes
Serves 4–6

4 slices bacon
2 tablespoons oil
50 g (1¾ oz) butter
300 g (10 oz) small button
  mushrooms, halved
1.5 kg (3 lb) chicken pieces
2 onions, chopped
2 cloves garlic, crushed
400 g (13 oz) can tomatoes
1 cup (250 ml/8 fl oz) chicken stock
1 cup (250 ml/8 fl oz) cream
2 tablespoons chopped fresh parsley
2 tablespoons fresh lemon thyme
  leaves

1 Chop the bacon into large pieces. Place a large, heavy-based pan over medium heat. Brown the bacon, then remove and set aside on paper towels.
2 Heat half the oil and a third of the butter in the pan until foaming, then stir in the mushrooms and cook until softened and golden brown. Remove from the pan with a slotted spoon.
3 Add the remaining oil to the pan with a little more butter. When the oil is hot, brown the chicken pieces in batches over high heat until the skin is golden all over and a little crisp. Remove from the pan.
4 Heat the remaining butter in the pan. Add the onion and garlic and cook over medium-high heat for about 3 minutes, or until softened. Pour in the tomatoes, stock and cream. Return the bacon, mushrooms and chicken pieces to the pan and simmer over medium-low heat for 25 minutes. Stir in the herbs, season with salt and freshly ground pepper and simmer for another 5 minutes before serving.

NUTRITION PER SERVE (6)
Protein 70 g; Fat 40 g; Carbohydrate 7 g; Dietary Fibre 3 g; Cholesterol 215 mg; 2650 kJ (630 cal)

When the oil and butter are foaming, add the mushrooms and cook until soft.

Brown the chicken pieces in batches over high heat until the skin is golden and crisp.

Add the tomatoes, stock and cream to the softened onion and garlic.

BRAISED CHICKEN WITH CHICKPEAS

Preparation time: 35 minutes
Total cooking time: 1 hour 35 minutes
Serves 4

50 g (1³/₄ oz) butter
1 onion, roughly chopped
3 cloves garlic, crushed
1 carrot, finely chopped
¹/₂ celery stick, finely chopped
1.5 kg (3 lb) chicken pieces
  (about 8 portions)
¹/₃ cup (80 ml/2³/₄ fl oz) Marsala
1 cup (250 ml/8 fl oz) chicken stock
2 tablespoons lemon juice
¹/₂ cup (40 g/1¹/₄ oz) fresh
  breadcrumbs

300 g (10 oz) can chickpeas, rinsed
  and drained
200 g (6¹/₂ oz) button mushrooms,
  sliced
2 tablespoons shredded fresh mint
2 tablespoons chopped fresh parsley

1 Heat half the butter in a large, heavy-based pan and cook the onion over medium heat until soft and golden. Add the garlic, carrot and celery and cook over gentle heat for 5 minutes. Remove from the pan and set aside.
2 Melt the remaining butter in the pan and brown the chicken in batches over high heat. Return all the chicken to the pan with the carrot and celery mixture. Quickly add the Marsala and stir well, scraping the sides and base of the pan.

Add the stock and lemon juice, and bring to the boil. Reduce the heat and simmer gently for 1 hour, stirring occasionally.
3 Remove the chicken; keep warm. In a food processor, purée the contents of the pan, then add the breadcrumbs and blend for another 15 seconds.
4 Return the chicken to the pan, pour in the purée, add the chickpeas and mushrooms and simmer, covered, for 15 minutes. Season to taste, and scatter with mint and parsley to serve.

NUTRITION PER SERVE
Protein 120 g; Fat 30 g; Carbohydrate 50 g;
Dietary Fibre 15 g; Cholesterol 260 mg;
3900 kJ (930 cal)

Gently fry the garlic, carrot and celery in the butter for 5 minutes.

Pour the Marsala over the vegetables and chicken, stirring well.

Add the fresh breadcrumbs to the puréed vegetable mixture and process until smooth.

COQ AU VIN

Preparation time: 20 minutes
Total cooking time: 1 hour
Serves 6

2 fresh thyme sprigs
4 fresh parsley sprigs
2 bay leaves
2 kg (4 lb) chicken pieces
plain flour, seasoned with salt and
    freshly ground pepper
1/4 cup (60 ml/2 fl oz) oil
4 thick bacon rashers, sliced
12 pickling onions
2 cloves garlic, crushed
2 tablespoons brandy
11/2 cups (375 ml/12 fl oz) red wine

11/2 cups (375 ml/12 fl oz) chicken
    stock
1/4 cup (60 g/2 oz) tomato paste
250 g (8 oz) button mushrooms
fresh herbs, for sprinkling

1 To make the bouquet garni, wrap the thyme, parsley and bay leaves in a small square of muslin and tie well with string, or tie them between two 5 cm (2 inch) lengths of celery.
2 Toss the chicken in flour to coat, shaking off any excess. In a heavy-based pan, heat 2 tablespoons of oil and brown the chicken in batches over medium heat. Drain on paper towels.
3 Wipe the pan clean with paper towels and heat the remaining oil. Add the bacon, onions and garlic and cook,

stirring, until the onions are browned. Add the chicken, brandy, wine, stock, bouquet garni and tomato paste. Bring to the boil, reduce the heat and simmer, covered, for 30 minutes.
4 Stir in the mushrooms and simmer, uncovered, for 10 minutes, or until the chicken is tender and the sauce has thickened. Remove the bouquet garni, sprinkle with fresh herbs and serve with crusty French bread.

NUTRITION PER SERVE
Protein 80 g; Fat 20 g; Carbohydrate 7 g;
Dietary Fibre 2 g; Cholesterol 180 mg;
2420 kJ (580 cal)

Wrap the thyme, parsley and bay leaves in a small square of muslin.

In batches, brown the chicken in the hot oil over medium heat.

Return the chicken to the pan with the liquids, bouquet garni and tomato paste.

MAJORCAN CHICKEN

Preparation time: 30 minutes
Total cooking time: 1 hour 30 minutes
Serves 4

2 tablespoons olive oil
30 g (1 oz) butter
1.5 kg (3 lb) chicken pieces
1 orange
1 red onion, thinly sliced
2 cloves garlic, chopped
3/4 cup (185 ml/6 fl oz) chicken stock
1/2 cup (125 ml/4 fl oz) white wine
1 tablespoon plain flour
1 red capsicum, quartered
12 stuffed green olives
1/4 cup (15 g/1/2 oz) chopped fresh
    parsley

1 Preheat the oven to moderate 180°C (350°F/Gas 4). Heat the oil and butter in a large pan. Brown the chicken in batches over high heat and transfer to a flameproof casserole dish.

2 Cut two large strips of rind from the orange and set aside. Remove the pith from the orange, then slice the orange into thin rounds. Set aside.

3 Cook the onion and garlic in the pan for 3 minutes over medium heat, or until softened. Combine the stock and wine. Stir the flour into the pan, then slowly add the stock and wine and stir until the mixture comes to the boil. Add the orange rind strips, then pour over the chicken. Cover and bake for 1 hour.

4 Meanwhile, grill the capsicum, skin-side up, for 8 minutes, or until black and blistered. Place in a plastic bag, seal and allow to cool. Peel away the skin and cut the flesh into strips.

5 Remove the chicken from the dish; cover and keep warm. Bring the sauce to the boil on the stove top, skimming off the fat. Boil for 5 minutes to thicken slightly. Add the capsicum strips, orange slices, olives and parsley. To serve, remove the orange rind, season to taste and spoon the sauce over the chicken.

NUTRITION PER SERVE
Protein 90 g; Fat 25 g; Carbohydrate 10 g;
Dietary Fibre 4 g; Cholesterol 205 mg;
2700 kJ (645 cal)

Peel two strips of orange rind. Remove the pith and slice the orange into rounds.

Combine the chicken stock and wine and add to the softened onion mixture.

Grill the capsicum, skin-side up, until the skin is black and blistered.

Stir the capsicum strips, orange slices, olives and parsley into the sauce.

Curries

GREEN CHICKEN CURRY

Preparation time: 20 minutes
Total cooking time: 25 minutes
Serves 4

1 tablespoon oil
1 onion, chopped
1–2 tablespoons green curry paste
1¹/₂ cups (375 ml/12 fl oz) coconut milk
500 g (1 lb) chicken thigh fillets, cut into bite-sized pieces
100 g (3¹/₂ oz) green beans, cut into short pieces
6 kaffir lime leaves
1 tablespoon fish sauce
1 tablespoon lime juice
1 teaspoon finely grated lime rind
2 teaspoons soft brown sugar
¹/₄ cup (7 g/¹/₄ oz) fresh coriander leaves

1 Heat the oil in a wok or a heavy-based pan. Add the onion and curry paste to the wok and cook for about 1 minute, stirring constantly. Add the coconut milk and ¹/₂ cup (125 ml/4 fl oz) water and bring to the boil.
2 Add the chicken pieces, beans and kaffir lime leaves to the wok, and stir to combine. Simmer, uncovered, for 15–20 minutes, or until the chicken is tender. Add the fish sauce, lime juice, lime rind and brown sugar to the wok, and stir to combine. Sprinkle with fresh coriander leaves just before serving. Serve with steamed rice.

NUTRITION PER SERVE
Protein 32 g; Fat 28 g; Carbohydrate 8 g; Dietary Fibre 3 g; Cholesterol 63 mg; 1702 kJ (407 cal)

NOTE: Chicken thigh fillets are sweet in flavour and a very good texture for curries. You can use breast fillets instead, if you prefer. Do not overcook fillets or they will be tough.

Add the coconut milk and water to the wok and stir with a wooden spoon.

After simmering, stir in the fish sauce, lime juice, lime rind and brown sugar.

CHICKEN AND PEANUT PANANG CURRY

Preparation time: 25 minutes
Total cooking time: 30–40 minutes
Serves 4

1 tablespoon oil
1 large red onion, chopped
1–2 tablespoons Panang curry paste
1 cup (250 ml/4 fl oz) coconut milk
500 g (1 lb) chicken thigh fillets, cut
   into bite-sized pieces
4 kaffir lime leaves
1/4 cup (60 g/2 oz) coconut cream
1 tablespoon fish sauce
1 tablespoon lime juice

2 teaspoons soft brown sugar
1/2 cup (80 g/2 3/4 oz) roasted peanuts,
   chopped
1/2 cup (15 g/1/2 oz) Thai basil leaves
1/2 cup (80 g/2 3/4 oz) chopped fresh
   pineapple
1 Lebanese cucumber, sliced
chilli sauce, to serve

1 Heat the oil in a wok or large frying pan. Add the onion and curry paste to the wok and stir over medium heat for 2 minutes. Add the coconut milk and bring to the boil.

2 Add the chicken and kaffir lime leaves to the wok, then reduce the heat and cook for 15 minutes. Remove the chicken with a wire mesh strainer

or slotted spoon. Simmer the sauce for 5 minutes, or until it is reduced and quite thick.

3 Return the chicken to the wok. Add the coconut cream, fish sauce, lime juice and brown sugar. Cook for 5 minutes. Stir in the peanuts, basil and pineapple. Serve with the sliced cucumber on the side, some chilli sauce, as well as steamed rice.

NUTRITION PER SERVE
Protein 40 g; Fat 40 g; Carbohydrate 16 g;
Dietary Fibre 5 g; Cholesterol 63 mg;
2466 kJ (590 cal)

Add the red onion and curry paste to the hot oil and stir with a wooden spoon.

Remove the cooked chicken from the wok and set it aside while cooking the sauce.

Stir in the chopped peanuts, basil and pineapple just before serving.

VIETNAMESE CHICKEN CURRY

Preparation time: 30 minutes
Total cooking time: 1 hour
Serves 4

1.5 kg (3 lb) chicken pieces, such as thighs, drumsticks and wings
2 tablespoons oil
4 cloves garlic, finely chopped
5 cm (2 inch) piece ginger, finely chopped
2 stems lemon grass, white part only, finely chopped
2 teaspoons dried chilli flakes
2 tablespoons curry powder
2 brown onions, chopped
2 teaspoons sugar
1 teaspoon salt

1¹/₂ cups (375 ml/12 fl oz) coconut milk
fresh garlic chives, cut into long strips, to serve
fresh coriander leaves, to serve
roasted peanuts, to serve

1 Using a large heavy knife or cleaver, chop each piece of chicken into two, chopping straight through the bone. Pat the chicken pieces dry with paper towels.

2 Heat the oil in a large deep frying pan. Add the garlic, ginger, lemon grass, chilli and curry powder and stir constantly over medium heat for 3 minutes. Add the chicken pieces, onion, sugar and salt; toss gently. Cover, cook for 8 minutes, or until the onion has softened and then toss well to coat the chicken evenly with the

curry mixture. Cover again and cook for 15 minutes over low heat—the chicken will gently braise, producing its own liquid.

3 Add the coconut milk and water to the pan. Bring to the boil, stirring occasionally. Reduce the heat and simmer, uncovered, for 30 minutes, or until the chicken is very tender. Serve garnished with the chives, coriander and peanuts.

NUTRITION PER SERVE
Protein 60 g; Fat 26 g; Carbohydrate 11 g; Dietary Fibre 6 g; Cholesterol 125 mg; 2189 kJ (523 cal)

NOTE: Asian curry powders are available from speciality shops. There are different mixtures available for meat, chicken or fish.

Chop each piece of chicken into two pieces, or ask your butcher to do it.

Toss the chicken pieces through the curry mixture, using two wooden spoons.

Add the coconut milk and water to the curry and stir well.

CHICKEN DUMPLINGS IN GREEN CURRY

Preparation time: 25 minutes
  + 2–3 hours refrigeration
Total cooking time: 35 minutes
Serves 3–4

500 g (1 lb) chicken mince
3 spring onions, finely chopped
2 tablespoons small fresh coriander
  leaves
1 stem lemon grass, white part only,
  thinly sliced
1/4 cup (60 ml/2 fl oz) fish sauce
1 teaspoon chicken stock powder
11/2 cups (280 g/9 oz) cooked jasmine
  rice

1 egg, plus 1 egg white
2 teaspoons oil
2 tablespoons green curry paste
2 x 400 ml (13 fl oz) cans coconut milk
4 fresh kaffir lime leaves
1/2 cup (15 g/1/2 oz) fresh basil leaves
1 tablespoon lemon juice

1 Mix together the chicken mince, spring onion, coriander leaves, lemon grass, 2 tablespoons of the fish sauce, stock powder and some pepper. Add the rice and mix well with your hands.
2 In a separate bowl, beat the egg and egg white with electric beaters until thick and creamy and then fold into the chicken mixture. With lightly floured hands, roll tablespoons of the mixture into balls. Place on a tray,

cover and refrigerate for 2–3 hours, or until firm.
3 Heat the oil in a large frying pan, add the green curry paste and stir over medium heat for 1 minute. Gradually stir in the coconut milk, then reduce the heat to simmer. Add the lime leaves and chicken dumplings to the sauce; cover and simmer for 25–30 minutes, stirring occasionally. Stir in the basil leaves, remaining fish sauce and lemon juice. Serve with steamed rice.

NUTRITION PER SERVE (4)
Protein 37 g; Fat 46 g; Carbohydrate 30 g; Dietary Fibre 4.5 g; Cholesterol 110 mg; 2815 kJ (672 cal)

Beat the egg and egg white with electric beaters until thick and creamy.

Flour your hands and roll tablespoons of the mixture into balls.

When the sauce is simmering, add the lime leaves and chicken dumplings.

CHICKEN WITH CREAMY CURRY SAUCE

Preparation time: 25 minutes
Total cooking time: 40 minutes
Serves 4

1 tablespoon oil
50 g (1³/4 oz) butter
1 onion, chopped
2 cloves garlic, crushed
2 teaspoons grated fresh ginger
1 green chilli, seeded and finely
  chopped
1/4 teaspoon crushed cardamom
  seeds
1 teaspoon garam masala
1 teaspoon ground turmeric

1 tablespoon plain flour
1¹/2 cups (375 ml/12 fl oz) chicken
  stock
1/3 cup (80 ml/2³/4 fl oz) brandy
1/2 cup (125 ml/4 fl oz) cream
4 large chicken breast fillets, each cut
  into thirds and flattened with a
  meat mallet
flaked toasted almonds, to serve
chopped fresh coriander, to serve

1 Heat the oil and half the butter in a large, deep frying pan. Add the onion and cook over medium heat until soft and transparent. Add the garlic, ginger and chilli and cook for 1 minute. Add the cardamom, garam masala and turmeric and cook for 1 minute. Stir in the flour and cook for 1 minute.

2 Remove from the heat. Gradually mix in the combined chicken stock, brandy and cream, stirring constantly. Return to the heat. Cook, stirring, until the sauce boils and thickens. Cover and simmer over low heat for 15 minutes.

3 Meanwhile, heat the remaining butter in a frying pan and brown the chicken pieces. Add the chicken to the sauce and cook for a further 10–15 minutes to reduce. Season with salt and black pepper. Serve scattered with toasted almonds and coriander.

NUTRITION PER SERVE
Protein 40 g; Fat 35 g; Carbohydrate 5 g;
Dietary Fibre 2 g; Cholesterol 155 mg;
2295 kJ (545 cal)

Seed and finely chop the green chilli with a sharp knife.

Cook the onion over medium heat until it turns soft and transparent.

Gradually add the combined stock, brandy and cream, stirring constantly.

BUTTER CHICKEN

Preparation time: 30 minutes
  + 4 hours marinating
Total cooking time: 20 minutes
Serves 4

1 kg (2 lb) chicken thigh fillets
1 teaspoon salt
1/4 cup (60 ml/2 fl oz) lemon juice
1 cup (250 g/8 oz) yoghurt
1 onion, chopped
2 cloves garlic, crushed
3 cm (1 1/4 inch) piece ginger, grated
1 green chilli, chopped
3 teaspoons garam masala
2 teaspoons yellow food colouring
1 teaspoon red food colouring
1/2 cup (125 ml/4 fl oz) tomato purée
2 cm (3/4 inch) piece ginger, extra,
   finely grated
1 cup (250 ml/8 fl oz) cream
2 teaspoons sugar
1/4 teaspoon chilli powder
1 tablespoon lemon juice, extra
1 teaspoon ground cumin
100 g (3 1/2 oz) butter

1 Cut the chicken into 2 cm (3/4 inch) thick strips. Sprinkle with the salt and lemon juice.
2 Place the yoghurt, onion, garlic, ginger, chilli and 2 teaspoons of the garam masala in a food processor and blend until smooth.
3 Combine the food colourings in a small bowl. Brush over the chicken and turn the strips to coat the meat all over. Add the yoghurt mixture and toss to combine. Cover and refrigerate for 4 hours. Remove the chicken from the marinade and allow to drain for 5 minutes.
4 Preheat the oven to hot 220°C (425°F/Gas 7). Place the chicken in a shallow baking dish and bake for 15 minutes, or until it is tender. Drain off any excess juice, cover loosely with foil and keep warm.
5 Mix together the tomato purée and 1/2 cup (125 ml/4 fl oz) water in a large jug. Add the ginger, cream, remaining garam marsala, sugar, chilli powder, lemon juice and cumin, and stir to thoroughly combine.
6 Melt the butter in a large pan over medium heat. Stir in the tomato mixture and bring to the boil. Cook for 2 minutes, then reduce the heat and add the chicken pieces. Stir to coat the chicken with the sauce and simmer for a further 2 minutes, or until completely heated through. Serve with rice and garnish with some shredded kaffir lime leaves.

NUTRITION PER SERVE
Protein 55 g; Fat 60 g; Carbohydrate 10 g; Dietary Fibre 2 g; Cholesterol 330 mg; 3390 kJ (805 cal)

NOTE: The chicken can also be marinated overnight in the refrigerator. It is important to always use a non-metallic dish when marinating.

HINT: Kaffir lime leaves are available from most supermarkets, Asian food stores and good fruit and vegetable shops.

VARIATION: Chicken pieces can be substituted for the chicken thigh fillets. Score the thickest part of the meat with a knife and then bake for 30–40 minutes, or until tender.

Sprinkle the salt and lemon juice over the strips of chicken.

Process the yoghurt, onion, garlic, ginger, chilli and garam masala.

Brush the food colourings over the chicken, coating the meat thoroughly.

Drain any excess juice from the baked chicken pieces in the baking dish.

Add the ginger, cream, garam masala, sugar, chilli, lemon juice and cumin.

Add the chicken pieces to the pan and stir to coat with the sauce.

CHICKEN AND LIME CURRY

Preparation time: 30 minutes
Total cooking time: 45 minutes
Serves 4

SPICE PASTE
1 large onion, roughly chopped
6 red chillies, seeded and finely
    chopped
4 cloves garlic, crushed
1 teaspoon finely chopped lemon
    grass, white part only
2 teaspoons finely chopped fresh
    galangal
1 teaspoon ground turmeric

1.6 kg (3¼ lb) chicken
¼ cup (60 ml/2 fl oz) oil
1 cup (250 ml/8 fl oz) coconut milk
2 limes, halved
5 kaffir lime leaves, finely shredded
1 tablespoon fish sauce
2 tablespoons fresh coriander leaves
2 limes, quartered, to serve

1 To make the spice paste, finely chop the onion, chilli, garlic, lemon grass, galangal and turmeric in a food processor for a few minutes, or until the mixture is a rough, thick paste.
2 Cut the chicken through the bone into large bite-sized pieces. Heat the oil in a large heavy-based pan or wok and add the spice paste. Cook over low heat, stirring occasionally, for 10 minutes, or until fragrant.
3 Add the chicken and stir-fry for 2 minutes, making sure the pieces are well covered with the spice paste. Add the coconut milk, ½ cup (125 ml/4 fl oz) water, lime halves and shredded kaffir lime leaves. Simmer the mixture for 20–25 minutes, or until the chicken is tender, stirring regularly.
4 Discard the limes. Add the fish sauce, scatter with the coriander leaves and serve with the lime wedges and steamed rice.

NUTRITION PER SERVE
Protein 60 g; Fat 40 g; Carbohydrate 5 g;
Dietary Fibre 3 g; Cholesterol 195 mg;
2590 kJ (615 cal)

Finely shred the kaffir lime leaves with a sharp kitchen knife.

Process the ingredients for the spice paste to a rough, thick consistency.

Add the coconut milk, water, lime halves and shredded lime leaves to the pan.

Season the curry with 1 tablespoon of fish sauce before serving.

SPICED LIVER CURRY

Preparation time: 25 minutes
+ 2 hours marinating
Total cooking time: 20 minutes
Serves 4

1/4 cup (60 ml/2 fl oz) dark soy sauce
3 cloves garlic, crushed
1 tablespoon sesame seeds, toasted
1 teaspoon sesame oil
500 g (1 lb) chicken livers, trimmed
    and sliced
2 tablespoons olive oil
1 onion, sliced
1 red capsicum, sliced
1 teaspoon ground coriander
1 teaspoon ground cumin
2 tablespoons peanut oil
1/2 cup (125 ml/4 fl oz) chicken stock
100 g (31/2 oz) snow peas, trimmed

1 Combine the soy sauce, garlic, sesame seeds and sesame oil with 2 tablespoons water. Place the liver in a dish and pour over the marinade. Cover and refrigerate for 2 hours.
2 Heat half the olive oil in a large, heavy-based pan and cook the onion and capsicum over medium-low heat for 5–10 minutes, or until softened. Remove from the pan and set aside.
3 Sprinkle the liver with coriander and cumin and season well with freshly ground black pepper. Remove from the dish, reserving the marinade.
4 Heat the remaining olive oil and the peanut oil in a pan and add the liver. Cook over high heat, turning often, for about 3–5 minutes, or until firm but still slightly pink inside. Return the onion, capsicum and reserved marinade to the pan. Add the stock and snow peas, and simmer gently for 2–3 minutes. Serve immediately, with rice if desired. Garnish with toasted sesame seeds.

NUTRITION PER SERVE
Protein 35 g; Fat 35 g; Carbohydrate 5 g;
Dietary Fibre 2 g; Cholesterol 705 mg;
2042 kJ (485 cal)

Trim and slice the chicken livers, making sure to remove any membrane.

Mix together the marinade ingredients and then pour over the liver to coat.

Sprinkle the coriander and cumin over the liver and season well.

Add the chicken stock and snow peas, then simmer gently for 2–3 minutes.

SAFFRON CHICKEN

Preparation time: 25 minutes
Total cooking time: 1 hour 20 minutes
Serves 6

1 teaspoon saffron threads
2 tablespoons hot water
2 tablespoons oil
2 onions, chopped
3 cloves garlic, crushed
3 cm (1¼ inch) piece ginger, chopped
2 red chillies, seeded and sliced
1 teaspoon ground cardamom
1 teaspoon ground cumin
½ teaspoon ground turmeric
2 kg (4 lb) chicken pieces
2 cups (500 ml/16 fl oz) chicken stock

1 Fry the saffron threads in a dry frying pan over low heat for 1–2 minutes. Transfer to a small bowl, add the hot water and set aside.
2 Heat the oil in a pan over medium heat. Add the onion, garlic, ginger and chilli. Cover and cook for 10 minutes, or until very soft.
3 Add the cardamom, cumin and turmeric, and cook over medium heat for 2 minutes. Add the chicken pieces and cook over high heat for 3 minutes, or until the meat is well coated. Add the saffron liquid and the chicken stock. Bring to the boil, then reduce the heat and cook, covered, stirring occasionally, for 30 minutes.
4 Uncover, and cook for a further 20 minutes. Remove the chicken and keep warm. Reduce the stock to about 1½ cups (375 ml/12 fl oz) over very high heat. Pour over the chicken. Season with salt and pepper, to taste.

NUTRITION PER SERVE
Protein 45 g; Fat 15 g; Carbohydrate 3 g;
Dietary Fibre 1 g; Cholesterol 155 mg;
1445 kJ (345 cal)

Fry the saffron threads in a dry pan over low heat for 1–2 minutes.

Add the chopped onion, garlic, ginger and chilli and stir to combine.

Add the saffron threads with their liquid, and the stock to the pan.

Remove the chicken from the pan and reduce the stock over high heat.

LEMON CHILLI CHICKEN

Preparation time: 20 minutes
Total cooking time: 35 minutes
Serves 4

2 garlic cloves, chopped
1 tablespoon grated fresh ginger
2 tablespoons olive oil
600 g (1¼ lb) chicken thigh fillets
1 teaspoon ground coriander
2 teaspoons ground cumin
½ teaspoon ground turmeric
1 red chilli, chopped
½ cup (125 ml/4 fl oz) lemon juice

¾ cup (185 ml/6 fl oz) white wine
1 cup (30 g/1 oz) fresh coriander
  leaves

1 Blend the garlic, ginger and
1 tablespoon water into a paste in a
small food processor or mortar and
pestle. Heat the olive oil in a heavy-
based pan and brown the chicken in
batches. Remove with a slotted spoon
and set aside.

2 Add the garlic paste to the pan and
cook, stirring, for 1 minute. Add the
coriander, cumin, turmeric and chilli
and stir-fry for 1 minute more. Stir in
the lemon juice and wine.

3 Add the chicken pieces to the pan
and stir to combine. Bring to the boil,
then reduce the heat, cover and cook,
stirring, for about 20–25 minutes, or
until the chicken is tender. Remove the
lid and cook the sauce over high heat
for 5 minutes to reduce it by half. Stir
in the coriander and season with salt
and pepper to taste. Serve on a bed of
steamed jasmine rice.

NUTRITION PER SERVE
Protein 30 g; Fat 15 g; Carbohydrate 0 g;
Dietary Fibre 0 g; Cholesterol 105 mg;
1290 kJ (310 cal)

Brown the chicken in batches to stop the meat
from stewing.

Add the coriander, cumin, turmeric and chilli and
stir-fry for 1 minute.

Once the sauce has reduced, stir in the fresh
coriander leaves.

241

CHICKEN WITH CITRUS LEAVES

Preparation time: 30 minutes
Total cooking time: 45 minutes
Serves 4–6

1 cup (250 ml/8 fl oz) chicken stock
2 teaspoons tamarind concentrate
4 red chillies, seeded
80 g (2¾ oz) fresh galangal, roughly chopped
2 stems lemon grass, white part only, roughly chopped
5 spring onions, chopped
5 cloves garlic, roughly chopped
2 teaspoons ground turmeric

¼ cup (60 ml/2 fl oz) peanut oil
1.5–2 kg (3–4 lb) chicken pieces
410 ml (13 fl oz) coconut milk
5 citrus leaves (kaffir lime or lemon)

1 Heat half the stock in a pan. Remove from the heat and add the tamarind concentrate. Set aside, and allow the tamarind to dissolve.
2 Place the chillies, galangal, lemon grass, spring onion, garlic, turmeric and remaining stock in a food processor and combine well. Heat the peanut oil in a large pan. Add the chilli mixture and fry over low heat for 2 minutes, stirring constantly so the mixture does not stick to the bottom of the pan.

3 Add the chicken to the chilli paste, tossing to coat well. Cook for a further 3–4 minutes, or until the chicken is lightly browned. Stir in the tamarind liquid. Bring to the boil and add the coconut milk and citrus leaves. Reduce the heat and simmer for about 30 minutes, or until the chicken is tender. Remove the chicken and simmer the sauce until thickened. Serve the chicken and sauce with steamed rice.

NUTRITION PER SERVE (6)
Protein 65 g; Fat 50 g; Carbohydrate 5 g;
Dietary Fibre 5 g; Cholesterol 205 mg;
3000 kJ (715 cal)

Peel and roughly chop the fresh galangal with a sharp knife.

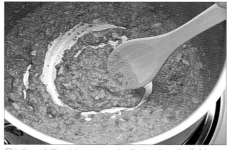

Stir the chilli mixture constantly to stop it sticking to the bottom of the pan.

Add the coconut milk and citrus leaves to the pan and simmer until the chicken is tender.

CHICKEN AND APPLE CURRY

Preparation time: 20 minutes
Total cooking time: 1 hour 5 minutes
Serves 4–6

1 kg (2 lb) chicken wings
1/4 cup (60 ml/2 fl oz) oil
1 large onion, sliced
1 tablespoon curry powder
1 large carrot, chopped
1 celery stick, sliced
400 ml (13 fl oz) can
   coconut cream
1 cup (250 ml/8 fl oz) chicken stock
2 green apples, chopped
1 tablespoon finely chopped fresh
   coriander
1/4 cup (30 g/1 oz) sultanas
1/2 cup (80 g/2³/4 oz)
   roasted peanuts

1 Pat the chicken wings dry with paper towels. Tuck the wing tips to the underside.
2 Heat 2 tablespoons of the oil in a large heavy-based pan and add the chicken in small batches. Cook quickly over medium heat for 5 minutes, or until well browned on both sides. Drain on paper towels.
3 Heat the remaining oil in the pan. Add the onion and curry powder and cook, stirring, over medium heat for 3 minutes, or until soft.
4 Return the chicken to the pan. Add the carrot, celery, coconut cream and stock, and bring to the boil. Reduce the heat and simmer. Cook, covered, for 30 minutes. Add the apple, coriander and sultanas, and cook for a further 20 minutes, or until the chicken is tender, stirring occasionally. Serve sprinkled with the peanuts.

NUTRITION PER SERVE (6)
Protein 27 g; Fat 37 g; Carbohydrate 20 g;
Dietary Fibre 5 g; Cholesterol 42 mg;
2133 kJ (510 cal)

VARIATIONS: Pear may be used instead of apple in this recipe. Curry paste may be used instead of curry powder.

Pat the chicken wings dry, then tuck the tips of the wings to the underside.

Cook the chicken in small batches over medium heat until well browned.

Cook the onion and curry powder, stirring, for 3 minutes, or until soft.

CHICKEN AND SPINACH CURRY

Preparation time: 25 minutes
Total cooking time: 1 hour 45 minutes
Serves 4

2 tablespoons ghee
1 kg chicken drumsticks and thighs
1 tablespoon hot curry powder
1 tablespoon curry paste
1/2 teaspoon black mustard seeds
1/2 teaspoon ground coriander
1 teaspoon paprika
1/4 teaspoon cinnamon
1/2 teaspoon cumin
1/2 teaspoon turmeric
1 tablespoon finely chopped coriander root
2 cloves garlic, crushed
2 cm piece fresh ginger, grated
1 onion, chopped
1 kg potatoes, quartered
1 1/2 cups (375 ml/12 fl oz) chicken stock
1 tablespoon lemon juice
2 x 425 g (14 oz) cans peeled whole tomatoes
250 g (8 oz) packet frozen spinach, defrosted
1/4 cup (60 ml/2 fl oz) coconut cream
shredded fresh coriander leaves, to garnish

1 Melt 1 tablespoon of ghee in a heavy-based pan, and cook the chicken in batches for 2–3 minutes, or until browned all over. Remove. Melt the remaining ghee in the pan, add the curry powder, paste and remaining dry spices, and cook over low heat for 1–2 minutes, or until fragrant. Increase the heat, add the coriander root, garlic, ginger and onion, and cook for 3–5 minutes, or until the onion is soft.

2 Return the chicken pieces to the pan, add the potato and gently toss in the spices to coat. Season generously with salt and pepper. Pour in the chicken stock, and stir to ensure that any spices on the bottom of the pan are incorporated. Add the lemon juice and tomatoes, bring the mixture to the boil, then reduce the heat and simmer for 1–1 1/2 hours, or until the potato is tender and the chicken meat is falling off the bones.

3 Carefully remove the chicken from the pan, let it cool slightly and pull the meat off the bones. Return to the pan. Stir in the spinach and coconut cream and cook for 3–5 minutes, or until heated through. Garnish with the coriander leaves and serve with rice.

NUTRITION PER SERVE
Protein 36 g; Fat 20 g; Carbohydrate 45 g; Dietary Fibre 12 g; Cholesterol 130 mg; 2115 kJ (505 cal)

Melt the ghee, then cook the chicken in batches until browned all over.

Cook the curry powder, curry paste and dry spices until fragrant.

Gently toss the chicken and potatoes in the spices to coat.

THAI POTATO AND CHICKEN CURRY

Preparation time: 20 minutes
Total cooking time: 30 minutes
Serves 4–6

250 g (8 oz) chicken thigh fillets
250 g (8 oz) orange sweet potato, peeled
300 g (10 oz) potatoes, peeled
2 tablespoons oil
1 onion, chopped
1–2 tablespoons Thai yellow curry paste
¼ teaspoon ground turmeric
1²/₃ cups (410 ml/13 fl oz) coconut milk
2 kaffir lime leaves
2 teaspoons fish sauce
2 teaspoons soft brown sugar
1 tablespoon lime juice
1 teaspoon lime rind
⅓ cup (10 g/¼ oz) coriander leaves
⅓ cup (50 g/1¾ oz) roasted peanuts, roughly chopped

1 Remove the excess fat from the chicken and cut into bite-sized pieces. Cut the sweet potato and potatoes into bite-sized pieces. Heat the oil in a large heavy-based pan or wok and cook the onion until softened. Add the curry paste and turmeric and stir for 1 minute, or until aromatic.
2 Stir in the coconut milk and 1 cup (250 ml/8 fl oz) of water and bring to the boil. Reduce the heat and add the potato, sweet potato, chicken and kaffir lime leaves. Simmer for 15–20 minutes, or until the vegetables are tender and the chicken is cooked through.
3 Add the fish sauce, sugar, lime juice and lime rind, and stir to combine, then add the coriander leaves. Garnish with the peanuts and serve with rice.

NUTRITION PER SERVE (6)
Protein 10 g; Fat 35 g; Carbohydrate 15 g; Dietary Fibre 3 g; Cholesterol 40 mg; 1805 kJ (430 cal)

NOTE: Thai yellow curry paste is not as common as the red or green but is available from most Asian food stores.

Peel the orange sweet potato and chop into bite-sized pieces.

When the onion has softened, stir in the curry paste and turmeric.

Reduce the heat and add the potato, sweet potato, chicken and lime leaves.

BURMESE CHICKEN CURRY

Preparation time: 45 minutes
Total cooking time: 1 hour
Serves 6

1 kg (2 lb) chicken drumsticks or
  thighs
2 large onions, roughly chopped
3 large cloves garlic, peeled
5 cm (2 inch) piece ginger, peeled
2 tablespoons peanut oil
1/2 teaspoon shrimp paste or
  3 tablespoons fish sauce (see Hint)
1 teaspoon salt
2 cups (500 ml/16 fl oz) coconut milk
1 teaspoon chilli powder, optional

TRADITIONAL ACCOMPANIMENTS
200 g (6 1/2 oz) bean starch noodles
6 spring onions, diagonally sliced

1/3 cup (10 g/1/4 oz) chopped fresh
  coriander leaves
2 tablespoons garlic flakes, lightly fried
2 tablespoons onion flakes, lightly fried
3 lemons, cut into wedges
4 dried chillies, fried in oil to crisp
1/4 cup (60 ml/2 fl oz) fish sauce

1 Pat the chicken with paper towels.
Place the onion, garlic and ginger in a
food processor bowl, and process until
smooth. Add a little water to help
blend the mixture, if necessary.
2 Heat the oil in a pan and add the
onion mixture. Add the shrimp paste
and cook, stirring, over high heat for
5 minutes. Add the chicken and cook
over medium heat, turning until
browned. Add the salt, coconut
milk and chilli powder. Bring to the
boil. Reduce the heat to a simmer
and cook, covered, for 30 minutes,
stirring occasionally. Uncover and

cook for 15 minutes, or until the
chicken is tender.
3 Meanwhile, place the noodles in a
bowl and cover with boiling water. Set
aside for 20 minutes. Drain, then place
in a serving bowl. Place the traditional
accompaniments in separate, small
bowls. Each person helps themself to
a portion of noodles, chicken and a
selection, or all, of the accompaniments.

NUTRITION PER SERVE
Protein 33 g; Fat 27 g; Carbohydrate 15 g;
Dietary Fibre 5 g; Cholesterol 62 mg;
1827 kJ (437 cal)

HINT: If fish sauce is used, add at the
same time as the salt and coconut
milk. Dried garlic flakes and dried
onion flakes are sold in jars at
supermarkets. Fry them lightly in oil
until golden.

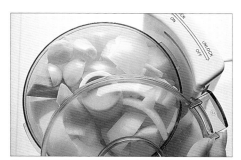

Place the onion, garlic and ginger into a food
processor bowl.

Add the salt, coconut milk and chilli powder to the
chicken mixture.

Cover the noodles with boiling water and leave to
soften for 20 minutes.

INDONESIAN CHICKEN IN COCONUT MILK

Preparation time: 15 minutes
+ 1 hour marinating time
Total cooking time: 50 minutes
Serves 4

8 large or 12 small chicken
    drumsticks
2 teaspoons crushed garlic
1 teaspoon salt
1/2 teaspoon ground black
    pepper
2 teaspoons ground cumin
2 teaspoons ground coriander
1/2 teaspoon ground fennel
1/2 teaspoon ground
    cinnamon
1/4 cup (60 ml/2 fl oz) oil
2 onions, thinly sliced
3/4 cup (185 ml/6 fl oz)
    coconut milk
1 tablespoon lemon juice or
    malt vinegar

1 Pat the chicken drumsticks dry with paper towels. Place the chicken in a large glass or ceramic bowl. Combine the garlic, salt, pepper, cumin, coriander, fennel, cinnamon and 2 tablespoons of the oil. Rub the mixture thoroughly over the chicken. Cover and marinate for 1 hour in the refrigerator.

2 Heat the remaining oil in a large pan. Add the onion and cook, stirring, until it is soft and golden. Add the chicken drumsticks and cook quickly over medium-high heat until they are well browned.

3 Combine the coconut milk, 1 cup (250 ml/8 fl oz) water and the lemon juice. Pour over the chicken, cover and simmer until the chicken is tender and the sauce is well reduced. (This should take about 40 minutes.) Serve the chicken with rice.

NUTRITION PER SERVE
Protein 44 g; Fat 28 g; Carbohydrate 4.5 g;
Dietary Fibre 2 g; Cholesterol 95 mg;
1870 kJ (445 cal)

Rub the garlic and spice mixture thoroughly over the chicken drumsticks.

Add the marinated chicken to the onion and cook over medium-high heat until well browned.

Combine the coconut milk, water and lemon juice, and pour over the chicken.

INDONESIAN SPICED CHICKEN

Preparation time: 15 minutes
Total cooking time: 1 hour
Serves 6

1.5 kg (3 lb) chicken thighs
1 large onion, roughly chopped
2 teaspoons crushed garlic
1 teaspoon grated ginger
1/2 teaspoon ground turmeric
1/2 teaspoon ground pepper
2 teaspoons ground coriander
1 teaspoon salt
3 strips lemon rind or 3 fresh kaffir lime
    leaves
400 ml (13 fl oz) can coconut milk
2 teaspoons soft brown or palm sugar

1 Wash the chicken under cold water, then pat dry with paper towels. Trim the chicken of excess fat. Place the onion, garlic and ginger in a food processor bowl or blender. Process until smooth, adding a little water if necessary. Place the chicken, onion mixture, turmeric, pepper, coriander, salt, lemon rind or lime leaves, coconut milk, sugar and 1 cup (250 ml/8 fl oz) water in a pan and bring slowly to the boil.
2 Reduce the heat to a simmer. Cook, covered, for 45 minutes, or until the chicken is tender. Stir occasionally. Remove the chicken from the pan. Discard the lemon rind or lime leaves.
3 Bring the sauce remaining in the pan to the boil. Reduce the heat to medium-high and cook, uncovered,

stirring occasionally until thick. Place the chicken on a cold, lightly oiled grill and cook under high heat, browning the pieces on both sides. Serve the chicken with the sauce poured over or served separately.

NUTRITION PER SERVE
Protein 58 g; Fat 20 g; Carbohydrate 4.5 g;
Dietary Fibre 1.5 g; Cholesterol 125 mg;
1778 kJ (425 cal)

VARIATION: The chicken pieces can be barbecued instead of grilled.

Place the chicken, onion mixture and the remaining ingredients in a pan.

Cook the chicken for 45 minutes, then remove from the pan.

Bring the sauce to the boil, then reduce the heat and cook, stirring occasionally, until thick.

CHICKEN CURRY WITH MANGO AND CREAM

Preparation time: 10 minutes
Total cooking time: 20 minutes
Serves 4

750 g (1¹/₂ lb) chicken breast fillets
2 tablespoons ghee or oil
2 large onions, thinly sliced
2 red chillies, seeded and sliced
1 teaspoon grated fresh ginger
¹/₄ teaspoon saffron threads
1 tablespoon hot water
¹/₂ teaspoon salt
¹/₄ teaspoon ground white pepper
¹/₂ teaspoon ground cardamom
¹/₂ cup (125 ml/4 fl oz) cream
2 ripe mangoes or 425 g (14 oz) can
    mango slices, drained

MINT AND YOGHURT RAITA

1 cup (250 g/8 oz) plain yoghurt
¹/₄ cup (15 g/¹/₂ oz) finely chopped
    fresh mint leaves
1 green chilli, seeded and chopped
1 teaspoon finely chopped fresh
    ginger
¹/₂ teaspoon salt

1 Wipe the chicken with paper towels. Cut the chicken into 3 cm (1¹/₄ inch) wide strips. Heat the ghee in a pan, add the onion, chilli and ginger, and cook until the onion is soft and golden.

2 Cook the saffron threads in a dry pan over low heat until dry and crisp, stirring constantly. Cool. Place the strands in a bowl and crush with the back of a spoon. Add the hot water and leave to dissolve. Add the chicken strips, salt, pepper and cardamom to the onion mixture in the pan and stir to coat the chicken with the spices. Add the saffron to the pan with the cream. Simmer, uncovered, for 10 minutes.

3 Peel the mangoes and slice the flesh, discarding the seeds. Add to the pan and cook for a further 4 minutes, or until the mango is heated through and slightly softened.

4 To make the mint and yoghurt raita, mix the yoghurt, mint, chilli, ginger and salt together. Serve chilled.

NUTRITION PER SERVE
Protein 47 g; Fat 28 g; Carbohydrate 14 g;
Dietary Fibre 1 g; Cholesterol 170 mg;
2086 kJ (498 cal)

Cook the onion, chilli and ginger until the onion is soft and golden.

Add the cream and saffron to the chicken mixture, and simmer, uncovered.

Peel the mangoes and slice the flesh, discarding the seeds.

Curry Accompaniments

CUCUMBER RAITA

Peel and finely chop 2 Lebanese cucumbers and combine with 1 cup (250 g/8 oz) plain yoghurt in a small bowl. Set aside. Fry 1 teaspoon each of ground cumin and mustard seeds in a dry pan for 1 minute, or until fragrant. Add the toasted spices to the yoghurt mixture with 1/2 teaspoon grated fresh ginger and mix well to combine. Season well with salt and black pepper and garnish with a pinch of paprika. Serve chilled. Makes about 2 cups.

COCONUT BANANAS

Peel 2 large bananas and cut into thick slices. Dip the slices into 1/3 cup (80 ml/2³/4 fl oz) lemon juice, then toss in enough desiccated coconut to coat each piece. Serve at room temperature. Makes about 2 cups.

NAAN BREAD

Sift 500 g (1 lb) plain flour, 1 teaspoon baking powder, 1/2 teaspoon bicarbonate of soda and 1 teaspoon salt into a large bowl. Add 1 beaten egg, 1 tablespoon melted ghee or butter, 1/2 cup (125 g/4 oz) natural yoghurt and gradually mix in approximately 1 cup (250 ml/8 fl oz) milk to form a soft dough. Leave in a warm place, covered with a damp cloth, for 2 hours. Preheat the oven to moderately hot 200°C (400°F/Gas 6). Turn onto a well-floured surface and knead for 2–3 minutes, until smooth. Divide the dough into 8 portions and roll each into an oval 15 cm (6 inches) long. Brush with water and place wet-side down onto greased baking trays. Brush the top of each naan with melted ghee or butter (you will need 2–3 tablespoons). Bake for 8–10 minutes, or until golden brown. Serve immediately. Makes 8.

SWEET MANGO CHUTNEY

Peel 3 large, green mangoes, remove the stones and chop the flesh into large slices. Sprinkle with salt. Remove the seeds from 2 red chillies and finely chop. Blend $1/2$ teaspoon garam masala with $1^1/2$ cups (330 g/11 oz) raw sugar and place in a large pan with 1 cup (250 ml/8 floz) white vinegar. Bring to the boil, then reduce the heat and simmer for 5 minutes. Add the mangoes, chillies, a finely grated 5 cm (2 inch) piece fresh ginger and $1/2$ cup (95 g/3 oz) finely chopped dates. Simmer for 1 hour, or until the mango is tender. Pour into warm sterilized jars and seal. The chutney can be stored in the refrigerator for up to 1 month. Makes about 3 cups.

STEAMED FRAGRANT RICE

Wash $2^1/2$ cups (500 g/1 lb) long-grain rice in a sieve until the water runs clear. In a large saucepan, fry 1–2 crushed cloves garlic and 2 tablespoons finely grated fresh ginger in 2 tablespoons oil, ghee or butter. Add 3 cups (750 ml/24 fl oz) water, bring to the boil and cook for 1 minute. Cover with a tight-fitting lid, reduce the heat to as low as possible and cook for 10–15 minutes, or until steam tunnels form on the surface and the rice is soft and swollen. Turn off the heat and leave the pan, covered, for 10 minutes. Fluff the rice with a fork. Serves 6–8.

LIME PICKLE

Cut 12 limes into 8 thin wedges, sprinkle with salt and set aside. In a dry pan, fry 2 teaspoons each of turmeric, cumin seeds, fennel seeds, fenugreek seeds, and 3 teaspoons brown or yellow mustard seeds for 1–2 minutes. Remove from the heat and grind to a fine powder in a mortar and pestle. Over low heat, fry 5 chopped green chillies, 4 sliced cloves of garlic and a grated 2.5 cm (1 inch) piece fresh ginger in 1 tablespoon oil until golden brown. Add 2 cups (500 ml/16 fl oz) oil, 1 tablespoon sugar, the lime wedges and spices. Simmer over low heat for 10 minutes, stirring occasionally. Spoon the pickle into warm sterilized jars and seal. Store in the refrigerator. Makes 4–5 cups.

TOMATO AND ONION RELISH

In a medium bowl, combine 2 large, chopped tomatoes, 2 tablespoons chopped fresh coriander, 2 small, thinly sliced red onions, 2 tablespoons lime juice and 1 teaspoon soft brown sugar. Season with salt and black pepper. Mix well. Cover with plastic wrap and refrigerate for 15 minutes before serving. Makes about 2 cups.

From left to right: Cucumber raita; Coconut bananas; Tomato and onion relish; Lime pickle; Sweet mango chutney; Naan bread; Steamed fragrant rice.

Index

USEFUL INFORMATION

The recipes in this book were developed using a tablespoon measure of 20 ml. In some other countries the tablespoon is 15 ml. For most recipes this difference will not be noticeable but, for recipes using baking powder, gelatine, bicarbonate of soda, small amounts of flour and cornflour, we suggest that, if you are using the smaller tablespoon, you add an extra teaspoon for each tablespoon.

The recipes in this book are written using convenient cup measurements. You can buy special measuring cups in the supermarket or use an ordinary household cup: first you need to check it holds 250 ml (8 fl oz) by filling it with water and measuring the water (pour it into a measuring jug or even an empty yoghurt carton). This cup can then be used for both liquid and dry cup measurements.

Liquid cup measures

$1/4$ cup	60 ml	2 fluid oz
$1/3$ cup	80 ml	$2^1/2$ fluid oz
$1/2$ cup	125 ml	4 fluid oz
$3/4$ cup	180 ml	6 fluid oz
1 cup	250 ml	8 fluid oz

Spoon measures

$1/4$ teaspoon	1.25 ml
$1/2$ teaspoon	2.5 ml
1 teaspoon	5 ml
1 tablespoon	20 ml

Nutritional information

The nutritional information given for each recipe does not include any garnishes or accompaniments, such as rice or pasta, unless they are included in specific quantities in the ingredients list. The nutritional values are approximations and can be affected by biological and seasonal variations in foods, the unknown composition of some manufactured foods and uncertainty in the dietary database. Nutrient data given are derived primarily from the NUTTAB95 database produced by the Australian New Zealand Food Authority.

Oven Temperatures

You may find cooking times vary depending on the oven you are using. For fan-forced ovens, as a general rule, set oven temperature to 20°C lower than indicated in the recipe.

Note: Those who might be at risk from the effects of salmonella food poisoning (the elderly, pregnant women, young children and those suffering from immune deficiency diseases) should consult their GP with any concerns about eating raw eggs.

Weight

10 g	$1/4$ oz	220 g	7 oz	425 g	14 oz
30 g	1 oz	250 g	8 oz	475 g	15 oz
60 g	2 oz	275 g	9 oz	500 g	1 lb
90 g	3 oz	300 g	10 oz	600 g	$1^1/4$ lb
125 g	4 oz	330 g	11 oz	650 g	1 lb 5 oz
150 g	5 oz	375 g	12 oz	750 g	$1^1/2$ lb
185 g	6 oz	400 g	13 oz	1 kg	2 lb

Alternative names

bicarbonate of soda	—	baking soda
capsicum	—	red or green (bell) pepper
chickpeas	—	garbanzo beans
cornflour	—	cornstarch
fresh coriander	—	cilantro
cream	—	single cream
eggplant	—	aubergine
flat-leaf parsley	—	Italian parsley
hazelnut	—	filbert
plain flour	—	all-purpose flour
prawns	—	shrimp
sambal oelek	—	chilli paste
snow pea	—	mange tout
spring onion	—	scallion
thick cream	—	double/heavy cream
tomato paste (US/Aus.)	—	tomato purée (UK)
kettle barbecue	—	Kettle grill/Covered barbecue
zucchini	—	courgette

Published in 2000 by Merehurst Limited, Ferry House, 51–57 Lacy Road, Putney, London SW15 1PR
Editor: Justine Harding **Designer:** Annette Fitzgerald **CEO & Publisher:** Anne Wilson
ISBN 1-85391 941 1
A catalogue record of this book is available from the British Library.

Front cover, clockwise from top left: Red Curry Chicken Salad; Chicken and Vegetable Soup; Vietnamese Chicken and Noodle Casserole; New Potato, Chicken and Spinach Frittata; Roast Chicken with Country Sage Stuffing; Creamy Chicken, Sage and Tarragon Pie.